Beyond Tomorrow

BEYOND TOMORROW

Planning a New Civilization

Christopher Nye

FOREWORD BY
Otto Scharmer

WIPF & STOCK · Eugene, Oregon

BEYOND TOMORROW
Planning a New Civilization

Copyright © 2025 Christopher Nye. All rights reserved. Except for brief quotations in critical publications or reviews, no part of this book may be reproduced in any manner without prior written permission from the publisher. Write: Permissions, Wipf and Stock Publishers, 199 W. 8th Ave., Suite 3, Eugene, OR 97401.

Wipf & Stock
An Imprint of Wipf and Stock Publishers
199 W. 8th Ave., Suite 3
Eugene, OR 97401

www.wipfandstock.com

PAPERBACK ISBN: 979-8-3852-5250-3
HARDCOVER ISBN: 979-8-3852-5251-0
EBOOK ISBN: 979-8-3852-5252-7

VERSION NUMBER 11/24/25

Cover: *The Path* by Jane Morton Norton

Wendell Berry, "The Peace of Wild Things" from *New Collected Poems*. Copyright © 2012 by Wendell Berry. Reprinted with the permission of The Permissions Company, LLC on behalf of Counterpoint Press, counterpointpress.com.

Rumi, "The Guest House" from *The Essential Rumi*. Copyright © 2004 by Coleman Barks. Reprinted with the permission of Reid Boates Literary Agency on behalf of Coleman Barks.

Lines from Gwendolyn Brooks's "Paul Robeson" are from *The Essential Gwendolyn Brooks*, edited by Elizabeth Alexander. New York: Library of America, 2005. Copyright © 1970 by Gwendolyn Brooks. Used by consent of Brooks Permissions.

Unless otherwise noted, all Scripture quotations are taken from the King James Version (KJV), public domain.

Author website and Study Guide: https://chris-nye.com

To the one whose
love and encouragement
sponsor my best efforts.

*The eyes of the future are looking back at us
. . . praying for us to see beyond our own time.*

—Terry Tempest Williams

CONTENTS

Foreword by Otto Scharmer | ix
Preface | xi
Acknowledgments | xiii

Part One—Key Elements
Chapter One: Learning from the Future | 3
Chapter Two: Is Deep Freedom Possible? | 19
Chapter Three: What Does *Convivencia* Mean? | 38
Chapter Four: Love One Another | 53

Part Two—Education
Chapter Five: Educate the Whole Child | 69
Chapter Six: Freedom to Teach | 90

Part Three—Indications for Two Other Fields
Chapter Seven: A Healing Agriculture | 109
Chapter Eight: A Cooperative Economy | 133

Other Considerations
Chapter Nine: Seeking a Balance | 169
Chapter Ten: What Bees Can Teach and What They Can't | 183
Chapter Eleven: Centering on Education | 192

Epilogue—Developing an Inner Compass | 213

Appendix A: Inner Development Options | 219
Appendix B: Burley Tobacco Price and Production Management | 223
Appendix C: Gap Years | 225
Bibliography | 227
Index | 243

FOREWORD

STEPPING INTO THE FUTURE—into a future that is not merely an extension of the past—requires more than knowledge or strategy. It requires the capacity to sense and activate the deeper potential of what is wanting to emerge. It asks of us to shift our mode of attention—from reacting to presencing, from downloading to listening with open mind, heart, and will.

We are living in times of profound disruption—what I often refer to as "emerging complexity." These are moments when the familiar frameworks no longer hold, and the problems we face mutate faster than our capacity to define them. Whether it is the accelerated rise of artificial intelligence, global pandemics, social fracture, war, or climate breakdown, these phenomena confront us with challenges that outpace inherited solutions. In such moments, our habitual responses—be they technocratic, ideological, or purely reactive—fall short. What is needed is a different stance toward the future, one that is not based on control or prediction, but on connection and co-creation.

This is the terrain in which Christopher Nye's *Beyond Tomorrow: Planning for a New Civilization* is situated. The book invites us into a courageous inquiry: What might a renewed civilization look like if it were grounded in deeper values—care, mutuality, regeneration, and freedom? What are the seeds already sprouting around us, and what forms of education, economy, and agriculture might nourish them?

Drawing from decades of lived experience as an educator, Christopher becomes not only a guide but a companion on a journey that traverses ideas, practices, and lived examples. One of the most striking is Sekem, the pioneering Egyptian community that transformed desert sand into biodynamic farmland and vibrant social enterprise. Sekem is not just a case study—it is a living system where economic, ecological, educational, and spiritual renewal converge. It demonstrates what becomes possible when human endeavor is rooted in alignment with natural rhythms and higher purpose. It shows us that regeneration is not a theory—it is a practice, one that can be scaled when embedded in values and systems that support life, not extract from it.

And this is where education emerges as a bridge—perhaps the most vital one. If Sekem is a seed of the future, then learning and leadership belong to the soil. The question is not only what we teach and learn, but how we cultivate the capacities for young people to become stewards of such transformation. Education that emphasizes inner development, systems thinking, ecological literacy, and the courage to prototype new realities is essential. As Christopher argues, this kind of education prepares not just for making a living but for making a meaningful life—and more than that, for shaping a different civilization.

The kind of transformation Christopher evokes is not top-down or programmatic. It is rooted in a different form of leadership—one that moves from siloed expertise to systems sensing, from top-down imposition to bottom-up co-creation. In the language of *Theory U*, it is about cultivating the social field so that awareness-based collective action becomes possible. We see this happening in diverse contexts around the world—often in response to collapse, crisis, or necessity. But also, increasingly, as a conscious choice to align with a deeper intention.

And yet, as anyone who has sat in a partnership meeting knows, this shift is not easy. Ecosystem collaboration is fragile; it can be blocked when we default to control or fear. Christopher points us toward a foundational leverage point: a radical renewal of education that not only teaches us how to think, but how to see, how to sense, and how to co-create.

When systems collapse, we are returned to our relationships, to the land, to one another, and to ourselves. *Beyond Tomorrow* is not a map but a mirror. It invites each of us to reflect: Where do I stand in relation to the emerging future? What is mine to do now?

This book has elements of both a diagnosis and a doorway. May it be received, not as a conclusion but as an invitation to co-initiate the next step.

Otto Scharmer, Boston and Berlin, July 2025

PREFACE

Civilizations rise. Civilizations fall. Ours could be superceded by a rapidly ascending China. When historians of the future look back at our own time, they may well perceive a contest decided by military, economic, or political superiority. Or it could turn out to be a war of ideas, in which America and the West had so much to offer, and the Chinese Communist Party so little. However, the ideas of America and the West—democracy, a deeper understanding of freedom, an active caring and community—can only prevail if they come back to life in a form that grabs people's imagination and fires a desire for constructive change.

This can happen if we come together to frame an inspiring vision that allows ideas like these to regain vitality and become once again real. Consider this book a modest effort to begin the conversation, imagining that in the future the lives of millions could be affected by how compelling, complete, and honest that vision can be.

Join me in exploring how our highest and best selves can frame a future worth striving for.

ACKNOWLEDGMENTS

I received help from so many people that the book truly feels like a team project. Foremost among those helping was my wife, who served as my first-line critic. The steadfast editing of Chip Blake helped me through many revisions. Other readers whose insights were valuable included Kam Bellamy, John Bell, Philip Francis, Dave Hattem, Jared Haynes, Cheryl Heller, Jed Horowitz, Marion Gilliam, Jeremy Jeliffe, John Jeliffe, Mari Margill and Thomas Linzey, Mark Phillips, Moni McIntyre, Jacob Hundt, Grace Greenwald, Christine Kelly, Seth Jordan, Elizabeth Lynch, Tom McGuire, George Russell, Dick Shohet, David Stone, and Armando Zanecchia.

For my sections on Sekem, I thank Helmy Abouleish and all who generously gave their time and insights when I visited there, plus Christine Arlt in Germany for fact-checking.

Special thanks to managing editor Matt Wimer and the Wipf and Stock team for their role in having these ideas reach the public.

Part One—Key Elements

CHAPTER ONE: LEARNING FROM THE FUTURE

> *We have it in our power to begin the world over again.*
> —Thomas Paine

> *We are each other's harvest.*
> —Gwendolyn Brooks

> *The future ain't what it used to be.*
> —Yogi Berra

Looking Ahead

My wife says that I am peculiarly focused on the future. Of course, I don't think it's peculiar at all. Anyone in the teaching profession prepares the future. But she may have a point in that long before climate change was a term, I urged students in the college classes I taught to think about environment and the quality of life; in fact, that was the name of a program for college freshmen I helped found. Instead of blaming and criticizing the polluters and the past, why not take that energy and redirect it to first visioning a cleaner future and then bringing it to fruition? It seemed to me that often utopians like the Shakers were trying to love an envisioned future into existence. Even their failures were instructive. In the same program I taught a course called Strategies for Social Change and pushed students to think as boldly as they could. It is easy to take risks in thinking. There will be plenty of chances to correct and criticize before it is time to pour concrete.

Building on this future orientation, I thought it was important to write this book for several reasons. First, at a time when future prospects from a climate perspective look frightening, it can be helpful and hopeful to develop an alternative vision of the positive possibilities. Yes, it is conceivable that after climate catastrophes and social breakdown, society can descend into tribalism and disaster profiteering. But such a scenario is much more likely if there is a vacuum of vision into which negative elements will inevitably flow. Second, an enlivened awareness of the positive that wants to be born can give rise to new forms, new alliances, new initiatives that unlock human potential and quicken and inspire those with the potential to become midwives for the good. There are thinkers and techniques that can help this to happen. Third, it is too easy to overlook the power of ideals and ideas. The Civil Rights Movement in the United States provides an outstanding example of how sweeping changes can be effected when an uplifting ideal gets beautifully articulated and is able to move whole communities. We have yet to achieve Martin Luther King Jr.'s Beloved Community, but we have come a long way from "Whites only" water fountains and bathrooms.

This book is for people who are ready to entertain the audacious. I wrote it for readers open to looking at the big picture and taking the long view, people not content to simply oppose things like corporate greed, racism, and polarization. Rather, I want to understand the conditions of which these are symptoms and imagine bold alternatives. Beyond that, I want to explore ways for a more perfect world to promote human flourishing. A number of the ideas presented will seem utopian, too ambitious or radical to be practical. However, some utopian communities actually thrive. And we can learn from their successes. In October 2022 I traveled to Sekem in Egypt, an intentional community that in the span of forty-five years has turned desert sand and rocks into luxuriant farmland and thriving businesses—remarkably successful. An understanding of this endeavor and other experiments can become an inspiration for a future unencumbered by slavish adherence to the past and a fearful immunity to change. Let us free our imaginations.

Significant and sustainable change requires a compelling vision of the future. Picture what could happen with an entirely new civilization, a place and a time to be determined, when human motives have matured to a point where, for example, it doesn't take a flood or an emergency for people to go out of their way to help one another. I am projecting a time beyond tomorrow, when a different set of expectations exists for what it means to be a complete human being. Of course, proposing that such a thing is even possible involves the risk of being perceived as a utopian nutcase. But many years as an educator have taught me that raising the stakes often promotes learning. Imagining a different future can unlock opportunities for the present. Looking foolish is a small price to pay if a path can be opened to a revitalized, creative, and purposeful society, one in which the hidden potential in all individuals has a chance to flourish. An over-the-horizon view can bring perspective to the present, as the Iroquois knew when, in making decisions, they considered consequences down to the seventh generation.

Despite my being an early model year (1937), with high mileage (to most states and twenty countries), I still want to be a vehicle for positive change and a better future. I have enough experience on the planet to be able to learn from the past and to provide the perspective of an elder. I choose to focus on the future and see the tremendous potential for young people to remake the world. This book provides some energy to help their quest.

Visioning

Tinkering with existing systems to make incremental changes fails to satisfy me. And now, as a climate crisis looms over us, democracy unravels, and truth appears to be a casualty of the scramble to get ahead, the urgency of thinking boldly and turning over the apple cart of conventional assumptions screams louder than ever. I hear it from high school and college students—half measures won't cut it. The country needs to go beyond bold; it needs a revitalizing vision commensurate with the size of the problems. As educator and unconventional thinker Zak Stein puts it, "We must find a way to break open into a new civilization based on new frontiers of human potential."[1] The pace and complexity of our world has outstripped our ability to understand and manage it. There are ways to address this, but not if we persist in seeing our reflection in a stagnant pool. Fresh visioning can in a sense free us. Recall the caveat from King Solomon (about 700 BC): "Where there is no vision, the people perish" (Prov 29:18 KJV).

---

1. Stein, *Education Between Worlds*, 14.

Visioning calls us to be *for* something. There is plenty to criticize. There is plenty to oppose. But negativism will not get us where we need to go. Being *against* can be essential, especially in the face of imminent danger, but the thrust here will be *for*. And while it would be presumptuous to provide a blueprint for a generation that has not yet been born, I aim to open vistas of possibility that can fuel change. May suitable ideals inspire plans and actions that leap over incrementalism and engender true transformation.

In order for wisdom to grow enough to manage and counterbalance the power and complexity of our current culture, it's essential to cultivate a vision of how to change both ourselves and society. This need not be one single prescription but preferably a rich variety of possibilities coupled with qualities of leadership that can actualize the possibilities. To give a small example of one way this can happen, my wife and I have undertaken to sponsor gap year programs that expose recent high school graduates to deeply transformative learning, the sort of thing that can happen when one goes alone for a wilderness experience. We hope that through challenging experiences and exposure to fresh ideas, they will develop an inner compass to guide them toward service to humanity in whatever way they believe suits their skills and who they want to be. See appendix C for more on this. We envision a population of energetic young leaders with the resilience and sense of purpose to handle the trials ahead. This book can provide thought-food for the intelligent general reader, but more important, it is designed to stimulate discussion for groups of all ages and persuasions.

A deeper understanding of three key concepts will help navigate a challenging future. A deeper understanding of freedom, community building, and love have always been important but never more than now. The next three chapters take up those subjects in turn. As the title of this introductory chapter indicates, a fresh look at the present can be gained by going forward, imagining a brighter future, and then looking back. Mindful that the major changes of Franklin Roosevelt's New Deal would never have been possible without the societal disruption of the Great Depression, I intend to contribute something to this visioning by imagining what could be accomplished *after* a seismic event, such as global climate catastrophe. Let the prospect of catastrophe be a catalyst for freeing the imagination. One hopes for not just an awakening in the matter of cognition but also a changed and awakened attitude. Open mind, open heart, and open will can fling wide the door to future possibilities.

CHAPTER ONE: LEARNING FROM THE FUTURE

The great unraveling is already happening, in slow motion. Its other name is the Metacrisis.[2] It involves, not just the environment but the fact that the world mankind has created exceeds our capacity to make sense of it. AI, vast cities, corporations with more wealth and power than most countries, the speed and complexity of modern life—these and other factors combine to challenge our ability to stay centered and hopeful enough to continue being productive. Certain navigational aids can help people find their way through this thicket of challenges, not be overwhelmed by the Metacrisis, and emerge whole on the other side. They take the form of ideals, historical examples, personal openness, and sources of inspiration.

There is nothing like having your car float away down the street or seeing the roof blown off your house to get your attention.[3] I invite intelligent readers, to whom this book is directed, to join me in stretching to imagine how we might reinvent the way we live and work together. Since I have been thinking about these things for decades, I decided to give it a try.

Why not? With a PhD in American Studies, experience in many jobs from garbage collector to CEO, and a deep concern for young people, the ones who will inherit this troubled planet, why should I not pull together thoughts that prove helpful? I have been active in the environmental movement since the 1960s, helped start *Orion Magazine*, and promoted organic farming and gardening when it was a fringe movement. As cofounder of Educate the Whole Child,[4] I see plenty of well-meaning schools preparing kids to make a living. What about preparing them to make a meaningful life?

Learning must also occur beyond classroom walls. And not just in education but in all areas we need to aim higher. In response to the climate crisis, we strive for sustainability. Why not raise the bar? We can do much better than just getting by, just sustaining ourselves. Envision the tremendous human potential waiting to be tapped. In Chapters 5 and 6 you will see how a radically different approach to education can open up great possibilities.

---

2. This term and its implications have been insightfully explored by Jonathan Rowson. See Rowson, "Four Ways of Knowing."

3. Kim Stanley Robinson's *The Ministry for the Future* envisions catastrophe on a scale guaranteed to get people's attention.

4. Learn more at Educate the Whole Child's website: educatethewholechild.org.

Any readers concerned about the world in crisis their children will inherit can improve their prospects by joining in this visualization of possibilities. Not only can it provide rays of hope in a time of alarming prospects; it can help parents see how the education their children currently receive can become a true growth experience, rather than a transactional one in which test scores and grades reward performance. Decades as an educator have led me to believe education is the key. Or as Zak Stein says as the title of an essay, "If Education Is Not the Answer, You Are Asking the Wrong Question."[5]

Education and Self-Change

Education in the broadest sense is the cornerstone of an enhanced vision of the future. And what can be accomplished through a truly nurturing education gives ample reason for hope. Visioning or the planning referenced in this book's title are meant to be an invitation to learn. An alternative title could be "Success Factors for Community Building and Meaning-Making." Any blueprint for a new civilization would take volumes and would be an unreasonable undertaking for one person. I offer instead building blocks—a vision, concepts, and attitudes—that can make a strong and sustainable civilization possible. Many of these elements apply as well to present society. "Community building," too, can be taken in the broadest sense because success depends on incorporating factors like a deeper understanding of freedom in both political and personal senses, as well as love for the other, both human and nonhuman. The factors apply to communities of all sizes, from the smallest to a potential civilization with global reach. "Meaning-making," a term I learned from entrepreneur-turned-activist Tomas Björkman, carries the implication for him that if you want enduring social change, begin with yourself. Ongoing personal, inner development is essential. This is not to say that those of us who want to work for a better world must first perfect ourselves before social change can occur. Imperfect people have accomplished amazing things throughout history. However, the intensity of purpose in individual lives mortars a group together. One sees this in the lives of such figures as Rosa Parks, Cesar Chavez, Nelson Mandela, and, today, Volodymyr Zelensky.

---

5. Stein, "If Education."

Each of these building blocks can also serve as a point of departure for lively discussion by groups concerned about the kind of society they would like to live in if the road ahead were truly to open up. In fact, the best way to flesh out ideas for social change is for groups representing various points of view to come together, brainstorm, and seek common ground, rather than having one individual hand down completed plans, as it were, from Mount Olympus.

And is thinking utopian such a bad thing? You will find in subsequent chapters some discussion of the Shakers, the Mondragón Cooperative movement, and Sekem in Egypt—all utopian communities, and all successful in different ways. Utopians are often bold adventurers, trying things conventional thinkers would not consider. The people who sailed from Europe to found what became the United States could be seen as opportunistic, but they were also in some senses utopians for their time.

Exploring radically different paradigms and solutions will require articulating ideals that give moral integrity to our thinking and subsequently our acting. This does not guarantee success. The intentional communities of Shakers were deeply dedicated to higher purposes, but that did not keep them from diminishing away like an endangered species when changes wrought by the Industrial Revolution caught up with them. Nevertheless, I contend that ideals, higher principles, and purposes must be part of any re-visioning of a new civilization if it is to have staying power. Existing examples of this have endured for decades, like a number of Camphill communities (established in 1939) dedicated to caring for people with special needs in the United States and around the globe, and Sekem (founded in 1977), a thriving intentional community based on Islamic principles. The title of a book by Alan Wiseman about a community in Colombia captures the spirit at work here: *Gaviotas—a Village To Reinvent the World*. It is less important what those ideals and principles are than that they exist and become incorporated into an ethic of individual self-change and a social fabric that is indeed *filled with intention*. Some of these communities are associated with a spiritual practice. Some are not.

Years ago, when I was setting up the curriculum for a non-traditional college program for adults, one of the first courses to be established was called Self-Change as a Living Philosophical Principle. The professor who taught it had already discovered that thinkers going all the way back to Plato had found that taking one's own life in hand was the first step to becoming a change agent. The import of "Be the change you want to see in the world"[6] makes perfect sense. By finding and realizing one's authentic self, one earns the right, so to speak, to motivate others.

Often in America those in a position to prompt change have become anesthetized by their own wealth, perceived importance, and outer success. Caring is limited to their immediate circle or family. The United States is a resourceful country with food surpluses, but one out of every six children here does not get enough to eat. Would childhood hunger be so hard to fix? Plenty of other developed countries have already done it, not just the powerful ones but many of us fail to heed what Gwendolyn Brooks tells us: "We are each other's harvest."

Let us begin our journey. But first I would like to take up three questions:

1. Why plan for a new civilization—why now?
2. What kind of thinking does such planning require?
3. Why is education central to the undertaking?

Why Plan—Why Now?

The future seems to be racing toward us—a climate going berserk, pandemic casting its shadow, democracies being replaced by dictatorships around the world, and the chasm between haves and have-nots growing ever wider. The rich use money to make more money, while poor children go hungry. At the same time, something as fundamental as truth gets devalued so that opinion often manages to trump facts. These deteriorating conditions leave us feeling more like the victims of destiny than its masters. Young people I speak with are often eager to contribute, to make a difference, but typically they lack a sense of how they can help or how their efforts could fit into a broader vision of a more just, purposeful, and caring society. It is increasingly difficult for citizens to find examples of moral courage among our political leaders. More often, behind the red tie we find self-assertion and expediency, with words like "freedom" and "democracy" sounding like empty phrases.

Yet, as Martin Luther King Jr. liked to say, "There is nothing more powerful than an idea whose time has come."[7] The changes wrought by

---

6. Often attributed to Gandhi, who did not originate the idea. See Quote Investigator, "Be the Change."

7. Attributed to Victor Hugo; quoted in King, "Keep Moving."

the Civil Rights Movement in the United States prove this. Formulating and internalizing potentially transformative ideas is job one. With these, there is a basis for counterbalancing the decisions about spending and priorities made by government that serve short-term advantage but do not change the destiny of the country or alter the momentum of an often-predatory capitalism. Such a foundation or moral grounding might lead one to question, for example, spending talent and treasure going to Mars, when those resources and ingenuity poured into space might be applied directly to mitigating climate change or feeding the hungry here on Earth.

Current trend lines point toward dicey times, with millions forced to migrate away from heat, wildfires, and coastal flooding,[8] and society a sea of violent conflict with everyone out for himself.[9] Arguably, parts of some American cities are already there. As noted above, these deteriorating conditions—our abuse of nature, our failing political systems, our decadent popular culture—give us the opportunity to see that our conventional thinking and stock answers no longer work. This in turn can prompt us to imagine better ways and to think beyond dealing with symptoms by, for example, hiring more police. Fresh visioning, together with the courage to try things that may fail, can completely change the calculus of what is possible.

Another reason for embarking on this journey of visioning and a radically different future as soon as possible is that many young people experience a sense of hopelessness. Their elders have not only created these problems, they have failed to help them find inner compass and higher purpose. Subject to anxiety and depression, these young people turn to forms of escape that actually intensify a sense of isolation and in some cases end in suicide. If they see no life purpose beyond fulfilling their own desires, and if the world is headed for climate catastrophe anyway, why go on living? Moreover, if creation is just a series of accidents winnowed down to an existence that only *appears* to make sense, what are the prospects? What is the point? But hope can spring up anew. Not a shallow optimism, but hope grounded in meaningful ideals, a plan, a process, a reason to belong, and a sense of agency in the world can be strong motivators to develop a pragmatic idealism and to stay alive to work for something better.

8. Bittle, *Great Displacement*, 274–79.

9. For a picture of how social collapse could occur, see Bendell and Read, *Deep Adaptation*, 1–12.

What Kind of Thinking Does This Planning Require?

It may be helpful to imagine a new civilization less as a destination and more as a journey, one that many people participate in, stretching their thinking to include models and initiatives that in today's world might not be possible. But even so, thinking is hard work, and feels risky. Human nature being what it is, often people have trouble letting go of the familiar, and even more difficulty with changing patterns of thought. What would it take if, instead of tracking familiar paths, people were able bring a vitality, an inner initiative to their thought?

Massachusetts Institute of Technology (MIT) professor Otto Scharmer offers a technique that can make this easier. He travels the world teaching people how to think and solve problems that reach well beyond technology. In seminars and his books like *Leading from the Emerging Future* and *Theory U*, he breaks open our habitual thinking patterns and ways of tackling obstacles. His work is particularly relevant here because he teaches a technique for pulling the best ideas, not from the past but from the future. He gives it the name *presencing*, and it is one of the things this book strives to do. He defines it this way: "Presencing, the blending of *sensing* and *presence*, means to connect to the Source of the highest future possibility and to bring it into the now."[10] It takes some work to understand this skill and then to be able to use it. In a sense it is the mental equivalent of what famous hockey player Wayne Gretzky meant when he explained his success: don't go after the puck, but "skate to where the puck is going to be." But how do you acquire the ability to know where the puck will be? Scharmer explains that you need to step back and pay attention to your attention, i.e. mindfulness. It helps to cultivate your creative side. And you will need to "tune" three inner instruments of knowing. Those are: open mind, open heart, and open will. This is explained further in connection with the chart on page 14 and a taxonomy Scharmer developed on how we can attack problems.[11]

An example can help show how presencing works. One day when I was in my office at *Orion Magazine*, a total stranger appeared: a retired teacher and arts coordinator from New York City schools. He informed me that the three-ring binder he was carrying contained the material for a book *Orion* should publish. He already knew that we had published the basic book on place-based education. I was dubious but agreed that he could leave the binder with me for a week to see if there was a

---

10. Scharmer, *Theory U*, 16.
11. Scharmer, "Theory U—Learning."

possibility. There wasn't. When he returned the next week I said to him, "You don't want to write a book; you want to start a movement." And we began to brainstorm the main thrust of his approach to teaching, which was essentially "Educate the whole child." I had taught in college but never in a K–12 public school, but more or less on the spot we agreed to see if we could stir up what Congressman John Lewis called "good trouble." Other allies appeared, as if sent to us by fate. We extended our thinking and let the momentum grow until it became Educate the Whole Child, a national initiative described later in this book. This was only possible because we were, in Scharmer's words, open to and "leading from the emerging future."[12]

Scharmer's problem-solving framework has proved useful in workshops I have led with teachers who want authentic education reform. At the first level of addressing problems you treat *symptoms*. In some cases this suffices. You cut yourself peeling an apple. Wash the cut, first aid cream, Band-Aid; simple. But suppose that isn't sufficient. Let's say you have a child with attention deficit disorder (ADD).

The second level of problem solving involves digging deeper to address the *structures* or causes of the problem. Thus, instead of medicating children with short attention spans, devise holistic projects that get them out of static rows of desks, that allow them to move around and invest more of themselves in learning. Scharmer makes the point that most problem-solving never goes beyond these two approaches. What if neither of these methods work?

The third solution level involves *thinking differently*. Einstein famously asserted that you can't solve a problem with the same kind of thinking that created it. This is borne out in public education, where the system expects conventional teaching, enforced with standardized curriculum, and measured quantitatively in tests. When this approach fails because it doesn't engage the whole child, the response has been to amp up testing and accountability. But we need to find new paradigms and new ways to think about the problem. Possibly, we can look to giants in the field from the past, turning to innovators and paradigm-shifters who might, for example, attune present education strategies to producing the creative individuals who will be needed to cope with the future.

Scharmer breaks new ground with the fourth level of problem-solving—*presencing*.[13] The term itself shifts the paradigm. To problem-solve

12. This idea became the title for an important book: Otto Scharmer's and Katrin Kaufer's *Leading from the Emerging Future: From Ego-System to Eco-System Economics*.

13. Applications of presencing are developed at the Presencing Institute. Learn more at Presencing Institute, "Presencing."

with presencing means to change yourself. With practice, you can learn to connect with future possibilities. Then these possibilities can be translated and connected with one's own authentic self in the present. Other ways exist to learn from the future, but I believe presencing is the most nuanced and complete, once you learn how to apply it.[14]

Formidable obstacles stand in the way of presencing. Scharmer identifies three of them. Opposing the process of developing a truly *open mind* is our well-honed ability to criticize and judge. Don't we love our skill in finding defects and pointing them out? Opposing having a truly *open heart* is cynicism. "That's utopian; it couldn't possibly work." "It's been tried before." "We lack the resources to implement what you're proposing." Opposing what Scharmer calls *open will* is fear. This undermines a great many worthwhile initiatives, even prevents them from being tested out. My chapter on love will have more to say about this. The following chart shows how these levels of problem solving relate to each other and how they work in practice with three sample problems.

SOLUTION LEVELS

PROBLEM:	Treat the symptoms	Make structural change	Reorient thinking	Employ presencing
Restless child	Give Ritalin	Provide more activities, time outdoors	What insights can we use from Whitehead or Thich Nhat Hanh?	Start by asking what kind of adult the future will require. 000wil Kinwi00l0lwill
Test-dominated education	Fewer tests	New forms of accountability	A new paradigm: Whole Child Education	As above. Find ways to return creativity and agency to teaching.
Impending climate crisis	Solar, wind, and nuclear power, electric cars, energy conservation	Walkable cities, carbon tax	Clarify thinking about the three spheres of society and economic/corporate excess	Education that re-shapes human wanting and develops a social conscience.

Figure 1. Based on Otto Scharmer, *Theory U: Leading from the Future As It Emerges*, 42–45.

14. Another avenue for developing skill in presencing is cultivating that capacity young children have for experiencing wonder. See Keltner, *Awe*.

This chart was created for educators. In using it, I emphasize that in education, as well as many other fields, solutions never get beyond the first two levels. Whole child education, on the other hand, as will be discussed in subsequent chapters, attempts much more. It anticipates the future by nurturing in each individual student open mind, open heart, and open will.[15]

As Scharmer explains it, presencing begins with an unvarnished appraisal of the present. Use deep listening to get beyond one's preconceptions and historical ways of making sense.[16] That is the *letting-go* portion of presencing. The *letting come* can happen when we make the choice to be open, serve the evolution of life, and tune our instrument to be able to hear or perceive what the future wants us to know. For example, in the farming area, it doesn't take a genius to "hear" the earth saying, "Stop poisoning me; stop letting my topsoil wash away. Otherwise, I won't be able to feed you and other life in years to come."

There is a further dimension of presencing, which Scharmer describes as "linking with and acting from one's highest future Self." Out of self-knowledge and empowerment one becomes "a vehicle for bringing forth new worlds."[17] This accords with what theologian Frederick Buechner was getting at when he defined a person's true calling as "the place where your deep gladness and the world's deep hunger meet."[18]

The concept and practice of presencing become particularly important when envisioning a transformed future and the uses we can make of utopian experience. The quality of thought that supports presencing and visioning is *intuition*, the key that unlocks creativity and the faculty that both Steve Jobs and Albert Einstein asserted was at the heart of their success. Einstein called it "a sacred gift."[19] Also, to grasp the meaning of mighty terms like freedom, community, and love we need a more holistic knowing than intellect alone can provide. But what is intuition?

Art educator Betty Edwards, in a book called *Drawing on the Right Side of the Brain*, believes that people who think they can't draw, in fact can by cultivating the largely neglected creative parts of their brains. She characterizes intuition as the ability to make leaps of insight, often based

---

15. For more on whole child education and why it works, see educatethewholechild.org.
16. Senge et al. *Presence*, 13.
17. Senge et al. *Presence*, 234.
18. Buechner, *Wishful Thinking*, 118.
19. Quote Investigator, "Intuitive Mind."

on incomplete patterns, hunches, or visual images. Intuition, she says, is able to imagine totally new things, to synthesize, to put things together to form wholes. This is not intellect, which analyzes and divides in order to understand. Intuition can manifest through artistic creativity; this kind of consciousness shines forth in inspired works like Rembrandt's *Night Watch*, Shakespeare's *King Lear*, and Handel's *Messiah*.

But intuition can take another form. It can be a comprehending consciousness that connects us in an instant with more than we realized we knew, at times even to the more-than-human. One example of this intuitional, big-picture, flash-of-insight comprehension occurred on January 15, 2009, when pilot Sully Sullenberger suddenly had to decide what to do when his plane with 155 people aboard struck a flock of geese and lost power in both engines shortly after takeoff from LaGuardia Airport in New York City. He realized immediately that he lacked enough altitude to glide either to LaGuardia or nearby Teterboro airport. In a matter of seconds he decided to land the plane on the Hudson River, which he did, successfully saving the lives of all aboard. There wasn't time for the pilot to employ a logical, systematic, analytical process; he was thinking clearly, but he was using a faculty that enables athletes to make instantaneous decisions, jazz musicians to improvise, and some parents to know whether forbearance or discipline is appropriate in responding to a child's misbehavior.

Intuition illuminates the whole landscape, like a floodlight or a lightning flash. On the other hand, intellect is more likely to be penetrating but narrow like a headlight. Both intuition and intellect are needed to marshal the breadth and depth required to creatively imagine a new civilization.[20] For presencing and to think into the future, we need that gift. It can help going forward if we explore the possibility of fostering a freedom grounded in community and love.

Why Make Education Central?

There are several reasons to focus on education, particularly as it is handled in the United States in public schools, which over 90 percent of children attend.

---

20. To dig deeper into this subject, see Winkler, "Training in Intuition." Or, for a contemporary and exhaustive exploration that relates this quality of thought to brain physiology, see McGilchrist, *Master and His Emissary*.

A first reason is that schools today need to change. They do a mediocre job of preparing young people for the world that they will encounter after graduation, and even less for a world wracked by climate chaos. Do they teach resilience, creativity, problem-solving, interpersonal skills, and agency? Not typically. Instead they teach content acquisition (often memorized) analysis, and performance on tests. The chapter titled "Educate the Whole Child" tells what to do about this.

A second reason education must be central to envisioning a new civilization is that what we teach today becomes the world tomorrow. And not only what we teach but how it gets taught is important. A new civilization demands a different consciousness and sense of self than prevails today. Individuals will need to develop a more active caring, and a sense of belonging that extends beyond our own skin, and perhaps our family, to the community, nature, and the world. Because this system change will take time, and because it will take even more time for the children to grow up to become responsible adults, we need to get started immediately. Encouraging efforts in this direction already exist, as we shall see.

The last reason is that a democracy succeeds or fails in no small part on the effectiveness of the education provided to its citizens. When graduates emerge from school unable to tell the difference between a fact and an opinion, when they have so little regard for truth that they will believe lies they like and reject truths they don't, when their capacity to care about other people has never been recognized and cultivated; then you get the kind of election results and voter manipulation that one sees in this country and others where autocracy is on the rise.

Part one of this book addresses the principles without which thinking about the future is likely to be shallow and unsatisfying. An understanding of the principles of freedom, community, and love forms a foundation on which the following section about education can rest. Part two, the core of the book, will show what can be accomplished when our education paradigm changes and we think of learning as something that takes place throughout life and not only within school walls. Part three, "Indications for Two Other Fields," takes up other areas crying out for radical rethinking—agriculture and the economy. In these later chapters I try to look beyond the horizon and suggest promising paths forward, paths intended to promote lively discussion and innovation.

Throughout, I hope to offer ideas that will stimulate readers to answer for themselves the questions, *What kind of people do we aspire to be? And what kind of an evolved society would be best to support this development?* Remember those questions. They will come up in what follows. Material from the chapters on freedom, community, and love, plus the experience of Shakers and others should be helpful in framing one's own answers.

I hope this book will unite us in a common visioning, and that it will give you tools for planning the new civilization. Use Scharmer's technique of presencing. Future chapters will return to it. Try out your ideas on friends. Expect to be shot down. Try again. "Forget what is possible right now," says Zak Stein. Ask, "What in our hearts do we want for our children and ourselves?"[21]

---

21. Stein, *Education in a Time*, 201.

CHAPTER TWO: IS DEEP FREEDOM POSSIBLE?

> *Freedom is not a destination but a journey.*
> —Anonymous

> *The strength and health of a free society depend on individual citizens cultivating their capacity for inner freedom.*
> —Steven Rockefeller

> *We have Paleolithic emotions, medieval institutions, and godlike technology.*
> —E. O. Wilson

> *We are free to err. . . . We can, if we wish, retreat into a comfortable materialism requiring no burden of responsibility on our part.*
> —Steven L. Talbott

FROM THE PERSPECTIVE OF the final phase of my life, as I look back on my journey, I see a progression in which more and more I have not wanted to be the passenger in the body and mind I inhabit. I want to be the driver. Of course, the ways through many of my challenges and choices have not been consciously self-directed—learning to walk, discovering the pronoun "I," getting into different kinds of trouble, teen love, and so on into adulthood—but gradually one learns to drive instead of being driven. Over time, in obvious and subtle ways, one can become the driver without being diverted by impulses from within and distractions from without. Reflecting on this, it occurs to me that nothing is more closely aligned with the process of becoming fully human[1] than self-mastery or inner freedom.

Sometimes the opportunity to act freely fleets away almost as soon as you notice it. Especially in any challenging situation, between the stimulus and one's response exists a space. In that space—often overlooked—exists the opportunity to choose one's attitude and frame one's response. Therein lies the opportunity to grow freedom.[2]

I devote a whole chapter to freedom and place it here in the book because nothing is more important for coming to understand what we are capable of as individuals and as communities than grasping its deeper meaning. The word *freedom* gets used and abused a great deal, but I believe at a deeper level it is a core value humans seek to evolve toward. If that is so, it is key to understanding human evolution, so much so that it can serve as a cornerstone objective for a future civilization. Both in a personal sense of inner self-command, and in a social sense of a society that allows democracy to operate effectively, a focus on freedom can help readers keep in mind the intangibles that give meaning and purpose to a civilization. This will be particularly true as the planet enters a period of extreme duress.

It makes a difference whether people opt for freedom *from* (negative freedom) or freedom *for* (positive freedom). This distinction, developed by Timothy Snyder in his book *On Freedom*, allows people to steer away from thinking of freedom as the absence of barriers and instead focus on what freedom makes possible.[3] People Snyder spoke with in Ukraine during the Russian invasion told him that repelling the Russians was "a necessary condition for freedom not the thing itself."[4] This distinction may prove particularly important in coming decades if social unrest, climate catastrophe, and other disturbances call on people to clarify what they are fighting for. Without suggesting that the

---

1. For a Native American perspective on this, see Topa (Four Arrows) and Narvaez, *Restoring the Kinship Worldview*, 191–92.
2. See Frankl, *Man's Search*, 104.
3. Snyder, *On Freedom*, 277.
4. Snyder, *On Freedom*, xii.

coming developments can be predicted by straight-line projections, it is nevertheless clear enough that the future is beckoning with a message. Growing dysfunction across multiple spheres portends stormy weather, in fact, a virtual typhoon.

Otto Scharmer's *presencing* technique helps reveal what the future can tell us. In order to survive and prevail, we will need, among other things, extraordinarily capable leaders, who understand freedom as an organizing ideal. Leadership informed by intellect and intuition is crucial particularly when things are not going well and other systems of governing offer panaceas built on security and prosperity, not freedom. In order to grasp the big picture as it emerges, the floodlight of intuition will be essential, in addition to the spotlight of intellect, with its penetrating but narrow focus.

Elements of Freedom

In *The Second Mountain*, commentator David Brooks asks how one can balance inner and outer personal ambition and service to humanity. Prompted by a seismic change in his own life at about age fifty, Brooks came to realize that conventional career success built around scaling the mountain of ego and outer success is hollow. He had climbed the wrong mountain.[5] Brooks disavows his thesis in an earlier book, that building character is a regimen similar to going to the gym: address your weaknesses and get in shape. That turns out to be somewhat narcissistic. In the later book he revised his view. "Good character," he writes "is a by-product of giving yourself away."[6] The first mountain is self-centered; the second is other-centered.

His analysis applies to societies as well as to individuals. Refuting Machiavelli, Hobbs, Freud, and countless economists, Brooks argues against organizing society around the principle that people are basically selfish. "The central journey of modern life is moving from self to service,"[7] he writes. Scharmer calls it moving from Ego to Eco, and it relates to becoming capable of the deeper form of freedom explored in this chapter.

---

5. Brooks, *Second Mountain*, xvi.
6. Brooks, *Second Mountain*, xix.
7. Brooks, *Second Mountain*, 301–2, 304.

Elsewhere in the book he maintains that communities should be defined by altruism and focus on those with great needs, their treatment of the least among them. Instead, capitalism has normalized selfishness by rewarding the quest for money, status, and power. Governments can shift spending priorities but cannot cause people to care. That requires a moral commitment from leaders to awaken conscience and guide people to properly define and apply their freedom. Brooks faults the political Right for their version of freedom, which he characterizes as being unburdened by government regulations and constraints on capitalism. He faults the Left for their version of freedom, opting for a self-indulgent lifestyle, as in those who eschew relationship commitment in order to keep their options open.[8] The second mountain—scaled by those who counsel altruism and shedding self-centeredness—is the beginning of wisdom for future leaders.

Brooks indicates that self-centeredness is an obsolete notion for the civilization of the future. Civility demands we get beyond *me* to *we*. First, the forerunners or more evolved individuals, then the rest, will need to expand their circle of belonging, those about whom they care. In contrast to being fully present, open, and flexible, as Scharmer would have us be, the *me-first* person succumbs to the habit of self-centeredness. Habits, because they have a life of their own and normally manifest without conscious choice, are antithetical to freedom.[9]

As you read into this book, hold this thought. It is not a matter of whether or not freedom exists; rather, the better question to ask is, Could there be a part of me—think of it as an inner Self—that, if developed, can become free? If the answer to that is "yes" or "maybe," that constitutes an invitation to consider how development of that slumbering Self can begin.

The preparation for true inner freedom must start early—with homelife, schools, and programs that nurture the whole child to achieve a healthy balance of thinking, feeling, and will. The challenges and responsibilities of adult life offer many opportunities to continue this growth. But many choose not to. Consider this: a survey of people who were

---

8. Brooks, *Second Mountain*, 10.

9. On this point, John Dewey undermines his own advocacy of freedom because he ascribes enormous power to habits, calling them "the sole agents of . . . foresight and judgment." See Dewey, *Human Nature*, 176.

dying found their greatest regret to be a lack of courage to lead the lives they desired rather than conceding to what *others* expected of them.[10]

From the perspective of geologic time, the enterprise of human evolution can be seen as an experiment in freedom. This was true in the distant past, when robed prophets walked the earth, and will continue through the post-apocalyptic future, when remnants of our present civilization may get another chance. But bear in mind: major crisis can lead to constructive change, particularly if people are prepared.

As with any experiment, the desirable outcome is not guaranteed. Create these two-legged beings, endow them with some intelligence, agency, and the capacity for free choice, and see what they can do with it. And even after all this time, it is not possible to write the last chapter of that book.

Freedom—Inner and Outer

During World War II, Viennese psychotherapist Viktor Frankl became prisoner 119,104 in a Nazi concentration camp and was hired out as a virtual slave to a construction company laying railroad track. He was treated with contempt, fed starvation rations, and endured unspeakable conditions. Yet, as described in his book *Man's Search for Meaning*, under these most extreme circumstances he affirmed his inner freedom by staying true to his moral compass and displaying a constructive approach to these challenges. "There is only one thing that I dread," he wrote, quoting Dostoevsky, "not to be worthy of my sufferings."[11] The key to survival under these conditions, he wrote, was his conscious choice to find a higher purpose beyond self-preservation.

> We who lived in concentration camps can remember the men who walked through the huts comforting others, giving away their last piece of bread. They may have been few in number, but they offer sufficient proof that everything can be taken from a man but one thing: the last of the human freedoms—to choose one's attitude in any given set of circumstances, to choose one's own way.
>
> And there were always choices to make . . . [choices] which determined whether you would or would not submit to those

10. Björkman, "Peaceful Change."
11. Frankl, *Man's Search for Meaning*, 105.

powers which threatened to rob you of your very self, your inner freedom; which determined whether or not you would become the plaything of circumstance.

It can be said that [these generous-hearted individuals] were worthy of their sufferings; the way they bore their suffering was a genuine inner achievement. It is this spiritual freedom—which cannot be taken away—that makes life meaningful and purposeful.[12]

In more recent times, Malala Yousafzai was born in the Swat Valley of Pakistan. When the Taliban took control of the region and closed all schools for girls, her father, a poet and teacher, educated her at home. At age eleven she began to speak out for girls' right to attend school. Her first such speech was to a local press club in Peshawar. She is credited with getting the girls' schools reopened, and she was awarded a prize by the prime minister. But this visibility made her a target. One day, as she was returning home, a Taliban member boarded the bus and shot Malala through the head, neck, and shoulder. Her life in the balance, she was transported to Birmingham, England, where she was able to recover, complete secondary education, and be accepted to Oxford. On her sixteenth birthday, she addressed the United Nations. When she was seventeen years old, she became the youngest person ever to receive the Nobel Peace Prize. The most remarkable part of her story, however, was how she exercised her freedom in choosing her attitude toward the person who tried to kill her. She said "Islam teaches forgiveness." Instead of nursing anger toward her attacker or a desire for vengeance, she said of him, "He made a great mistake."[13]

We often hear of another kind of freedom, a counterfeit that amounts to *I do as I please*. People who refuse to wear masks at the height of a pandemic are indeed making a choice, but it is a choice not of self-governing, but of self-centeredness. This perspective does not move human evolution forward but rather backwards toward the barbarism of every man for himself. "So much of our lives," writes David Brooks in *The Second Mountain*, "is determined by the definition of freedom we carry around unconsciously in our heads." On the second mountain,

---

12. Frankl, *Man's Search for Meaning*, 104–8.
13. Rossi, "Malala Yousafzai."

what was unconscious can become conscious. One makes choices knowing they may require restraints and sacrifice.[14]

What is it that drives men and women to fight and even die for freedom? It is helpful to distinguish between political freedom, which involves the right to choose one's leaders and other democratic practices, and personal freedom, the ability to take command of one's own thinking, feeling, and actions, as Viktor Frankl and Malala Yousafzai did. Both are forms of self-government, the one outer and applying to a society, the other inner and involving only oneself. Both forms of freedom need to be optimized for the new civilization we seek. Since the days of ancient Greece, an understanding and cultivation of freedom as an extraordinary and distinctly human gift has defined what it means to be civilized.

In the book *For Freedom Destined*, another Austrian-born doctor, Franz E. Winkler, describes human evolution toward greater degrees of personal, inner freedom. In ancient periods, he explains, individuals had far more intuitive capacities; they were open to a direct and personal experience of the divine and of spiritual realities. Nature pulsed with meaning and intent, offering wisdom from which they could draw guidance for their lives. But this intuitive consciousness faded, to be replaced by intellectual knowing.

One can trace this evolution, for example, in the Bible. In Genesis, it is stories—of creation, the fall, Noah, and so on—that fertilize a more intuitive apprehending of how to live and behave. A more pictorial consciousness can grasp what guidance is offered. By the time we get to the Ten Commandments in Exodus, written considerably later, one sees rules and laws targeted for a different consciousness that responds to explicit instructions. This approach suited a people that had developed some intellectual faculties but still needed to be told what to do. In the New Testament, later still, Jesus enjoins people to reach into themselves, by conscious choice, and learn to appreciate the meek, the persecuted, those without the wealth and power valued by the outer world. By this point in human evolution it is possible, Winkler avers, for people to get beyond being told what to do and to make moral choices on their own.[15]

Human consciousness continues to evolve.[16] Some people move ahead faster than others, and there are times and places where human

---

14. Brooks, *Second Mountain*, 58.

15. Winkler, *Man*, 115–37.

16. Pierre Teilhard de Chardin developed the idea of evolution of consciousness from a Christian perspective. For more, refer to both Teilhard de Chardin, *Christianity*

consciousness seems to slip backwards.[17] But historically the broad arc tends toward greater and greater degrees of inner activity and toward personal freedom of the sort Frankl and Winkler describe. These two physicians of the soul largely align on this subject. They differ in that for Frankl in the Nazi camps, freedom could operate only in a limited way: he could choose how to face the hideous injustice and cruelty with a freely chosen equanimity. For Winkler, writing and practicing medicine in New York City long after the war, freedom seemingly had far greater opportunities for expression. For the human individual, "his freedom is so great that he can reshape himself either in the image of the spirit, or in the image of the beast or robot." Winkler points out the harm done when, for example, educators presume an image of the human being that sees the child as "an animal to be tamed or conditioned."[18] I would add a different and equally unhelpful reductionism, one prevalent in cognitive science and learning theory: seeing the child's mind as a computer.[19]

Cultivation of freedom begins with the individual. "Be the change you want to see in the world,"[20] says the familiar saying. The outer, political freedom and the inner, personal kind relate to each other in this way. The more a person becomes capable of inner self-government, the better citizen she or he can be in a democracy. Ralph Waldo Emerson in 1840 pondered this connection and asserted that those who rule themselves do not need rulers. "One man is a counterpoise to a city," he wrote in his essay, "Politics." He developed this idea further, with characteristic hyperbole:

> With the appearance of the wise man, the State expires. The appearance of character makes the State unnecessary. The wise man is the State. He needs no army, fort, or navy—he loves men too well.
>
> That which all things tend to educe; which freedom, cultivation, intercourse, revolutions, go to form and deliver, is character.[21]

---

and Evolution and Ockham, "Noosphere."

17. The role of social media deserves mention but would take us into a different briar patch.

18. Winkler, *Man*, 149.

19. Sachs, "Mind as Computer Metaphor."

20. Gandhi embraced this idea but did not state this quote, often attributed to him. See Jacob, "Be the Change." See also Quote Investigator, "Be the Change."

21. Emerson, "Politics," 215–16.

Of course, societies like those in Europe and America today are a long way from the withering away of the state, and Emerson was writing for a young nation still pushing out the frontier. But the essential point remains: the more individual self-government, the less outer, civil government becomes necessary. Those who clamor for smaller government with cries of "kill the beast" typically fail to see that the essential corollary is development of a more caring and responsible electorate. But how can an individual who wants to become truly self-directing achieve that goal? How can inner freedom be part of the answer to the question: What kind of person do I want to be?

The Ascent Toward Freedom

Many paths wend up this mountain. For Emerson, writing in the nineteenth century, developing a capacity for self-reliance was the way to inner freedom. Today people who are self-aware are more apt to ask, "What kind of a person do I want to become?"[22] Those who embrace self-change have plenty of options. One can stop smoking, embrace yoga, Transcendental Meditation (TM), centering prayer, the Buddhist Eightfold Path. Those with children may strive to become the best possible parents. Typically, people exercise their freedom only intermittently as when, facing a challenging situation, one says, "I choose not to be upset by this." It is as if each of us is born with a gene for using freedom in order to become our best, to grow through this lifetime in ways that make us worthy of the gift of life. The challenges destiny throws in our path help with this. But perhaps fearful of what they perceive as the awesome responsibility that comes with freedom, many people choose security and comfort instead. Particularly as people see systems breaking down, who can blame them? The problem comes when people choose comfort at the expense of deeper responsibilities.

A further threat to developing inner freedom relates to the desire for comfort but comes from another direction. Depression in America has reached epidemic proportions. It particularly affects the young. In

---

22. Though beyond the scope of this book, some psychologists have described levels of moral development and mental complexity that go beyond the basic capacity for self-governing. In *The Evolving Self*, Robert Kegan identified the additional phases of self-authoring and then self-transforming. At these levels one assumes greater responsibility, first for self-change, then for using what one has achieved to help others and the community. See Kegan, *Evolving Self*.

2023, Centers for Disease Control and Prevention reported that 30 percent of high school girls seriously considered attempting suicide. This is up 60 percent from a decade before.[23] The trend existed before but was exacerbated by COVID-19. To deal with anxiety and depression, stress and lack of hope, many girls and boys, women and men, self-medicate or turn to drugs. This is a vast topic, and I do not propose to dive into it; but it is important to note that to the extent one uses drugs for immediate relief, one risks eroding the longer-term ability to cope. The drug culture is no friend of freedom.

Looking internationally, one sees how nations respond to stress and anxiety. When civil order breaks down, or when climate disaster strikes and vast portions of land become uninhabitable, the appeal of authoritarian regimes that promise stability and survival will be hard to resist. Two great models for civilization, represented pre-eminently by China and the United States, will compete to shape and control much of the world in the future. China believes individual freedoms can be dispensed with in order to provide the greater good for the greatest number. A dictatorship can be ruthless and highly efficient in advancing its agenda. Moreover, looking at how the communist regime, embracing a controlled capitalism, has been able to lift millions out of poverty, those leaders can plausibly argue that their system is actually more compassionate than ours.

On the other side stand those who value individual freedom and the immense potential of that freedom. One can make a very strong case for letting freedom, well-understood and optimized, carry human evolution forward. But not unless people get beyond a superficial understanding of this mighty ideal, and then take up their responsibilities to make it work. As important as it is to take one's own psycho-spiritual development in hand, therein lies a trap for those who rest satisfied that working for their own well-being is enough. No one is saying this will be easy amid political turmoil and polarization, plus growing inequity and injustice, on a warming planet.

Three Lenses to See Society

To see how inner growth relates to the prospect of a better world, it is helpful to understand three key elements essential to the founding of this country, and incorporated particularly in the Declaration of

---

23. Tanner and Gecker, "CDC Data Shows."

Independence. This can also begin to address the question: What kind of evolved society would support my becoming a better person? In an unpublished manuscript called "The American Dream," a book he did not live to complete, Franz Winkler asserted that achieving the dream the founders envisioned would depend on our grasping the meaning and relationship of three key elements that were the core ideals of the French Revolution—*liberté, egalité,* and *fraternité*.[24] I paraphrase the way he characterized these elements:

1. Freedom pertains basically to the mind, which can unfold its higher potential only if free from the manacles of dogma and all forms of rigid thinking.

    However, it would be a tragic mistake to believe that freedom can start with unrestricted actions. If every individual were to do as they please, they would necessarily interfere with the freedom of others. True freedom for all can only be achieved within a framework of laws—laws which should ideally be the fruits of free thought.

2. Equality concerns one's status before the law. It demands that *everyone* receive the same kind of justice and protection. And this requires perfecting of the legal framework enough to safeguard and pursue justice.

3. Mutuality or cooperation relates to a person's love for others. An individual's greatest gift is the capacity for love, compassion, and affirming others. This is the ingredient that makes our system different.[25]

The usefulness of these three ideas reaches far beyond the shores of France. Exploration of how each aligns with a particular sphere of society will help us envision the optimal foundation for a future civilization.[26]

Society can be viewed as consisting of three components or spheres—the cultural life, the economic life, and the life of rights, laws, and politics. Culture is the sphere of ideas, including education,

24. The French *fraternité* literally translates as "brotherhood," but I prefer to use "mutuality," "community," or the Spanish *convivencia* as roughly equivalent. "Solidarity" is another possible synonym.

25. Winkler, "American Dream," 1.

26. These three elements and their distinctive demands are explored in this book as follows: *liberté* in this chapter, *fraternité* in the next chapter and its economic implications in chapter 8, *egalité* at the end of chapter 3 and in my forthcoming article, "Toward a New Kind of Constitution."

literature and the arts, religion, and pure science. The inner life of an individual or a people, including their vital thought landscape, belongs here, along with values held in common.

The economic sphere exists in a polar relationship with culture because it is more outer. This includes the world of commerce, the value and exchange of commodities. Thus a painting, insofar as it has a dollar value and can be auctioned or sold, belongs to the economic sphere. However, the same painting as art, as a thing of beauty or offering a perspective on life and culture, belongs to the cultural.

Between the cultural and economic spheres, and in a sense regulating the potential excesses of each, lies the sphere of rights, of laws achieved through a political process. Laws or regulations must be established for the economy to function and to ensure order and stability in which culture can thrive. For those who misuse their freedom and harm others, there need to be consequences, equitably applied.

The following graphic, developed by inventor David Stone, elegantly shows the main influences of the three spheres on one another in an ideal system. Bear in mind that the relationships between spheres are far more complex than this intentionally-simplified graphic shows.

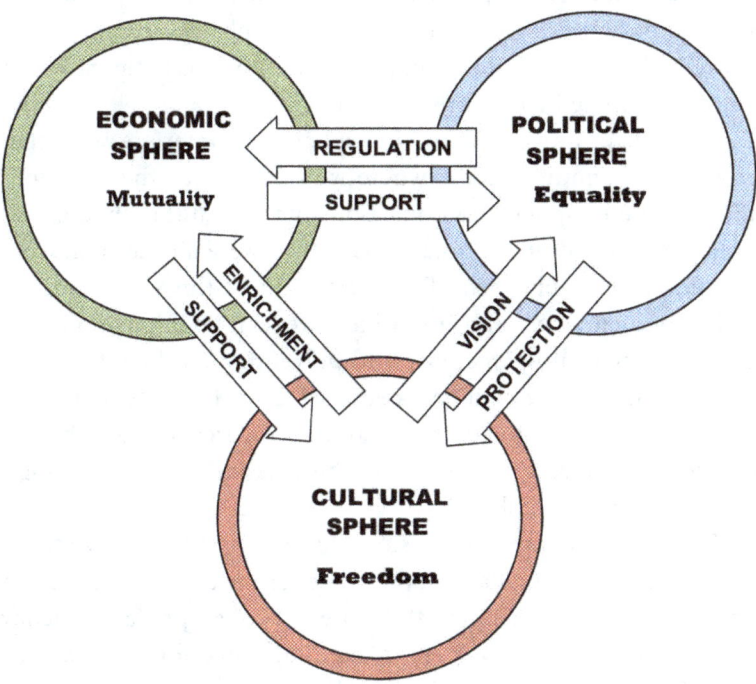

Figure 2. THREE SPHERES—DISTINCT BUT WORKING TOGETHER.
Design by David Stone, used with permission.

Each of the three spheres of society—the cultural, the economic, and the political—has an ideal that is inherently suited to it alone. Each functions best when aligned with the appropriate ideal. These ideals are the very ones Winkler names above. Thus the ideal of *freedom*, liberty, and all that relates to the ample unfolding of the individual belongs with the cultural sphere. The ideal of what Winkler, writing in the 1960s, called brotherhood and what today we can call *mutuality* or *solidarity*, implies cooperation, trust, and those qualities necessary for the production and distribution of commodities. This belongs to the economic sphere. The ideal of *equality* fits perfectly between these two and belongs with the political or rights sphere. The protections to freedom and to the ordering of commerce must be applied across the board and equitably. An understanding of the importance of how these different spheres are distinct, and how they need their independence, helps us understand how societies get into trouble, for example, when the moneyed interests of commerce and the economic sphere exert their hegemonic power over politics and the rights of citizens. The three spheres need to exist in a balanced relationship. If, for example, capitalism runs rampant, one cure would be to strengthen the other two spheres.[27]

Another example of how one sphere can interfere with the effectiveness of another occurs where we see equality, the ideal for the political sphere, applied to education in the cultural sphere. When this happens, children are treated as if they were all the same, like so many interchangeable parts. To a certain extent this exists today with standardized curricula and inflexible bureaucratic imposition of state control, extinguishing creativity and preventing teachers from taking initiatives that allow individual talents to thrive. The state should vigorously defend equal opportunity and protect the *right* of each child to an education. But having the political sphere design and run schools has led to problems, as we shall see.[28]

For purposes of this discussion, it is important to realize that this ideal of freedom is singularly appropriate for the cultural sphere. Apply it in the economic sphere, and you are apt to get predatory behavior running rampant within a "free market," unsuited for a modern complex society. Apply it in the political sphere, and you get the rights of the elite given more weight than those with less power and influence, thus undercutting equality. In the cultural area, on the other hand, freedom uncorks the energies and interests of creative individuals and fosters individual talents and undreamed-of possibilities. Think of jazz, music that combines elements of gospel, blues, calypso, ragtime, zydeco, and classical music. At its best, jazz is unpredictable and inspiring. Duke Ellington called it "the only unhampered, unhindered expression of complete freedom yet produced in this country."[29]

Thus freedom is tightly entwined with the cultural sphere in at least two ways. From the one side, freedom functions as the appropriate ideal that can enable and energize the open flow of ideas, creativity, and individual development. From another side, a vital cultural sphere can

---

27. This will be discussed in Chapter 9.

28. See chapter 5. Those wishing to pursue implications of the three spheres and the ways they affect one another may wish to read Charles Waterman's *The Three Spheres of Society*. For a contemporary discussion of threefolding see Seth Jordan's *The Whole Social* podcast (thewholesocial.substack.com/s/audio). The subject deserves a book-length treatment that far exceeds what can be provided here.

29. Quoted in Saunders, *Seed + Spark*, 189.

help ensure that freedom itself is not compromised or co-opted. The freedom ideal confers stature and purpose to its sphere, while a healthy, strong cultural sphere can safeguard freedom.

It would be a mistake to characterize the cultural sphere as the weakest of the three. It lacks the military might of government and the immense economic power of multinational corporations and the world of commerce; but in fact, ideas have tremendous power to shape history. Think of how the ideas of Marx and Engels led to the Russian Revolution, or how fascism's warped ideas fueled what became the Second World War. The ideas of Nelson Mandela, conceived in confinement on Robben Island, made possible South Africa's peaceful transition away from apartheid. We think of freedom as the United States' great idea, but it is insufficiently understood in this country.

Written in the middle of the twentieth century, when communism was expanding its reach (China and North Korea in 1949, North Vietnam in 1954) Russell Davenport's book *The Dignity of Man* grappled with how the United States could prevail against the appeal of presumed security and egalitarianism of communism. He believed that Americans were failing to prevail in the battle of ideas with communism, not because they didn't have the greater ideal of freedom but because they understood it only superficially and therefore could not communicate its power. Quoting St. John—"You shall know the truth, and the truth shall make you free" (John 8:32)—he maintained that if one meditates on this proposition, one will "begin to understand contemporary issues in a new way and gain a new sense of purpose."[30] He insisted that freedom is unattainable without truth. But how does this work?

Consider a corollary—untruth leads to unfreedom. Think about how autocrats came to power in what had been a democracy—Hitler, Urban, Erdoğan. Isn't it typically by means of false hopes, distortions, and outright lies? For a lynching to occur, any interest in truth has to be completely sidelined. Mobs have no time for that. Something else takes over, and it wants action. No one acts out of freedom. In the United States on January 6, 2021, the mob assaulting the Capitol was motivated by the lie that the 2020 election was stolen from Donald Trump. We think of insanity as something that possesses individuals. It can also happen to a group.

---

30. Davenport, *Dignity of Man*, 268.

But, as Davenport states, "The mere *search* for truth changes the whole situation." Because the search implies that truth exists, "Light is always born. And it is only in such light that we can intelligently speak of freedom." This light dispels dark passions and, I would add, the mental laziness that often leads to loss of freedom.[31]

I am reminded of a painting by Raphael in which St. George, patron saint of England, is depicted slaying with his spear a particularly reptilian dragon. St. George, in my mind, stands for integrity, courageous leadership, and truth. This is an appropriate image for truth besting snaky, slippery falsehood because a determined commitment to honesty requires courage. Often it is much easier to avoid unpleasantness or confrontation by lying instead of saying what is true and dealing with the consequences.

America's failure to prevail in the battle of ideas with Marxism can be attributed, in Davenport's view, to our lackluster efforts to develop this inner dimension of ourselves and our understanding of freedom. He hammers Americans: "Because we have failed to define or have taken for granted our ideas about man's inner nature . . . America emerges [in the world's eyes] not as a revolutionary force that has transformed an absolute capitalist system into a true economic democracy, but as a reactionary power dedicated to the pursuit of happiness in terms of the selfish acquisition and use of private property."[32]

Freedom and Individualism

Understanding freedom also requires clarity about how it connects with individualism. Feminist writer Gertrude Reif Hughes distinguishes between two types of individualism. One applies to "egomaniacal virtuosos, ruthless go-getters, rugged survivors, and prevailers," people who succeed based on the work and sacrifice of others who are often women and marginalized individuals. I would call this Individualism 1.0. Such people cannot truly be said to be free. Nor do they nurture freedom in those on whom they depend as they ascend to prominence. The behavior of the go-getters is typically coerced by their drives, temperament, or ambition. Nevertheless, when these ego-driven people are bright, talented, and charismatic, they often accomplish great things. For example, the

---

31. Davenport, *Dignity of Man*, 269.
32. Davenport, *Dignity of Man*, 121.

ruthless drive and intelligence of Jack Welch made General Electric (GE) for a time the largest corporation in the world, aptly detailed in David Gelle's book *The Man Who Broke Capitalism*.

The second type of individualism lacks egotism. Its practitioners consciously choose to act from clear thinking, truth, and a commitment to the greater good. A descriptive term for this is "ethical individualism." It corresponds to Emerson's self-reliance. I would call it Individualism 2.0. Hughes describes it as "conduct based not on obedience but love." Because it is *ethical*, it takes into account the needs and welfare of others. Thus, this concept avoids the individual versus community duality. It is social, as opposed to ego-centered individuality, which is anti-social. An active, healthy thought life and mindfulness of one's own thinking processes help make ethical individualism possible. This in turn builds the kind of freedom that was exercised by Victor Frankl, Nelson Mandela, and Franz Winkler.[33]

A way to implement this second form of individualism was brilliantly laid out by Steven Rockefeller, the moving force behind The Earth Charter.[34] He perceives American democracy as not just a political arrangement but a culture. The revitalization of that culture is captured in the title of his 2001 book *Spiritual Democracy and Our Schools: Renewing the American Spirit with Education for the Whole Child*. As we shall see later in this book, such an education lays the foundation for developing inner freedom, which in turn confers strength to a free society.[35]

---

33. Hughes, "Rudolf Steiner's Activist," 245–47. In 1979, at a time when OPEC was curtailing oil production and there was an energy crisis, President Jimmy Carter gave his "Crisis of Confidence" speech. He said,

> We are at a turning point in our history. There are two paths to choose. One is a path I've warned about tonight, the path that leads to fragmentation and self-interest. Down that road lies a mistaken idea of freedom, the right to grasp for ourselves some advantage over others. That path would be one of constant conflict between narrow interests ending in chaos and immobility. It is a certain route to failure. All the traditions of our past, all the lessons of our heritage, all the promises of our future point to another path—the path of common purpose and the restoration of American values. That path leads to true freedom for our nation and ourselves. We can take the first steps down that path as we begin to solve our energy problem.

For more, refer to the address in its entirety at Carter, "President Carter Address."

34. Learn more on the Earth Charter's website: earthcharter.org.

35. Rockefeller, *Spiritual Democracy*, 90.

These issues involving freedom often come into bright focus at the end of one's life. Parker Palmer, in *Healing the Heart of Democracy*, articulated it this way:

> I cannot imagine a spiritual pain deeper than dying with the thought that during my sojourn on earth, I had rarely, if ever, shown up as my true self. And I cannot imagine a spiritual comfort deeper than dying with the knowledge that I had spent my brief time on this planet doing the best I could to be present as myself to my family, my friends, my community, and my world.[36]

The choice to show up with your real self is freedom. It means breaking out of the prison of one's own egotism, and the other prison of knuckling under in blind obedience to external authority. It is not a destination but a process of growth. One might ask, once a degree of inner freedom has been achieved, How shall it be optimized and used? A key point to remember will be that the cultural sphere bears a great responsibility for its own integrity and authenticity, for it is from this sphere that values and formative ideas flow to and bless the other spheres, shaping not only who each of us chooses to be but the kind of relationships, laws, and institutions we found and sustain. In concluding this chapter, I offer a poem of mine that captures some of the obstacles to allowing freedom to manifest:

A Beginning

In the gentle beginning in the mind of God
from a single thread of melody and then
a texture soft as merino wool
spins an idea: create a planet
different from the others—
temperate, endowed, burgeoning—
to support new beings, split off from the hierarchies
and given, ultimately, the freedom to ignore,
reject, even revile the creator himself.
With these blessings
you can imagine
the new beings would draw toward
the music out of which they were created.

---

36. Palmer, *Healing the Heart*, 189.

But the path to this fully formed freedom,
one even angels cannot follow,
is long and leads through
a wilderness of distractions
so perilous that
the muscle of moral choice
can't help but develop.
Expect self-created tempestuousness,
egos swelling like bladders
of foul-smelling air,
the need to show who's in charge,
the lust for lust and land,
the greed for glitter and the pronoun *my*—
to pile up like waves thrashing themselves
on beaches and rocky headlands,
their energy spent but not their substance,

until with each life less frantic
in a distant future,
after the complex rhythms of storms
have played themselves out
and echoes of the beginning
can be heard again
the melody and simple chords
and arpeggios sound—quietly
like a peaceful valley
in the sunshine.

CHAPTER THREE: WHAT DOES CONVIVENCIA MEAN?

With all things and in all things, we are relatives.
—Sioux proverb

Our goal is to create a beloved community and this will require a qualitative change in our souls as well as a quantitative change in our lives.
—Martin Luther King, Jr.

If we have no peace, it is because we have forgotten that we belong to each other.
—Mother Teresa

It's amazing how much you can accomplish with imperfect people.
—Anonymous

Sometimes a not-fully-translatable word is just the ticket. So it is with *convivencia*.[1] To translate it simply as "coexistence" or "commu-

---

1. The African term *ubuntu*, sometimes translated as "I am because we are" or "humanity towards others," similarly has no exact translation but overlaps *convivencia*.

nity" would be a vast oversimplification, practically a crime. You will see as this chapter unfolds how the term developed a special meaning in medieval Spain, of a mutually affirming living together of Muslims, Christians, and Jews. These three streams of devout but divergent citizens did more than tolerate each other. They blended their differences into a richly creative society.

Granada Circa 750 to 1492

In his book *Granada—A Pomegranate in the Hand of God*, Steven Nightingale describes this city in the south of Spain in a remarkable period leading up to 1492, when Ferdinand and Isabel chose to extend their dominion, unify and Christianize the Iberian Peninsula, and persecute Jews and Muslims. Prior to this raw exercise of power, famously known for the Inquisition, Granada enjoyed a degree of mutuality and harmony that can teach something about how a true sense of community can be achieved.

Speaking about the period when Muslim rule covered most of the Iberian Peninsula, Nightingale asserts,

> In Al-Andalus, for eight centuries, communities of Muslims, Jews, and Christians lived side by side or intermingled the one with the other. There was no precedent for so extended an experiment in the history of Europe, and it has not been equaled since, for daring, brilliance, or productivity.[2]

He credits this climate of tolerance to Islam's acceptance of Abraham and Jesus as prophets preparing the way for Muhammad, with the three religions joined in fellowship as "the people of the book."

> From 711 to 1009, the three principal religious communities of the Mediterranean settled down to live together: to learn new languages, trade, start businesses, farm, travel, intermarry, and slowly learn from one another. The project had its difficulty, conflict, animosity, and spasmodic, wretched violence. . . . But overall, during this early period, and in fact during the nearly eight hundred years of Al-Andalus, under Muslim emirs and caliphs and Christian kings, and with the assistance of an active and powerful Jewish community, three great religions of

---

2. Nightingale, *Granada*, 119.

the Mediterranean had their chance to settle down together and make a go of it.[3]

For this condition, Nightingale uses the delightful, musical-sounding word *convivencia*. It is usually translated as "coexistence."[4] But the social climate he describes was more than merely tolerating those of a different persuasion. It was an active appreciation of and engagement with the very differences which, under other circumstances led to prejudice, division, and even war. Religion and the group egotism of various sects can produce conflict. But in this instance religious impulses toward love and understanding appeared to have a unifying effect.

To explain how this was possible, the author cites Ibn 'Arabi (1165–1240), mystic, poet, philosopher, and scholar. This wise and influential man taught a principle called the "Unity of Revelation." It holds that the founders of these three religions all tapped into a core truth. It is accessible to anyone who has the interest and the capacity for it. And "we can be transformed by love that brings us into connection with the divine."[5] For centuries, there was enough of this impulse in southern Spain around Granada to promote a period of incredible flourishing—in philosophy, medicine, artistic tile work, agriculture, poetry, and other fields. As with other spiritual impulses, it had a profound effect, not only in the region but upon Sufism, that more mystical branch of Islam, which incorporates this influence and related teachings to this day. Nightingale asserts,

> The aim of this teaching is to transform the self, by means of love, so as to know a living reality present on earth in its full beauty and permanence. In such a transformation, love and knowledge come together, and a person can thereafter be of the most timely, secret, and fabulous help to others, and to life itself.[6]

In the balance of this chapter, I will be talking about three communities—Sekem in Egypt, Chautauqua in western New York State, and the Shakers, who at their peak had nineteen communities east of the Mississippi. It may be hard to see how a remote Egyptian village, an upscale retreat community, and a nearly extinct religion can inform contemporary thinking, but I am convinced that they can. I include them because each one was or is ahead of its time, and each one has things to

---

3. Nightingale, *Granada*, 120.
4. See Frankl, *Man's Search for Meaning*, 105.
5. Nightingale, *Granada*, 264.
6. Nightingale, *Granada*, 270.

teach. Each community reifies ideals that deserve consideration today, and even more as one imagines a more perfect future. Ideals—like sharing, making beauty through music, and pouring purpose into the work of one's hands—do not wear out.

Sekem Today

In what could be considered almost an echo of this remarkable *convivencia* centuries ago, an intentional farming community called Sekem exists today in Egypt. In 1977, Ibrahim Abouleish returned to his native Egypt from Austria, where he was research director for a pharma company. Standing alone at a barren spot in the desert, he experienced an epiphany and resolved to establish a farm right there in this inhospitable place. His family, friends, the Bedouin, and even government officials told him he was crazy. Not only did this place hold no potential, he was not even a farmer. Yet he exercised his freedom and went forward. He drilled a well, hired farmers, and began what became not just a farm but a community.

Sekem will be discussed in later chapters, but here is what Abouleish had to say about how communities can hold together and accomplish good things for the world:

> Ever since the first people, both Egyptian and European, came to work on the farm, I wondered how to ensure that this growing community remained a living organism with dynamic development. A beautiful saying of Goethe's expresses my highest ideals with regard to social forms of working together: "And neither time nor power can destroy forms which have been shaped and have developed in a living way." This quote reveals how the ideal community of people cannot be destroyed by any power in the world if it is willing to mature continuously and employ the necessary spiritual activity.[7]

He goes on to credit the success of this community, despite incredible obstacles and many frustrations, to a kind of partnership between those on earth and beneficent forces beyond.

> The help of the spiritual world is required to achieve a living form, which is revealed to people who are open to inspiration through their own spiritual work. Because of this there has been continuous spiritual work among the Sekem employees

---

7. Abouleish, *Sekem—A Sustainable Community*, 211.

from the start. This ongoing work radiates into all areas of our dealings and creates the solid foundation for the future development of Sekem.[8]

Chautauqua

A very different tradition gave rise to a new movement in nineteenth-century America. In 1874, at Chautauqua Lake in western New York, two men from Cleveland—a Methodist bishop and an inventor-businessman—established a summer encampment for the purpose of training Sunday school teachers. They aimed to improve the quality of instruction in various Protestant churches by exposing these teachers to Bible study, church music, teaching techniques, and other relevant knowledge. What began as a few tents pitched by the shore, has evolved into what today is a virtual spa for the mind for nine weeks in the summer. Once inside this august Chautauqua Institution, one finds an amphitheater that seats over four thousand; two symphony orchestras; schools of dance, music, and theater; courses in writing and the arts; brilliant lectures on current events and religion; restaurants and a grand old hotel; along with various recreational facilities. The village is laid out for walking, not for cars. A climate of goodwill and congeniality prevails. Prompted by the quality of the speakers at the daily lectures, there is an openness to new ideas that is not present in society at large. That has been my experience, having attended Chautauqua over the years.

A unifying force is the outreach of the Chautauqua's Department of Religion, headed until recently by retired Episcopal bishop Gene Robinson. His predecessor initiated The Abrahamic Initiative, a conscious effort to build interfaith understanding among Jews, Christians, and Muslims. In addition to helping Christians relate to their faith in deeper ways, the department offers lectures and workshops to correct misunderstandings of mainstream Islam and promote an appreciation of common elements of these three religious streams that trace back to Abraham.

The different denominations have houses that provide lower-cost lodging for their congregants than the many rental units and inns. There is a kind of playful competition between them. At the Lutheran House, they serve only Lutheran punch at their weekly social hour, and claim they have the best cookies. A deep strain of goodwill and mutuality exists

---

8. Abouleish, *Sekem—A Sustainable Community*, 211.

among Catholic, Protestant, and Jewish groups, all of which have their houses. While Muslims are encouraged to attend, there is not yet a critical mass for them to have their own building.

It could be argued that Chautauqua is a privileged, gated community, that the cost of attending is out of reach for many, that it exists only as a vacation destination for nine weeks of favorable weather. But seeing Chautauqua as an artificial hothouse of harmony for the affluent misses the point. Rather, we need to ask what can be learned from this successful but admittedly limited experiment in community-building.

1. A spirit of *convivencia* prevails at Chautauqua. As with Granada in its golden age, a religion-inspired milieu that goes beyond toleration to mutual affirmation seems to have something to do with this.

2. Also mirroring Granada, the arts play an important role here. In music alone there is chamber music with its own building, an opera workshop, a full symphony orchestra, and a second orchestra comprised of students from Chautauqua's summer school of music. In concerts, lectures, and galleries, at Chautauqua and the world at large, one can see that, take people to a space beyond argumentation, where one perceives with a fresh perspective, and they may come to appreciate what is moving and beautiful. Art has even been known to puncture the shell of dogmatic religion.[9]

3. Because it is a vacation venue, Chautauqua affords time for people to live in a non-competitive, more relaxed, and inquisitive mental climate that pushes out the frontiers of understanding. I believe there is no reason why, with determined effort, some of this climate could not be cultivated to enrich life, even after returning to work.

4. From the first day of its founding, Chautauqua has been dedicated to self-improvement, initially to be a better Sunday school teacher, and today to become more informed or a more complete, aware person, a global citizen. Self-change can be undertaken at any age.

5. Perhaps the most important factor: Chautauqua is a community built on ideals. The current mission statement reads:

> Chautauqua is dedicated to the exploration of the best in human values and the enrichment of life through a program that explores the important religious, social, and political issues of our times; stimulates provocative, thoughtful involvement of

---

9. See Francis, *When Art Disrupts Religion*.

individuals and families in creative response to such issues; and promotes excellence and creativity in the appreciation, performance, and teaching of the arts.[10]

An ideal is usually not a destination but rather a guiding, navigational principle like the North Star. For an attorney, seeking justice would be an ideal; winning the case would be an objective. In the medieval guilds, the typical ideal was brotherhood. For a labor union, ideals could be seeking fairness and building a spirit of solidarity; while prevailing in negotiations for higher wages would be an objective. Ideals lend higher purpose, lifting people out of immediate, often self-centered, short-term gains. Ideals typically involve a *giving*; objectives, which may be worthwhile, are more apt to involve a *taking*. Ideals can be profoundly unifying, as is evident in the discussion of the Shakers that follows.

The American Shakers

Various intentional communities have existed throughout history that illustrate what principles help groups hold together or grow. The Shakers, at the peak of their membership, flourished in nineteen communities across the eastern United States. Of the many utopian experiments in the New World, this one lasted the longest, over two hundred years. What can be learned from them about building community?

Far ahead of their time, the Shakers valued all people equally, including women and people of color, opposed war as a means of settling international disputes, and established for their nineteen communities what amounted to a guaranteed income. Thus, even though they faded out due principally to their celibacy and strict rules, the end of a craft economy, and the loss of men to paid work in industry and cities, they were original thinkers in many respects.

In 1774, Ann Lee, a perceptive but illiterate blacksmith's daughter, had a vision that she and fellow believers should leave Manchester, England, for America to escape persecution and in search of religious freedom. During the next seventy-five years, their membership in the Shaker order waxed to around five thousand and waned to a total of three today. These utopians, who believed they were creating heaven on earth, earned the distrust of both colonists and loyalists during the Revolutionary War

---

10. Chautauqua Institution, "About."

CHAPTER THREE: WHAT DOES *CONVIVENCIA* MEAN?

because, as pacifists, they refused to take sides. In addition to pacifism, they believed in the following:

- Men and women are equal.
- All races are welcome.
- Slavery should be abolished.
- All property should be held in common.
- Work is a form of prayer and should be offered freely without compensation.
- God should be worshiped as both Mother and Father.
- Religious joy should be expressed through dancing and singing.
- Celibacy promotes a spirit-informed focus on the work to be done.
- Simplicity should be valued in form and function.
- Creativity and innovation breathe life into work.

Some of these values seem self-evident, particularly with respect to equality and access. Other beliefs, such as celibacy, still seem outside the pale. For our purposes, their efforts and tenets related to community building are most important.[11]

The Shakers held themselves apart from "the world's people," but did so in a kindly way, despite having been persecuted. Their communities had no poverty so that no one had to live in fear or be degraded by want. In the Shaker villages there was no crime to speak of; there were no

---

11. Wanting to make Shaker values relevant to today, the board of Canterbury Shaker Village in New Hampshire in August 2021 approved the following values for their historic site, intending that Canterbury become a place for "renewal of the human spirit." Three themes were articulated, with quotes from Shakers themselves:

- Community grounds us in basic kindness and respect for all, welcoming and celebrating divergent beliefs and traditions.

  "We make thee kindly welcome."

- Simplicity keeps us focused on what's most essential, with an overriding spirit of humility in all that we do.

  "'Tis a gift to be simple. 'Tis a gift to be free."

- Innovation guides creative problem-solving and continuous improvement in our stewardship of the Village and our services to others.

  "Do all your work as if you had a thousand years to live and as if you knew you must die tomorrow."

An excellent overview of Shaker life is Flo Morse's *The Story of the Shakers*.

jails.[12] They lived according to the teachings of the Gospels. When poor farming families near Shaker villages presented themselves as winter set in, the Shakers welcomed them to the community so long as they lived by the rules and contributed to daily work. These "Winter Shakers," as they came to be called, typically disappeared in spring and returned to their farms. When it was discovered that vegetables were being stolen by neighbors, the Shakers simply planted extra rows.

Shaker simplicity took the form of basic and unpretentious clothing, absence of ornamentation in the interior and exterior of their buildings, and a genuine humility. Some of their inventions and achievements could have given rise to intense pride, but they had rules against anything that would elevate one person at the presumed expense of another. For example, they did not sign their chairs or Shaker boxes, even though each was in a modest way a work of art. Their humility was a manifestation of their devotion. As Trappist monk Thomas Merton wrote in *Seeking Paradise: The Spirit of the Shakers*, "The peculiar grace of a Shaker chair is due to the fact that it was made by someone capable of believing that an angel might come and sit on it."[13] The heart of why their communities endured as long as they did, according to Merton, was that everything the Shakers did, from waking, through the day in work and song, until sleep, was considered opportunity to be in union with the divine.[14]

The Shakers lived in what Merton called "a cosmos of creativity and worship,"[15] and they would probably say their worship gave rise to creativity. In any case, they were responsible for some remarkable inventions—the clothes pin, the flat broom, seeds in packets, an industrial washing machine, and other things. The worship part of the "cosmos" Merton speaks of was in part an expression of the Protestant revival called the Second Great Awakening (1790 to 1840). The religious fervor of the time is captured in the Shakers' official name, The Society of Believers in Christ's Second Appearing.

Despite their communal way of life, their celibacy, and their millennial beliefs, the Shakers' earnest embrace of Christian principles offered an alternative to American values based on individualism, materialism, and competition. Their communal way of life and concern for one another held enough appeal for them to establish communities from Maine

12. Morse, *Shakers*, xx.
13. Merton, *Seeking Paradise*, 81.
14. Merton, *Seeking Paradise*, 85.
15. Merton, *Seeking Paradise*, 44.

CHAPTER THREE: WHAT DOES *CONVIVENCIA* MEAN? 47

and to as far west as Indiana. Their demise has been attributed to two causes: the shift from an agrarian and craft economy to an industrial one, and their insistence on celibacy so that over time they died out.

What can we learn from the Shakers about achieving *convivencia*?[16]

- The glue that held them together was shared, life-affirming, spiritual purpose.
- This glue created a climate of equity and freedom from racial and gender discrimination.
- In ways not really understood, their beliefs and way of life seemed to engender creativity.
- There are alternatives to work-for-money.

Shakers would have been familiar with "My yoke is easy, and my burden is light" from the Bible (Matt 11:30 KJV). The focus and rhythm of their days conveyed the message that when work is shared, and when it is deemed part of a higher goal, even menial tasks are not a burden.

---

16. For another perspective on what can be learned from the Shakers, a friend asked Google's AI application, BARD, this question: "What can the lives and lessons of a Shaker community . . . teach students today?" This was the answer from BARD:

"The lives and lessons of a Shaker community can teach students today a lot of things, such as:

- **The importance of community.** Shaker communities were based on the idea of communal living, where everyone worked. Together for the common good. This can teach students the importance of community and cooperation.
- **The importance of equality.** Shaker communities were also based on the idea of equality where everyone was treated equally, regardless of gender, race, or social class. This can teach students the importance of equality and respect for all people.
- **The importance of simplicity.** Shakers lived a simple life, focused on their faith and their work. This can teach the importance of simplicity and living a life that is free from materialism.
- **The importance of sustainability.** Shakers were very conscious of the environment and how they could live sustainably. This can teach students the importance of sustainability and living in harmony with nature.
- **The importance of creativity.** Shakers were very creative people, and they expressed their creativity in their art, music, and furniture. This can teach students the importance of creativity and using their imaginations."

A Sense of Belonging

Individuals in all three communal experiments described in this chapter shared a *sense of belonging* to their communities. This sense can grow like a plant. Two people in a strong and mature marriage share a mutual belonging that provides not only a warming glow but an abiding foundation for the relationship. Is it unrealistic to imagine that an analogous sense of belonging could be actively cultivated that would extend out to others so that concentric circles of belonging could ripple out into the world? In *The Nordic Secret*, their book that describes the sweeping impact of the Danish Folk Schools, Andersen and Björkman describe how these schools were able to expand students' circle of concern so that they felt more attachment to community and then to nation. A diagram of what they call "circles of solidarity" consists of concentric circles with Ego at the center, followed by Family, In-group, Nation, Culture Zone, Humanity, and Planet.[17] Singing together, hearing stories, and learning folklore from their own traditions helped feed the sense of belonging so it could grow.

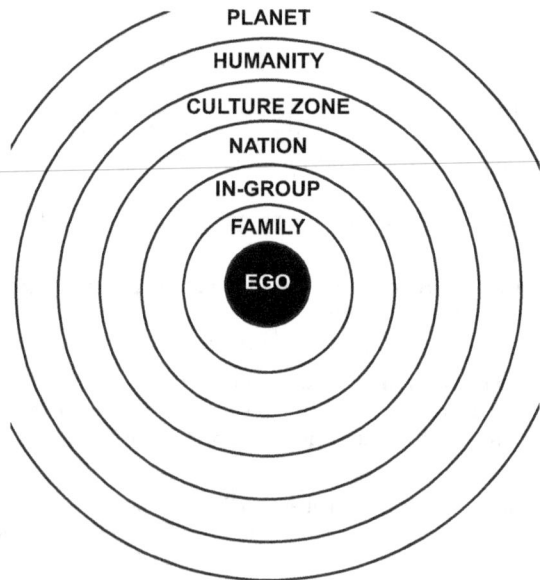

Figure 3. CIRCLES OF BELONGING. Used by permission of Christian Welzel; enhanced by David Stone.

17. See Andersen and Björkman, *Nordic Secret*, 38. The authors credit lectures by Christian Weizel for the Circles of Solidarity concept.

CHAPTER THREE: WHAT DOES *CONVIVENCIA* MEAN?

Today, some feel an intense loneliness, a manifestation of not belonging anywhere. Why do bored or troubled teens join gangs? At least in part because they are seeking a sense of solidarity. I know because at that age I was just such a person—alienated, seeking challenge and adventure, and getting into trouble with a gang. That raises another consideration. The motive that drives belonging greatly influences how it manifests. Belonging that has the motive of love behind it will bring a healing force to the earth. Unwholesome motives bring the opposite. One sees this in countries like Afghanistan where tribalism prevails, making them almost ungovernable. One also sees it in US hate groups like the Proud Boys or in drug gangs. Tribalism, as well as toxic nationalism, are really egotism but of the group.

With a sense of belonging comes a sense of responsibility. Thus, from being responsible just for oneself, one can consciously expand with circles that move toward the ideas of "I am my brother's keeper" or "We are each other's harvest." This in turn can become a sense of responsibility for one's country and eventually even abstract values like human rights.

What made the community of Granada work so well is that Muslims, Christians, and Jews felt they belonged together and carried a shared responsibility for their community. At Chautauqua, although widely divergent belief systems dwell in the same space, denominations and religions known to have persecuted and killed each other in different settings, pull together, united in the affirmation of ideas and the process of sharing that makes for a better world. Even the Shakers, some of whose beliefs seem strange by today's standards, shared a sense of belonging, not only to their own communities but also to an immense and largely unfathomable world beyond.

Many Indigenous people, who are still immersed in their own culture, have a beautiful way of expressing this when they speak of their "relations."

> I have been considering the phrase "all my relations" for some time now. It's hugely important. It's our saving grace.... It points to truth that we are all related, that we are all connected, that we all belong to each other. The important word is "all." Not just those who look like me, sing like me, dance like me, speak like me, pray like me or behave like me. That means every person, just as it means every rock, mineral, blade of grass, and creature. We live because everything else does. If we were to choose

collectively to live that teaching, the energy of our change of consciousness would heal each of us—and the planet.[18]

By strengthening each individual's capacity for sharing and caring, and by extending that through relatedness and responsibility, all can grow. And at the same time, finding common denominators that give meaning and purpose to life can build sustainable communities. But when motivated by *giving* rather than *taking*, belonging can be the glue that holds individuals together and creates a Beloved Community. Therein lies solidarity and sustainability.[19]

The sense of belonging that accompanies and prompts altruism can be found not just in isolated communities but among ordinary folks living in cities and towns when disaster strikes. *A Paradise Built in Hell*, by Rebecca Solnit, explores how a higher expression of our human nature can arise when catastrophe knocks the blocks out from under everything one normally expects from government, commerce, and infrastructure. Citing the 1906 San Francisco earthquake, 9/11, Hurricane Katrina in New Orleans, and other major crises, Solnit quotes "disaster sociologists" who assert that pro-social responses outweigh looters and antisocial responses.

> The history of disaster demonstrates that most of us are social animals, hungry for connection, as well as for purpose and meaning. It also suggests that if this is who we are, then everyday life in most places is a disaster that disruptions sometimes give us a chance to change. They are a crack in the walls that ordinarily hem us in, and what floods in can be enormously destructive—or creative. Hierarchies and institutions are inadequate to these circumstances; they are often what fails in such crises. Civil society is what succeeds, not only in an emotional demonstration of altruism and mutual aid but also in a practical mustering of creativity and resources to meet the challenges. . . . Power devolves to the people on the ground.
>
> Two things matter most about these ephemeral moments. First they demonstrate what is possible or, perhaps more accurately, latent: the resilience and generosity of those around us and their ability to improvise another kind of society. Second, they demonstrate how deeply most of us desire connection, participation, altruism, and purposefulness. . . . After the psychiatrist

---

18. Wagamese, *Embers*, 36.

19. Jeremy Lent's *The Web of Meaning* very thoughtfully illuminates paths to finding meaning and purpose, with an emphasis on the Tao and Oriental wisdom.

Viktor Frankl survived Auschwitz, he concluded that retaining a sense of meaning and purpose was in many cases decisive in who survived and who did not.[20]

The urgency of other people's need in a disaster can pry us out of our self-centeredness and bring to the fore our inner altruism. It cannot be bottled for future use, but we can choose to make it a part of who we are in our daily lives. This will count all the more if, as has been predicted, the world enters a period of cascading catastrophes.[21]

Inequality

One other factor deserves mention in any discussion of how a sense of community can be strengthened or undermined. Two English researchers, Richard Wilkinson and Kate Pickett, in their book *The Spirit Level*, make a strong case that inequality not only weakens prospects for building community, it also significantly bears on a range of social and health ills including crime, suicide, mental health, obesity, teen pregnancy, ability to learn in school, diabetes, and other health concerns. Their exhaustive research shows remarkable correlations between the prevalence of these ills on the one hand, and the degree of inequality in various countries on the other.

Thus, in countries like Japan, Norway, Sweden, and Finland that lie on the more equal end of a continuum, one finds few of the social and health malfunctions. At the other end of the continuum, where the United States, Britain, and Portugal have the greatest inequality of countries studied, these problems are many times more prevalent. And the problems are not confined to the poor; they affect all levels of society. The order of magnitude of the differences is startling. For example, the incidence of mental illness is five times more prevalent in unequal countries over more equal ones. The same pattern pertains not only with nations but with states. The relentless drive for profit maximization they see as a key factor in driving inequality.[22]

---

20. Solnit, *Paradise Built in Hell*, 305–6.

21. Another factor may be relevant—gratitude. In a situation where others have lost their homes or their lives and we are still standing, we may find deep gratitude in the mix of strong emotions. Gratitude is healing.

22. Wilkinson and Pickett, *Spirit Level*, 61, 262.

The inequality problem needs to be addressed, they suggest, both with top-down strategies like taxing the rich, and with bottom-up equalizing efforts like health insurance for all.[23] The question they chose not to take up adequately is; Does a common factor exist that creates both inequity *and* all or most of the social ills they study? I suspect that another whole book could be written exploring the psychological, spiritual, and moral factors that contribute to what the Shakers would call the worship of Mammon. A Buddhist meditator might call this an inability to find one's center, and a modern holistic psychologist might deem it a set of amorphous personal values and a failure to care. Whatever the terminology, I believe a deeper look at causation of both inequality and social ills is warranted.

It may be helpful to remember that human evolution is anything but a straight-line ascent. A civilization thrusts forward for a time, as in Granada, and falls back, as with the Inquisition. Human creativity seems to wing upward for a period, as in the Enlightenment, then falls to Earth. Taking the long view provides reason for hope.[24] The divine right of kings eventually gives way to other forms of governing. Chattel slavery gets set aside. Institutionalized racism is pushed back by a successful civil rights movement. Today the rights of nature surface as an issue.[25] The struggles continue, but over the long term the trend line is positive.

---

23. Wilkinson and Pickett, *Spirit Level*, 254.

24. Eisler, "Caring for People," 71–79.

25. Cutting-edge Rights of Nature work is being done by the Center for Environmental and Democratic Rights. Learn more on their website at centerforenvironmentalrights.org.

CHAPTER FOUR: **LOVE ONE ANOTHER**

Love is the most powerful and still most unknown energy in the world.
—Pierre Teilhard de Chardin

First we must fall in love. Then we can make the world over.
—N. F. S. Grundtvig

Anything will give up its secrets if you love it enough.
—George Washington Carver

To love a person is to see them as God intended them to be.
—Fyodor Dostoevsky

A TRUE STORY: IN a college baseball game, a player hits a ball out of the park for a clear home run. However, as she rounds first base, she twists her knee so badly she cannot stand up. The umpire will not score this as a run because she has not rounded the bases. Two players of the opposing team pick her up and carry her past second, third, and home, so her run can be counted.[1]

1. Retif, "Integration of Sport."

If one thinks of a continuum, with love and empathy on one end and thoroughgoing self-centeredness on the other, this clearly belongs on the loving end. The young women of the opposing team—the carriers—probably didn't think of it in those terms at the time. They likely acted without thinking at all; they just quickly decided to do the right and generous thing. Has anything like this dynamic ever existed, not as a one-off event in sport but in a whole society?

In those centuries when Muslims prevailed in the Iberian Peninsula and Muslims, Christians, and Jews for the most part affirmed and supported one another, the spirit of *convivencia* existed. One could say that at least empathy prevailed, perhaps even universal human love. Of the four types of human love identified by the ancient Greeks, in Granada *philia* was evident. This is often translated as "friendship" or brotherly love, as in the name William Penn chose for Philadelphia, the city of brotherly love. Its opposite is *phobia*.[2]

The overlapping but not synonymous concept of empathy also has a range of expressions and permutations. At the risk of causing confusion, I include it in this chapter because both love and empathy are what psychologists call pro-social. For the time they are active, they move the parties closer in a constructive relationship. You have probably heard the story of the opposing Allied and Axis troops who, on Christmas Eve 1914, climbed out of their trenches, sang carols together, shared cigarettes, and fraternized for a time before returning to their posts to resume battling each other the next day.[3] In this remarkable, if temporary, coming together there was empathy, I would say, but not love. To give another example, I can have empathy for cows locked in a barn their whole lifetime and treated as if they were milk-producing machines without holding any affection for an individual animal or the herd. Empathy serves as a precondition for love.

When formulating what elements hold the greatest promise for allowing a newly conceived civilization to work, one must at least try to see how the mighty powers of love and empathy can open the eyes to new possibilities. The updraft from these mysterious powers also counters the egotism that so often pulls individuals, families, communities, and nations down and apart. Aren't we in a race to evolve our consciousness

---

2. Greeks identified the other types of love as the following: *eros*, love of a sexual nature; *storge*, familial love, especially of parents for children; and *agape*, divine or selfless love.

3. Rifkin, *Empathic Civilization*, 5.

and capacity for empathy before it is too late? More broadly speaking, can our moral development catch up with AI and other complex technical achievements that humanity has achieved? For me, if love and extending empathy can pour healing, creative forces into the world, then could an abundance of them inform a new civilization?

How far can communities of various sizes move in that direction?[4]

Love through Different Lenses

Turning to the Shakers again, these earnest people have been ridiculed for their celibacy. But given their belief structure, this sacrifice can be seen as an extraordinarily loving thing to do. For they believed that the world would soon end and that the passion and energy that went into bearing and raising children would better be directed toward serving the greater good, perfecting themselves, and preparing for the life to come. No matter how quirky their beliefs seem from a twenty-first-century perspective, one can see in those Shaker boxes, chairs, and buildings what love looks like when translated into enduring work of the hands. There was a deep intentionality in the way they integrated their values, beliefs, and work, captured in their motto—"Hands to work and hearts to God."

> [Job Bishop, one of two leaders of the Canterbury, New Hampshire Shaker village] believed that every aspect of life must be mindful and consistent with the teachings of Mother Ann and the Shaker leadership—as Brother Josiah Edgerly learned one Saturday after a four-mile trip to buy grain for the village. He had found himself a few cents short and pledged to return on Monday with what he owed. When Bishop learned of this, he sent Edgerly back to repay the debt immediately. He believed that men should owe nothing to each other but love.[5]

A kernel thought that helps one understand love and its role in shaping how people come together begins with the smallest possible universe—two people in love. This thought holds that *the most enduring love comes, not when a couple stares into one another's eyes but when they look together toward a shared ideal.* Romantic love, beautiful and nourishing, can inspire

---

4. Robert Kagan's *The Jungle Grows Back* provides a glimpse of the post–World War II period in which the goodwill manifest in the Marshall Plan and American foreign relations transformed Germany and Japan into peace-loving and prosperous global citizens.

5. Travis, *In Union*, 11.

great art, self-change, and the most intense feeling of being alive. But it is both a giving and a taking. When two pursue a shared ideal together, shifting the energy more toward giving, it provides a capacity to endure that relationships need. When the going gets tough in a marriage or partnership, as it inevitably will, that is when you want a commitment to a purpose beyond yourself. In a traditional family, parents are apt to be held together by love for their children. A shared ideal serves as a kind of glue, whether it involves preserving a beloved part of nature, saving neglected and abused animals, fighting for a political cause, commitment to one's spiritual or religious life, or pursuing sobriety through A.A.

Another cluster of ideals can form around justice. Cornel West repeatedly remarks, "Justice is what love looks like in public." For some people, helping others is a driving force, as in a civil rights struggle like Black Lives Matter. For others it could be correcting economic inequality that has gone so far that it becomes a matter of injustice. The possibilities are endless. The ideal may be all-consuming or just have a marginal influence on one's life. Of course, many people have no ideals whatsoever. The point is that where some ideal exists, not only with couples but with family groups and even larger ones, this can be the glue that holds people together because a shared ideal transcends anger and other centrifugal forces. It gets individuals beyond their personal self-interest, gives direction to their existence and strength to their lives together.

What is an ideal? Think of it as the North Star—a reference point that provides direction. It confers the power of aspiration, moral commitment, and hope. As Václav Havel reportedly said, "Hope is not the conviction that something will turn out well, but the certainty that something is worth doing, no matter how it turns out." That kind of certainty bespeaks an ideal, whether it originates in the Buddhist tradition of universal compassion, or the Christian one of *not I but Christ in me* (Gal 2:20), or other fundamental precepts. Even though not necessarily something one expects to achieve, an ideal provides inestimable value in aligning one's striving to higher purpose.

An ideal can provide direction for an individual, a relationship, or a society. Hitched to a consciously formulated *intention* it can help one power through to an ambitious goal. A favorite quote often attributed to Goethe states, "The moment one definitely commits oneself, then Providence moves too. Whatever you think you can do, or believe you can do, begin it. Action has magic, power, and grace."[6] I interpret this to mean that the act of forming an intention brings with it forces to help reify that intention. In order for love to thrive, either in a personal relationship or in society, a formed commitment or intention can turn ideals into deeds. Love wants to be more than a noun; think of it as a verb.[7]

Love and Egotism on a Continuum

The forces that pull people apart and polarize groups and parties manifest not only on a small scale, as in marriages, but on a much larger one, as when nations go to war. One can think of a scale or continuum with self-interested forces and egotism on one end, and love, empathy, and concern for others in common purpose on the other. History is replete with examples of civilizations regressing to self-centeredness and finally narcissism. Much of what happens in commercial transactions, labor negotiations, and foreign affairs involves moving groups or individuals far enough along the scale toward common purpose so that harmony can be restored and normal work and rhythms of the day can proceed. But complex forces often break people apart so that no reconciliation is possible. This can happen with individuals when self-centeredness or sub-clinical mental illness locks them in their own world. This can happen within a whole group or tribe. I call it group egotism. Or it can manifest on a still larger scale, for what is jingoistic nationalism if not egotism of the group or nation?

An example of what can happen to a country under the influence of a profoundly egotistical and unloving leader was already apparent in Donald Trump's first term. In foreign relations he unapologetically advanced an agenda of "America First," much to the distress of allies and our own corps of professional diplomats. But burnishing his own image and advancing his interests lay at the top of his agenda. His willingness to put himself ahead of the interests of others and the country became starkly apparent time and again. Thus, according to Carol Leonnig and Phillip

---

6. The actual author was Scottish explorer W. H. Murray. See Wikiquote, "W. H. Murray."

7. Psychologists Justine and Michael Thomas refer to "the genius of intention," and describe other elements of how it works. "When you are clear about your intention and at peace with yourself, aligned and moving with purpose in your work, then magic happens. People appear, affinity projects emerge, and support from unimagined quarters suddenly manifests." See Macy, *World as Lover*, 241.

Rucker, who wrote *Only I Can Fix It* about Trump's final year in office, the president's only regret about the year 2020 was not that so many lives were lost due to the bungled response to COVID-19, but rather that he didn't call out federal troops to put down Black Lives Matter protests in Portland, Oregon, and other cities. A show of force served his need to appear strong, which also explained his refusal to wear a COVID mask. Aides confided that he felt it would make him look weak.

Interviewed on CNBC, these authors responded to the question "What was the principle that drove Donald Trump?" as follows: "It's really simple. The principle was . . . how do I better my political fortunes? . . . How do I look better for Nov. 3, for the election? And he set aside the other concerns."[8] Unfortunately, Donald Trump was not only a regressive leader, he was also a *symptom* of a strong tendency in the country—looking out for number one.

Beside the continuum that has egoism on one end of the scale and concern for others at the opposite end, there is another. This one has fear at one pole and love at the other. In her book *Who Do We Choose to Be?*, Margaret Wheatley views our present civilization as reaching the last of the six stages of growth and decay. A key ingredient of this cycle is a progression from fearlessness to fearfulness as civilizations become more established, comfortable, and soft. Drawing on the work of John Glubb, Wheatley outlines the six stages as follows:

1. **The Age of Pioneers.** Fearless, courageous and without restraint, invaders surprise the dominant civilization . . . shared purpose, honor, and a strict moral code bind them.

2. **The Age of Conquest.** More disciplined military interests take control. Often . . . a strong religious imperative [drives] their conquest.

3. **The Age of Commerce.** With strong military protection . . . explorers embark in search of wealth creation. The rich build palaces.

4. **The Age of Affluence.** Service ethics disappear. The young and ambitious seek wealth, not honor or service.

5. **The Age of Intellect.** Arts and knowledge flourish in the midst of decline. Incessant talking substitutes for action. Internal factions seek to destroy one another.

---

8. Phil Rucker, interviewed on CBS *Face the Nation* on July 25, 2021 (see Leonnig and Rucker, "Transcript").

6. **The Age of Decadence.** Narcissism, consumerism . . . high levels of frivolity. A celebrity culture worships athletes, actors, and singers.[9]

Wheatley describes American civilization today as one in a pattern of collapse that involves both moral decay of individuals and "institutional rot":

> Increasing disorder is fueled by money replacing service as the core motivator, hierarchical leaders focused on maintaining power at all costs, the disappearance of the future from decision-making, the preservation of the status quo by the few elites who prosper from it. As things deteriorate, relationships disintegrate into distrust, self-protection, and opposition. Internal conflicts increase, and no one even notices threats to the whole as they fight for their tiny piece of the pie. *Leaders use fear to control and manipulate people,* and everyone moves into self-protection. Distractions, entertainments, and entitlements become primary instruments of allaying people's fears and for controlling them.[10]

Of course, fear can be seen as a form of self-centeredness, but there is enough difference to place it on its own continuum.

Wheatley's pessimistic view of modern-day civilization warrants a closer look. It would be hard to argue that the country is not in a period of moral decay. The appalling frequency of mass shootings;[11] the consumption of pornography (now a $12 billion per year industry in the United States alone);[12] and the epidemic of loneliness identified by the surgeon general as a major health risk[13] confirm the story. Even if one regards this decline as a kind of sickness, together with the hedonism, violence, and drugs saturating much popular culture, appetites in the developed world for constant overconsumption, and its impact on the environment—these trends clearly constitute a decadence of startling proportions.

Wheatley's assessment highlights historical patterns and warns us of weaknesses that have the potential to destroy so much that has been accomplished. But as in nature, so with civilizations; there are cycles of death and decay, followed by new life and rebirth. Moreover, one can already detect the seeds of new life today. These are pregnant ideas,

---

9. Wheatley, *Who Do We Choose*, 35.
10. Wheatley, *Who Do We Choose*, 54 (emphasis added).
11. Zaiets et al., "Mass killing database."
12. Fight the New Drug, "20 Must-Know Stats."
13. Murthy, *Our Epidemic of Loneliness.*

inspiring people, promising young leaders, and what Otto Scharmer calls "islands of coherence."[14] These can be initial building blocks for a new civilization.

Can Love-Force Redirect a Civilization?

In addition to the descending line Wheatley traces, there is an ascending line in the contributions of leading individuals and thinkers in our time. These people, few in number, take the measure of our challenges, but also identify our strengths and offer ideas and initiatives that can actually move human evolution forward. Individuals worthy of mention, living and dead, could include Representative John Lewis, activists and writers Bill McKibben and Naomi Klein, poets Wendell Berry and Mary Oliver, educators Deborah Meier and Parker Palmer, scientists Carl Safina and Jane Goodall, spiritual leaders Joanna Macy and Joan Brown Campbell. Organizations associated with some of these names have attracted many individuals who seek to advance goals and ideas of these thought leaders. And most of us know individuals, some who earn their living with their hands, who possess a deep goodness or a certain wisdom that shows in their parenting and their dedicated lives. These people restore one's faith in humanity. They take a concern for others and make it real in the world. This is the kind of love a civilization needs, and it can be tremendously powerful, even if only a minority, an articulate minority, demonstrates this love by example.

How might the capacity to love be cultivated so that it is not just the gift of a few individuals but is part of the culture? And is there a kind of love that can hold a community, and by extension a new civilization, together?

There have been turning points in history when the sense of self held by the general population undergoes a major shift. Joanna Macy coined a term for this: "The Great Turning." She describes what is going on right now as "a reawakening, at last, to our interdependence and mutual belonging." At certain moments in history, "this recognition ['of our essential non-separateness'] breaks through on a more collective level. This is happening now in ways that converge to bring into question the very foundation and direction of civilization."[15] The redirecting of civi-

---

14. Scharmer, "2023 in Eight Points," sec. 8.
15. Macy, *World as Lover*, 188.

lization's development can be effected, according to Buddhist tradition, by the Shambala warriors. These are more mature individuals who, imbued with moral and physical courage, go to the heart of barbarism as it exists in the minds of leading figures in the society, and *change minds*. They operate largely unrecognized and unheralded. Their weapons are compassion and insight, applied with patience and persistence.[16] Macy herself, I believe, modeled this behavior. When asked why she worked so hard with talks and workshops to awaken people to the opportunities inherent in The Great Turning, she replied, "I'm doing it so that when things fall apart, we will not turn on each other."[17]

This deeply caring statement points to an important fact about love. People typically think of love and hate as polar opposites. But in my experience, there is another, parallel truth, which is that what most powerfully undermines love, also empathy, and what often gives rise to hate, is fear. In the post-Reconstruction South, for example, what produced extreme racism and lynching was fear that white control, order, and ultimately safety, was threatened by perceived power or lawlessness exercised by former slaves against the master class. Driven by this fear, relatively minor incidents could erupt into violence and lawlessness. At the same time, fear was used by the KKK to keep people of color "in their place."

An example of how the love-force Macy talks about can manifest occurred in Denmark in the middle of the nineteenth century when a small circle of thoughtful and leading individuals in Copenhagen decided that their country's population—overwhelmingly poor, uneducated, and superstitious peasants—deserved a chance for a completely new form of education. Under the influence of German Romanticism, which had advanced a faith in the potential of the common man, and of Johan Pestalozzi, the Swiss education reformer, this circle was able to spark a series of initiatives that led to the famous Danish Folk Schools. These schools are credited with so changing the sense of self in the prevailingly agricultural population, of firing up their individual and cultural identity, and of stirring up a social conscience, that they paved the way for democracy in Denmark and subsequently all of Scandinavia. The Folk Schools will be taken up in Chapter 5 on education, but they also belong here in this chapter on love as well, because they were a positive civilization-shaping force. Were the motives of the intellectuals

---

16. Macy, *World as Lover*, 210–11.
17. Macy, *World as Lover*, 213.

who sparked these changes 100 percent pure? We don't know, but there was enough genuine caring for others to enable the changes to take root and provoke dramatic and lasting improvement.

This bit of history also illuminates a relationship between love and equality. I like to imagine love as an engine pulling a train, the cars of which include equality and also justice. One key factor that led to the creation of Folk Schools was the recognition of the gulf between haves and have-nots. The grinding inequality of the time trapped the working poor in perpetual penury. If love is, among other things, a heartfelt concern for others, then its application must mean that those with the power to do so will try to relieve others' precarity.

Start with Children

The capacity for love and empathy are best built very early, even before a child goes to school. A perceptive Montessori teacher of young children, Priscilla Jeliffe, asserts that empathy is a skill, and it can be taught, even to very young children:

> Arguably one of the most important skills humans have, empathy is important for building relationships between individuals and groups, cultures and countries. Empathy is the ability to imagine how someone else is feeling in a particular situation and responding to that person with care and concern.

Jeliffe names several ingredients that can foster this skill:

- Most kids are drawn to animals, and animal stories and especially having a pet can teach empathy and responsibility. This can begin even before kids are verbal because they imitate adult behavior. As they learn to be gentle with an animal, they can also be growing their expressing and receiving language skills.[18]
- Naming feelings and acknowledging that you (as the adult) have similar feelings, helps children feel a sense of belonging and connection.... This connection is the beginning of empathy.
- After naming the feeling, it is important to help children know how to handle some feelings. For example, when a child is sad and hurt by the actions of a friend, they do not know how to behave,

---

18. Human relationships with animals can teach much. See Dungy, "Sanctuary."

and they can easily turn their feeling into anger (adults do this too!). By coaching the child, using a peace table where we model conflict resolution, we help children identify how they feel. As the children talk, the teacher can model how to communicate—both talking and listening.

- When talking with children about feelings, it is important to use "I" statements.... [For example] "I am sorry I am irritable today." This not only makes the communication more personal and immediate to a child, it is the foundation of self-awareness [first the awareness of a feeling, then the expression of that awareness].
- Listen without judgment as the child explains how they feel. Judging immediately discounts the feeling and breaks the trust and connection.
- Suggest to your child how they can be caring to another. For example, if a child fell and hurt themselves, you can suggest to your child that they might want to help that child get some ice for the injury.
- Validate the child's feelings and help each child acknowledge their part in any interaction. Giving children the power to see their own behavior and how it affects others allows them the opportunity to change, to reach out and connect to others by changing their behavior. This could be an apology or a change in how two children play and interact.[19]

As children begin their school years, the capacity to love that was nurtured at home can develop further. It can arise when engagement in a specific interest and curiosity about all of existence are encouraged. I will address the topic again in the education chapter, but as it relates to love—teaching with enthusiasm and nurturing the individual child's inherent enthusiasms deepens a child's interest in the world. The more this can happen, the less is the child locked in himself. This outward-shining light sustains learning to learn and loving to learn as well.

Another quality that can be cultivated in children and adults is gratitude.[20] Being grateful for what other people, nature, and society provide can be a gateway to love and empathy because it involves recognizing and

---

19. Priscilla Jeliffe, personal communication with author, Aug. 1, 2021, and Dec. 9, 2022.

20. The remarkable number of connections between gratitude and happiness are captured in a graphic posted at P., "Benefits of Gratitude."

affirming the simple gifts like friendship, food, and health that we tend to take for granted, as well as the miracles that we let slip by without seizing on the opportunities they provide. A beautiful poem by Wendell Berry never mentions gratitude or thankfulness but infuses a mood of profound appreciation that bespeaks a loving relationship with the environment.

> **The Peace of Wild Things**
> When despair for the world grows in me
> and I wake in the night at the least sound
> in fear of what my life and my children's lives may be,
> I go and lie down where the wood drake
> rests in his beauty on the water, and the great heron feeds.
> I come into the peace of wild things
> who do not tax their lives with forethought
> of grief. I come into the presence of still water.
> And I feel above me the day-blind stars
> waiting for their light. For a time
> I rest in the grace of the world, and am free.[21]

This poem says to me that not only can empathy be a path into nature, expressed here as coming into the peace of wild things, but nature can be a path into love and empathetic transcendence. And like all enduring poetry, it says a great deal more. When Wallace Stegner wrote his famous "Wilderness Letter," he made the point that the existence of wild nature did much more than provide a venue for recreation; it gave us "a means of reassuring ourselves of our sanity as creatures, a part of the geography of hope."[22] When children see their parents finding this path to sanity and belonging in nature, it can have a profoundly healing effect into the future.

To affirm and nourish a capacity to love in a child, one has to see that this individuality before you is more than a material object or an advanced animal. One needs to be able to perceive not only the child but oneself as "a spiritual being having a human experience"[23] because love, after all, comes out of one's spiritual nature. In a chapter called "Prerequisites of Love" in *Man—the Bridge between Two Worlds*, Franz Winkler asserts that children subconsciously resent teachers who view

---

21. Berry, "Peace of Wild Things."

22. Stegner, *Sound of Mountain Water*, 147.

23. Variously attributed to Pierre Teilhard de Chardin, Russian mystic Georges Gurdjieff, and psychologist Wayne Dyer.

them through a materialistic lens, as bundles of behavior, higher animals, or intellectual raw material. He observes that they may "react violently against their teachers and the dreary, soulless existence in which they believe." While pedagogy that denies the higher potential in children strengthens the subhuman element in them, the opposite is also true—"Nothing but belief in his spiritual nature, and appeal to his non-egotistical, nonbiological potentialities, can awaken in a child love for freedom and moral values."[24]

Winkler further urges parents to appreciate instances where a young child shows a generous or loving nature, even when it may be hard to appreciate. He cites:

> Acts of spontaneous self-renunciation, such as his offering to another person a thing which he himself craves. The already half-consumed lollipop landing at an unexpected moment on the nose, in the mouth, or on another sensitive area of a loved adult, will rarely arouse a feeling of gratitude toward the little donor; yet the one possessed of a stoic nature, or the mere bystander, may in such an instance catch a glimpse of another world.[25]

As children grow, other opportunities to cultivate empathy and love exist when the child asks questions. Instead of answering them with scientific explanations and abstract concepts, it helps to provide responses that encourage the intuitive side of the growing child. Thus, for example, in response to a question about why a plant grows upward, one could respond to the young child that the plant is a child of the sky to which it wants to return. Nurturing children's imaginative, creative faculties as long as possible can help them live into adulthood where, combined with trained intellect and will, they can make a heartfelt and fulfilling life.

Toward a Beloved Community

Before concluding this chapter, I would like to offer an exercise that builds the capacity for love in adults. It goes like this: Before going to sleep at night, take the time to review the day, backwards. Imagine a film running in reverse through a projector. This is surprisingly difficult, but it strengthens the will and allows seeing oneself from an objective angle.

---

24. Winkler, *Man*, 197.
25. Winkler, *Man*, 198.

Refrain from judging or evaluating; simply be pictorial. Over time you will be surprised with the results.

Civilizations do cycle through different phases. All weaken and decay to a point where an emerging one will supplant them. Stepping back, we can see how American civilization became dominant in the world, not through military conquest like Rome but through a vital culture, an energetic and successful economy, and ideas the world needed. Think of this country's role in rebuilding Europe after World War II. Instead of extracting retribution from defeated nations, we helped them become strong, prosperous, and democratic. The genius here was turning enemies into close allies—arguably not only an enlightened but a loving endeavor. A strong, sustainable civilization of the future must hold the intention to cultivate impulses of that kind. Absent that, an emerging civilization such as China's would be only too happy to pounce on our weakness and assume world leadership with very different social forms that allot state control to not just government but the culture and the economy as well. As tensions with China increase in the direction of open conflict, we forfeit a great opportunity to engage in a War of Ideas that can be fought and won without a shot being fired. The ideals and ideas America can offer, once developed, articulated, and reified at home, can win the hearts and minds of those who might otherwise be sent into battle by their autocratic government.

Finally, note the synergy that exists between freedom and love. The process of self-conquest, of taking one's own life in hand as described in the freedom chapter, empowers a person to grow in love. At the same time, developing a loving nature can strengthen the qualities that make for inner freedom. By cultivating empathy, we rebuild our connection with the rest of life. The faculties of *convivencia* have a role in this synergy as well. To get along harmoniously with neighbors very different from oneself, as was done in golden-age Granada, requires apprehending their highest and best selves, or in the Dostoevsky view, seeing them as God intended them to be. Is this not a form of love, of expanding the circle of belonging and moving toward Martin Luther King's "Beloved Community"? This great mystery deserves some time in quiet contemplation to ponder the two questions that recur throughout this book—what kind of people do we want to be, and what form of society will help us move in that direction?

Part Two—Education

CHAPTER FIVE: **EDUCATE THE WHOLE CHILD**

> *Civilization is a race between education and catastrophe.*
> —H. G. Wells

> *Those preoccupied with "fixing"... schools do not stop to ask... what are schools for, who do they serve, and what kind of a civilization they perpetuate.*
> —Zachary Stein

> *Creativity is as important in education as literacy, and we should treat it with the same status.*
> —Sir Ken Robinson

> *Find the YES in every child.*
> —Kate Bell

No area is more important, and more in need of fresh thinking, than education. In this field, we do not so much need to look to the future and apply the technique of presencing, as we need to explore alternatives already in existence that have proved highly effective. It is not just because I have been an educator for over fifty years that I believe this area provides the best leverage for the changes in consciousness that a truly fresh civilization would demand. Good minds going all the way back to Plato in *The Republic* have pointed out the necessity for an educated populace if democracy is to work.

As the thrust of this book turns now from abiding principles of freedom, community, and love to how they can function in practical applications, it is worth reminding readers not to expect a blueprint. Rather, find here a vision of possibilities. Should people get to a point where they are more open to change, these principles can strike root. At present, interlocking educational systems at the federal, state, and local levels have become so bogged down with the burden of accountability and measurement that even incremental changes often face stiff resistance. But that need not stop us from asking fundamental questions that can reframe people's perception of the world they want.

A Blighted Paradigm for Public Education

An October 2023 national survey of K–12 teachers conducted by the EdWeek Research Center found that almost 80 percent of respondents agreed that they were not likely to advise their own children to pursue a career in K–12 teaching.[1] Why is that? Several factors contribute to making teaching an unattractive job for so many leaving the profession. Among them are increasingly what kids bring to school today—trauma, unmanaged anger, and even weapons. But I would like to draw attention to one factor in particular because it relates to a main thread of this book.

For teaching to proceed in a way in which both students and instructors flourish, love needs to be present. Every one of those twenty-four or so individualities in a classroom can be helped along toward growth and learning in a loving climate. Instead, love may be the single ingredient the public school paradigm does most to undermine with its obsession with accountability, enforced with relentless testing.

Of course, there are many dedicated teachers who love their students. Individual students love their teachers when those are truly caring and nurturing people. But the system projects the opposite—fear that students will get low test scores, fear that they will misbehave, fear that teachers will not measure up, fear that a beloved neighborhood school that gets low scores will be closed. This is the antithesis of a supportive learning environment. The fear manifests in a profoundly

---

1. Heubeck, "Family of Teachers."

disempowering distrust of teachers that results in intrusive and excessive testing, standardized curriculum, scripted lessons, and a far-reaching accountability paradigm. No wonder teacher turnover is 20 to 26 percent in some districts—before and after COVID-19.[2]

With the best of intentions and bipartisan support, in 2001 No Child Left Behind (NCLB) attempted to close the achievement gap between public schools serving poor communities and the rest of the educational establishment. To achieve this, much control of curriculum and standards was taken away from local jurisdictions. Strict accountability for students, teachers, and schools was enforced by high-stakes testing. NCLB and successive federal legislation that uses the same paradigm did have some success, but at a cost. Especially in the schools this legislation was intended to help, a culture of compliance ensued in which people did what was needed to get acceptable scores and not attract attention. There is great irony in the name No Child Left Behind, which projects a caring for individual children. What could be more loveless than a regimen that makes the data more important than the child?

The real crime here rests in reducing the whole child essentially to their brain. And what is in that brain gets further reduced to what can be measured in a standardized test. Children learn when they are *engaged*; ideally that happens when not just head but heart and hands are involved. In your own education, compare the experience of cramming for a test with the opportunity to work on a project with a team. Consider the difference in what you retained from each. The testing and accountability model makes getting an education a competition. A student engaged with a team on a project, on the other hand, learns cooperation, patience, and communication, among other things.

In a brilliant talk at Google, the highly respected child and adult psychiatrist Jonathan Salk painted a picture of where we are in the evolution of human consciousness that explains why we see two paradigms in conflict within education. The one looks backward and stresses quantifiable skills and knowledge with an emphasis on competition and grades. The other is forward-looking and stresses creativity, interdependence, and constructing win-win activities. Toward the end of the twentieth century, developed countries reached an inflection point where two value systems began to struggle for the hearts and minds of people. The old value system stressed competition, ever-expanding growth and markets,

---

2. Will, "Some Positive Signs."

capitalist power, and technical fixes when things went wrong. The new values, however, stressed cooperation, steady-state economies, sustainable population numbers, and a seventh-generation ethic,[3] meaning do no harm now or unto the seventh generation.

Simplifying a bit, the old values could make *me-first* work pretty well; the growth under capitalism and technical advancement were phenomenal. But then advocates of the new system saw that there were finite limits. Climate change, for example, made this abundantly clear. Capitalism's thrust for continuous growth and its insatiable appetite for fossil fuels is driving global sustainability off a cliff. The new values advocates sought to replace *me-first* with *us-together*. People like Zak Stein in *Education in a Time Between Worlds* and Daniel Pink in *A Whole New Mind* wanted a different paradigm, one that could support a person's inner quest for meaning and a purposeful life. Perhaps no event better represents the new paradigm, a coming together to construct win-win action, than the Paris Climate Accord, in which over two hundred nations actually agreed on something. But then, no event better illustrates the destructiveness of the old, limitless growth dynamic more than the United States' withdrawal from this same accord. To the advocates of the new paradigm, this was *me-first* run amok, egotism on a national scale.

In the summer of 2020, during a peak time for the COVID pandemic, over 450,000 people descended on Sturgis, South Dakota, for the annual motorcycle rally. People posed for group selfies and congregated in bars without masks or social distancing. The predictable result, subsequently studied and documented: a major spike in COVID cases and anguished complaints about participants carrying the virus back to their home communities.[4] One has to ask: Presumably these people went through public schools, so what was the missing ingredient that would let them defy common sense and fail to have a social conscience? And further, did the consequences of the 2020 rally provide a learning experience? Apparently not. The next year, the Sturgis local government approved another "10 Days and Nights of Riding, Food, and Music." With COVID still raging, even more people showed up.[5] I interpret this entire display of *me-first* to defective education, even if it is in kindergarten or preschool where we learn to share our toys and consider others.

3. Salk, "New Reality."
4. Knowles, "Covid Cases Are Linked."
5. Huber, "South Dakota."

The seismic shift from *me-first* to *us-together* would mean a society that supports more loving solutions and outlooks, but the forces reinforcing *me-first* are potent and ubiquitous. Where would capitalism be without the concept of "competitive advantage"? Look at the appeal in ads to sell luxury goods. Consider smart phones. Former computer scientist and now education professor Lowell Monke asserts that in the hands of young people they encourage narcissism and numb users to those around them.[6] Despite enormous resistance to a different paradigm, one that can find joy and fulfillment, not in what we can take but in what we can give, one in the spirit of John F. Kennedy's famous "Ask not what your country can do for you, but what you can do for your country," there are measures that can greatly increase the chances for success in this needed change. And the mighty, transformative force that can accomplish this over time is a deeply caring education.

Imagine a School of Unselfishness. What would happen there? A lot of storytelling, including stories that illustrate this quality—by the teacher and made up by the children. Students would spend time in nature and in making a garden, the fruits of which could be shared. They would work in teams on projects. They would play sports but emphasize participation and teamwork rather than competition. Coaching would stress working together over winning. Singing together requires you to tune your voice to others. Each class would have an animal as a pet and share in its care. Feeling and expressing gratitude would be nourished. Age-appropriate service projects in the community would be part of the curriculum. To defuse the hold of materialism in so much of the dominant culture, strategies like this could be incorporated where possible for all subjects. The best gap year programs like those my wife and I are involved with are schools of unselfishness on a small scale. These reach students who are eighteen years old and above. The best time to learn to share is when the clay is soft and impressionable—cradle to kindergarten.

Democracy cannot work unless those doing the voting can make intelligent decisions and learn from their mistakes. Jefferson was acutely aware of this from the earliest days of the republic: "Educate and inform the whole mass of the people.... They are the only sure reliance for the preservation of our liberty."[7] It appears that democracy at the national level in the United States is no longer functioning as Jefferson, and later John

---

6. Burniske and Monke, *Breaking Down the Digital Walls.*
7. See Jefferson, "From Thomas Jefferson."

Dewey,[8] intended. Enough Americans vote for representatives who embrace special interests, promote polarization, drive gridlock, and tolerate voter suppression and gerrymandering so that democracy barely works at the federal level. The failures of our education system are by no means the only cause of this, but they manifest in the dysfunctional federal government, our winner-take-all economic system, and in popular culture that lionizes athletes, actors, and singers, while often neglecting thoughtful voices that could have profoundly helpful impact.

Alternative Paradigms That Educate the Whole Child

In what follows, I will first outline what a wiser primary and secondary education looks like: a nurturing of the whole child that could foster the growth of a caring, clear-thinking generation of citizen agents of transformation. The *funding and governance* of education will be covered in the next chapter. Here we look at the *content*, as well as the *motives* and *inner life* of teachers and learners.

The path toward wholeness begins very early. In *Miseducation: Pre-Schoolers at Risk*, David Elkind explains how forcing adult intellectualizing on young children actually weakens them and impairs their ability to grow and integrate into healthy adults.[9] Instead, these youngest ones need the nurturing of imaginative play, a predictable life rhythm, protection from digital media, time in nature, and a loving, supportive, family environment. "As children start to grow," says Ken Robinson in "Do Schools Kill Creativity?"—for a time the most watched TED Talk ever—"we educate them from the waist up, and then we focus on their heads, and slightly to one side."[10] At all ages, get them singing.

A variety of approaches operating independent of public education actually do educate the whole child. Each attends to the essential concepts in the three previous chapters of this book. These approaches

---

8. American philosopher of education. See Dewey, *Democracy and Education*.
9. Elkind, *Miseducation*, 3–4.
10. Robinson, "Do Schools Kill Creativity?"

CHAPTER FIVE: EDUCATE THE WHOLE CHILD

include Montessori,[11] Waldorf,[12] Reggio Emilia,[13] and Korczak.[14] They all originated in Europe. In the United States, we find place-based education,[15] expeditionary learning,[16] project-based learning[17], and in many cases homeschooling;[18] all of these can liberate learning from the unimaginative and mechanical routines that fail to connect with children. Working for many years in higher education, I noticed that my best students, the ones with the greatest creativity, initiative, and curiosity, were those who had been homeschooled. They were apt to be original thinkers, and their desire to learn carried over from the classroom to life. Obviously, theirs was not the homeschooling that consisted of sitting in front of a computer doing canned programs, nor did it consist of a narrow religious indoctrination. Rather these original thinkers were products of a world-as-my-classroom type of homeschooling.

In my experience the second most capable students came from the very holistic and now global system called Waldorf Schools.[19] They had almost as many of these same qualities and in a balanced way. The idealism of these schools carries forward into college and life; it is reflected in their motto: "Receive the children in reverence; educate them in love; send them forth in freedom." All the successful existing approaches have in common an emphasis, not on accountability and data but on *nurturing the whole child*. What does that mean?

Parents and educators can use the website of Educate the Whole Child as a place to start (educatethewholechild.org). It explains how whole-child education can work, and it supplies resources. As a way to understand the possibilities for rethinking schools, it proposes a framework that involves engaging students whenever possible on five different levels. The framework builds on the fact that children have multiple intelligences

---

11. See American Montessori Society's website: amshq.org.

12. See the Sunbridge Institute's website at sunbridge.edu. See also Harwood, *Recovery of Man*.

13. To learn more about the Reggio Approach, see Reggio Children, "Reggio Emilia Approach."

14. Learn more at Yad Vashem, "Janusz Korczak."

15. Sobel, *Place-Based Education*.

16. To learn more, go to the EL Education website at eleducation.org.

17. See Edutopia, "Project-Based Learning (PBL)."

18. Mason, *Original Home Schooling Series*.

19. Readers may wish to examine the seven basic principles of Waldorf education at AWSNA, "AWSNA Principles" or the version of principles for Waldorf-inspired public schools at the Alliance for Public Waldorf Education, "Core Principles."

(see below), and brain studies tell us that material can be learned and retained better the more parts of the brain become involved. Students can learn something from sitting in straight rows, hearing a lesson, reading the textbook, completing worksheets, and later taking tests. But suppose instead of this less-engaged brain learning, students work in a team on a project. This can require doing research and making calculations in order to build a model or simulation, culminating in a presentation or written report. Students become motivated and engaged because this would be a multi-level activity requiring teamwork and initiative.

The five intelligences Educate the Whole Child seeks to involve are the following:

1. Cognitive-intellectual activity, associated with the left brain
2. Creative-intuitive activity (usually the arts), associated with the right brain
3. Structured physical movement and unstructured, self-directed play
4. Handwork, making things that can be useful, sometimes beautiful
5. Engagement with nature and community

These efforts work best when the school culture is warm and supportive; in other words, promotes not just content learning. Activity in each of these intelligences needs to be rich in social and emotional growth. Teachers who have run projects beyond school walls or had students learning through service in their community know that when students are active in the fifth area, it is easy to engage them in the other four. We want them not just to absorb content; we want them to mature into better people. The tangible service in one's own place or community adds a purposeful dimension to learning, one where students build self-esteem because they can see they are contributing. Moreover, community members become stakeholders in the children's education.

The Peace Table

An instructive example of social and emotional learning would be the Peace Table used in Montessori classrooms.[20] In a quiet corner stands a small table with chairs, a vase, and a "peace flower," usually a silk rose. There may also be a smooth rock, seashell, or some other calming

---

20. See note 12, p. 75.

object. When discord breaks out between students, a teacher invites the children to the Peace Table. They sit down opposite each other and take a deep breath to calm down. The teacher then guides one, then the other, to speak about the cause of the upset and to use "I" statements. The person speaking holds the flower. The other needs to listen and not interrupt. Then roles reverse.

After the second child finishes, inevitably the first wants to respond. The exchange continues until it reaches a point of resolution, and both parties feel that they said all they need to say, and that they have been heard. The teacher then recaps what was said, guides the discussion to a conclusion, and asks the children if they agree.

The table is not used as a time-out or punishment. Rather, it transforms conflict into a teachable moment, it provides practice in a technique for solving differences; it helps students learn to take control of their anger, to listen, to understand another's feelings, and to move along a path toward empathy.

Place-Based Education

When students' learning occurs in the community or surrounding natural environment, that is called place-based education. This approach gets students out of the school to undertake projects, and it brings knowledgeable community members into the school to share what they know. It makes learning real; it builds community participation and support of the school; and it often provides experiences for students that require teamwork and other social and emotional skills that will serve them well in life.

This movement opens all kinds of possibilities. It became more widely known with the publication by the environmental magazine *Orion* of *Place-Based Education: Connecting Classrooms and Communities* by David Sobel in 2005. More recently, Sobel reported on an impoverished and polluted mining town in Appalachia that discovered how the school could be a change agent for the community. To a remarkable extent it succeeded:

> Crellin Elementary School utilizes place-based instruction that is both meaningful and relevant to students' lives. Problem-based activities give students experience in conducting

research, using higher level thinking skills, and working in cooperative groups.

Classroom instruction is also content interrelated. During a fifth-grade math class on area and perimeter, students create the space outdoors for the new Stewardship Garden. Students write and publish books about the Environmental Education Laboratory (EEL) for younger grades. These publications include information about components of the EEL such as the water treatment ponds, wetlands, boardwalk, vernal pool, Snowy Creek, and native gardens. They create field guides, write newspaper articles, and demonstrate their knowledge artistically.[21]

"Drill, Baby, Drill might be a good mantra for off-shore oil enthusiasts," said the *Baltimore Sun* in an article about the Crellin School, "but it's an impoverished mindset for good school reform." This article of July 22, 2010, noted that of 847 elementary schools in Maryland, Crellin had come from a disappointing performance on the state assessment to having the highest score in the state. The Bob Gliner film, *Schools That Change Communities*,[22] has a moving chapter on the Crellin story. At Crellin, and at any schools that seek to enrich learning with out-of-classroom experiences, parent participation and support can make the difference between success and failure. The point is to give children reasons to invest themselves in learning.[23]

Project-Based Education

Any well-conceived, project-based learning like this readily engages the whole child. For example, gardens, even on a vacant lot next to an urban school, provide tremendous opportunities to challenge children on several levels. In the winter, students plan, calculating how they will use the available space, the number and cost of seeds; they can learn about different nutrients plants need. In early spring they can start tomatoes and peppers in the classroom in discarded paper cups, tend the seedlings, later transplant them out, and watch them grow. Other seeds they plant directly in the ground. Drawing the plants as they emerge builds

---

21. Sobel, "Swimming Upstream."

22. The very idea that schools can change communities adds a dimension to school reform that deserves further development.

23. For a worthwhile discussion of student motivation in this connection see Smith and Sobel, *Place- and Community-Based Education*, 32–35.

powers of observation and artistic skill. In late spring, the students will be challenged to come up with a plan for getting their vegetables through the vacation so there is something to harvest when school begins again. Then, in late summer into fall, they can be astounded by the way tiny seeds have transformed and produced seeds of their own, as with pumpkins. Students can learn meal preparation with food they have harvested. In late fall they dry and prepare open-pollinated seeds for next year's crop, and they learn about recycling and making compost. They create a cookbook with recipes they have researched and tested. Other writing activities can be introduced along the way. And, finally, reflecting and writing about the gardening experience can form the basis for the following season's plans.

According to a RAND Corporation survey of American teachers, they worked an average of nine hours more per week than their counterparts in other professions, but they received approximately $18,000 less pay. Compared with other working adults, they often experienced burnout and had roughly three times the amount of job-related stress.[24] Couple working very hard, under stressful conditions, with having to follow a rigid, government-mandated curriculum, and you can see why there would be little time to be creative, provide students individual attention, or take initiative to explore new approaches to learning. Teachers valiantly try to humanize learning and find the time to take an interest in individual students, but the system works against this by piling on mountains of paperwork and testing aimed at focusing on weakness rather than developing strengths. Standardization for education builds from the mistaken notion that learning consists of pouring knowledge into children. This makes the process passive for them and therefore boring and unmotivating. Scripted lessons, designed to be "teacher proof," do not help.

With project-based learning, a better dynamic prevails. It engages students and frees teachers to innovate in ways that draws on kids' innate desire to learn. This dynamic resides in the etymology of the word *education*, which comes from the Latin *educere*, meaning "to lead outward." This happens, for example, in independent Montessori schools, where teachers determine what motivates and energizes students, and then, like jazz musicians, improvise. They connect relevant content to student interests.

---

24. Doan et al., "Teacher Well-Being."

Of course, certain basic skills need to be taught; but this can be done imaginatively and material made more memorable if the teacher's hands are not tied to an overreaching, one-size-fits-all curriculum. Moreover, each child is different, with varied interests and skills. As these are developed, self-esteem grows and leaders emerge. One student's aptitude for calculating can be strengthened in laying out and ordering seeds for the garden; another may shine in a play like "Jack and the Beanstalk."

Project-based learning makes kids inwardly active and alive. When this happens, and when creativity is encouraged, remarkable progress can be made, particularly in the young person's motivation to learn, to take initiative, and to grow his or her imagination.

A gratifying example of this occurred outside of school, when a nine-year-old boy named Caine in Los Angeles decided to set up an arcade constructed entirely of cardboard boxes in his father's used auto parts store. Caine's Arcade got some favorable publicity, and an eleven-minute documentary was made about it that went viral.[25] Before long, people were lining up outside to visit what this young person's imagination had created. Caine raised enough money to pay for his college education. Another outcome was founding the Imagination Foundation, which then started the Global Cardboard Challenge. Today over 250,000 children of all ages from sixty countries respond to the challenge to build anything they can imagine using cardboard and recycled materials.

The way creativity can enliven learning is beautifully illustrated in a film about Mission Hill, a public pilot school in Boston and one of the first in a network of Whole Child Certified Schools. For an all-school unit on ancient China the children not only constructed a large dragon, they did calligraphy and experienced Chinese dance and music, prepared and ate Chinese food, and illustrated what life was like during one of the dynasties. In the film *A Year at Mission Hill*, one sees the extent to which the children are *in* the learning.[26] The entire film is worth seeing. As the narrator states in the film, once you have experienced Mission Hill, you will never see public education the same again.[27]

Facing stiff competition from countries like China, American industries have promoted science, technology, engineering, and math or STEM programs in schools. The version that provides an extra measure

25. Mullick, "Caine's Arcade."
26. Valens and Valens, "Chapter 5."
27. Valens and Valens, "Chapter 1" (Boston Public Schools closed Mission Hill in 2022).

of engagement and cultivates creativity and innovation is called STEAM. These programs involve not only the scientific but also art. The tag line for Flying Cloud Institute in Massachusetts[28] is "where science meets art." They bring programs to local schools that use dance to teach physics concepts of kinetic and potential energy, speed, and energy transfer. Music and percussion are used to teach sound wave technology. Inspired by the wind, teams of students design turbines that generate electricity. The children then put on a celebration that showcases the various designs they have come up with. Holistic teaching like this has been particularly successful in sparking science interest for girls.

Nature and Nature Deficit Disorder

The final intelligence Educate the Whole Child identifies (p. 76) involves "engagement with nature and community." Having children learn ways to connect with nature has always been important, for reasons outlined below (see pp. 84–86) in the discussion of forest schools; but these connections to all other forms of life become doubly important as a way to counterbalance all the electronic paraphernalia that fills modern existence, including social media with their highly addictive algorithms. Nature is real; it can be touched; it is full of growing things that change with the seasons, that evoke wonder and mystery. From the vastness of the horizon at sunset or the night sky, to details of the veins in a wildflower leaf in spring to the way a housefly grooms its antennae, there is something to observe and learn from at every scale. This exposure is important for psychological balance and inner development. The child can begin to feel his or her way into a connection with the great chain of being; at the same time a child's time in nature can prepare the way for finding a kind of transcendence in future. When I was a teen, I remember how, after a long trek in the woods behind our house, I sat down to rest on a low ridge looking out over a small wetland. It was late afternoon in the fall and the oak leaves I was sitting on made a crisp noise when I stirred. The late afternoon light streamed in from the west through branches that were becoming bare. It was extremely quiet with little wind. A mood came over me of peace more profound than I had ever experienced. It was as if I were completely one with my surroundings and all life. My heart filled with gratitude for having been given this

---

28. Flying Cloud Institute, "S.M.Art Schools."

moment. And just as unobtrusively as it arrived, it was gone. I think this was only possible because I had spent enough time in the woods to be completely comfortable there. Others have had similar experiences. One of the best known was recounted by Jane Goodall, who experienced an epiphany in the chimpanzee reserve at Gombe.[29]

Some eloquent voices speak up for allowing children both unstructured time in nature and nature study. Foremost among them is Richard Louv, who coined the term "nature deficit disorder." His books and essays, along with *Orion Magazine* and an excellent collection of articles called *Children and Nature: Making Connections*, edited by George K. Russell, are all worth reading.

It is fair to ask how a teacher can become the kind of person who can implement innovative teaching, be creative, caring, and able to build a community of learning in the classroom, in nature, and in the community? How can the teacher develop and model the qualities she wants her students to acquire? Such questions lead to an axiom for whole-child education: personal growth of the teacher is a necessary ingredient for whole-child learning of the class. This is the educational analog to what applies for social transformation or preparing a new civilization: personal, inner change is the foundation for social change, or "be the change you want to see in the world." Joanna Macy casts the idea in more psychological terms: "To heal our society, our psyches must heal as well."[30] Teachers I have known who can do this earn the love and respect of students and community.

---

29. "Lost in awe at the beauty around me, I must have slipped into a state of heightened awareness. It is hard—impossible, really—to put into words the moment of truth that suddenly came upon me then. It seemed to me, as I struggled afterward to recall the experience, that *self* was utterly absent: I and the chimpanzees, the earth and trees and air, seemed to merge, to become one with the spirit power of life itself. The air was filled with a feathered symphony, the evensong of birds. I heard new frequencies in their music and also the singing of insects' voices—notes so high and sweet I was amazed. Never had I been so intensely aware of the shape, the color of the individual leaves, the varied patterns of the veins that made each one unique. Scents were clear as well, easily identifiable: fermenting overripe fruit; waterlogged earth; cold, wet bark; the damp odor of chimpanzee hair and yes, my own too. . . . There are many windows through which we humans, searching for meaning, can look out into the world around us." See Goodall, "In the Forests," 64–65.

30. Macy, *World as Lover*, 221.

The Inner Life of the Teacher

Taking your own life in hand, exercising your freedom to grow into the kind of person you deeply want to be, excites and liberates in its own right; but doing it for the sake of your students and to become an even stronger teacher makes it even better. Kids are like little barometers who can read sincerity, caring, consistency, and dedication. They also sense weakness, which is how some become master manipulators. The work you do on yourself will show. It can make you a more resilient and resourceful parent or teacher, less stressed by incidents that formerly would take their toll on your equanimity. The attributes discussed in previous chapters of this book should help. The teacher shapes the students by who he or she *is* as much as by what gets taught.

There are many paths toward the goal of self-change. Various psychologists offer guidance. Wayne Dyer[31] and Kathryn Lively are down-to-earth and readable.[32] Be prepared to fail; then make something of that failure. There are workshops specifically for teachers, for example, at Garrison Institute, the Cultivating Awareness and Resilience in Education (CARE) Program. Every major religion has ways toward self-improvement. I find something called the Six Month Exercises highly effective over time as a path toward psychological and spiritual health.[33]

A whole-child approach to education necessarily embraces social and emotional development for each of the five intelligences (p. 76), and the greatest impact will come from example. Thus, for instance, a conscious effort to replace habitual criticizing with sympathetic understanding, and even commenting on this to one's pupils, advances the aim of teaching people to care. This is not to say that being critical has no use but rather that habit can be replaced by conscious intention. Teaching provides extraordinary opportunities for self-change, prompted in many cases by the thoughts and behaviors of the students themselves.

An insidious assumption exists that growing and learning largely stop when you leave school. To counter that fallacy, I offer this short poem.

---

31. Dyer, *Power of Intention*.
32. Lively, "Six Saboteurs."
33. See appendix A.

Education

If you've ever watched anyone die,
especially over time,
you know that education
does not cease.

In fact, the process of decline
is a school,

and the final letting go
a revelation.

Lessons from Scandinavia

When it comes to implementing a whole-child approach, Scandinavian schools have much to teach us. Finland comes out consistently at or near the top of the list of the best schools in the world. An excellent video of why this is so has been put together by Harvard professor Tony Wagner.[34] Essential to the Finns' success in this area is that they have created a learning culture that empowers teachers, trains and pays them well, and gives them the status of other professionals. They also have the freedom, even encouragement, to take initiative and be creative in the classroom.

Scandinavian educators generally understand the need to promote freedom and individual development in their students; but at the same time they realize society will come apart if the different sectors and classes have no basis for communicating and understanding one another. To a certain extent, that unraveling has occurred in the United States where you have MAGA Republicans on the one hand and woke Democrats on the other, unable to communicate and compromise, as if they did not speak the same language. A common sense measure to address this is used in Nordic countries, where a required core of competencies is articulated for every young citizen. That means literacy, numeracy, and basic citizenship. How schools accomplish this should be up to them.

Another Scandinavian impulse that has been remarkably successful is Denmark's forest kindergartens. These seem to operate on the principle that there is no bad weather, only bad clothing, because children are typically outside all day in all seasons. Other schools in the

---

34. Compton, *Finland Phenomenon*.

Nordic countries ensure that children are outside and learning in nature for at least part of the day. Usually groups of no more than twenty learn in a forest setting with two or more adults. They climb trees and encounter hazards, but the point is to take risks and learn to handle them. Building a fire and cooking pancakes over it might be one activity. When children find a dead animal or bird, this provides a teachable moment and a chance to talk about the cycle of life. Children develop their own games and activities and an appreciation of nature that would be impossible in a classroom or just from a textbook. The benefits of the forest schools, now to be found all around Britain as well as Australia and New Zealand,[35] are worth enumerating:

- Children's confidence is developed by giving them the freedom, time, and space to learn and demonstrate independence.
- Social and emotional skills are increased by children gaining an awareness of the consequences of their actions on peers through team and paired activities that involve sharing, negotiating, and turn-taking.
- Children's communication and language development is increased through sensory experiences and using natural materials.
- Motivation and concentration are developed by children's fascination with nature; they are more attentive, have better powers of memory, and are less easily distracted.
- Physical skills are improved by children being outdoors, illustrated by evidence of better balance, agility, and strength.
- Children's health and immunity is strengthened through being outdoors regularly; they, along with practitioners, seem to be ill less often.[36]

In the United States, the more than one hundred forest schools are mostly independent. Parents seem to appreciate that children learn to handle risks in a supervised setting and an age-appropriate manner. If a child gets stung by a bee, falls out of an apple tree, or gets their feet wet in a brook, those are treated as teachable moments. On one hand, most

---

35. The US state of Wisconsin has a good many school forests as well as forest schools.

36. See both Williams-Siegfredsen, "Forest Schools," and Williams-Siegfredsen, *Danish Forest School Approach*.

public school officials have little appetite for risk, even if it can be highly educational. On the other hand, in the field of developmental disabilities the concept of the Dignity of Risk promotes allowing clients to take and learn from reasonable risks as a way to grow self-determination and confidence.

Yet another fruitful line of thinking comes from Swedish philosopher of social change Tomas Björkman. In *The Nordic Secret*, he asks how we can prepare young people to have sufficient self-confidence so that they will be active co-creators of a new consciousness and a new world. "How can we restore our ability as a civilization to make good collective choices?"[37] Björkman tells the story of how Denmark, Norway, and Sweden were able to transform from backward, undemocratic, and poor to arguably the most socially advanced, most democratic, most prosperous, and happiest nations in the world. This was accomplished through education, but not in the usual sense.

In the first half of the nineteenth century, a group of leaders and intellectuals met in Copenhagen and over time devised a way of providing younger members of the largely unschooled and rural population with opportunities for personal growth so that they could become participating citizens of a newly-imagined country. They instituted the retreat-like Danish Folk Schools, in which small groups from all social classes came together and not only learned crafts and certain basic skills, but also came to appreciate their national identity, build self-confidence, and discover their own leadership potential. They also did a great deal of singing. This movement was so successful in Denmark that it spread to Norway, then Sweden, and in a small way to the United States. The Highlander Center in Tennessee, which was so important in training Rosa Parks and other leaders in the Civil Rights Movement, was modeled on the Folk Schools.

In *The Nordic Secret*, Björkman and coauthor Lene Rachel Andersen ask,

> Can this historical experience regarding the transition from feudal absolute monarchies to industrialized democratic nation states help us as we are going through a transition from industrialized nation states to a digitized, globalized economy that must somehow become a global community?[38]

---

37. Björkman, "Tomas Björkman on Co-Creation."
38. Andersen and Björkman, *Nordic Secret*, 381.

The book answers this question with an emphatic "Yes!" Accomplishing this, however, will not be easy, for the world is a great deal more complex than it was in the nineteenth century. Moreover, the Nordic nations they write about were at that time largely unified culturally. Today, advanced nations are multicultural. Learning to live in and deal with complexity will be a key skill for citizens of a revitalized culture. Andersen and Björkman make an important point about what happens when people lack this ability to cope in the modern world. This is their view:

> As the means of production and thus the economy change, so do many other things around us. This has happened before, but the pace was slower back then. With the world changing rapidly, and our minds and meaning-making not keeping up, there is a substantial risk that we are heading in the wrong direction, not towards increased mental complexity and ego-development but going the other way. As globalization and technological development strip the middle- and lower classes of their jobs and paths to prosperity, people lose their hopes and quickly their savings too if they ever had any. They suffer anxiety and will eventually get angry, and they will search for simple answers and seek whatever sense of security and belonging they can find, even if it is meaning-making at an insufficient level of complexity. Or in plain English: people will be homesick for simple solutions and will vote for whoever promises them the level of complexity that makes sense to them. Typically in the form of national chauvinism. This has happened before and it is incredibly dangerous.[39]

One can see this danger manifesting on every continent, where even in developed nations large numbers of people turn toward leaders and parties that promise exactly what the authors describe.

The kind of education that can counter this, that can grow in individuals the three qualities discussed in the chapters on freedom, community, and love, will be a whole-child education. In some cases, adults can re-educate themselves with these qualities in mind. They can still learn to listen, to work in teams, to appreciate and empathize with others, to embark on lifelong inner development.[40] Many self-help programs work in this manner.

39. Andersen and Björkman, *Nordic Secret*, 419–20.
40. A recent report from the European Organisation for Economic Co-Operation and Development (OECD) calls for "Education for Human Flourishing." In a truly holistic spirit, it declares, "Education for human flourishing embodies the three principles on which future education systems should be built. It encourages a broader range of

Andersen and Björkman conceptualize this as a horizontal axis of content learning—literacy and numeracy, history, other conventional disciplines, and, at a more specialized level, technical command of one's field. They imagine a vertical axis that includes what will be needed for lifelong inner development—the ability to listen, to work in teams, to appreciate and empathize with others different from oneself. In this connection they talk about cultivating "circles of belonging."[41] Typically, people feel they belong only to family and friends, and somewhat less to a community or tribe. But for us to live successfully in a globalized, profoundly connected world, this sense of belonging needs to expand so that one can become ultimately a citizen of the world. It has been the very lack of a sense of belonging in and to nature that has led to incredible abuse of our planet, even to the climate crisis. This can change with a whole-child education, rich with social and emotional learning, designed to encourage caring and sharing, and with a pedagogy that instills resilience and the other personal qualities that will be needed in the challenging times ahead. The whole-person approaches outlined here rarely appear in higher education. Colleges tend to be politically liberal but pedagogically conservative. This deficit can be effectively addressed through gap year programs (see appendix C).

I would like to close with a poem I wrote that conveys what extending this sense of belonging feels like.

What Dreams Can Do
I dream I hold a cat that falls asleep in my arms.
Then I hold a baby that falls asleep in my arms.
Then I hold my Beloved and, as she falls asleep,

from her trust a net of belonging grows
like mycelia out into the world. Golden
fibers spread to include the cousins,

even those who voted for Trump. Mostly under
ground, the web of belonging spreads above as well.
It overcomes walls and fences. It can shut down

---

capabilities, spanning the academic, the caring and the creative. It nurtures the designers of fair and sustainable models for the future. And it restores meaning to people's lives." See OECD, "High Performing Systems."

41. Andersen and Björkman, *Nordic Secret*, 331–35.

Interstates. It swallows politicians like Jonah's whale.
I am in it, and it makes a place for me
in the community of nations.

I speak with Merkel; she draws a lesson from
the story of Rumpelstiltskin. Macron recommends
a good vintage of Bordeaux. We are welcome

to each other, and the sense of belonging burgeons
so that in the spirit of Whitman it accepts contradictions.
It embraces multitudes.

CHAPTER SIX: FREEDOM TO TEACH

The freedom of teachers to make decisions about their classrooms and their lives is essential for a democratic school.
—Deborah Meier

When you do the common things in life in an uncommon way, you will command the attention of the world.
—George Washington Carver

The complexity of our present trouble suggests as never before that we need to change our present concept of education. . . . Its proper use is to enable citizens to live lives that are economically, politically, socially, and culturally responsible.
—Wendell Berry

Contrasting Classrooms

PICTURE AN ELEMENTARY CLASSROOM in one of those states more stingy than most when it comes to paying for public education.[1] A substitute is attempting to teach reading. The class's regular teacher, a single mom, has called in sick today. In fact, she has an interview in another state and

---

1. For a chart of per-pupil spending by state, see Wisevoter, "Per Pupil Spending." The range is immense, with New York over $25,000 and Idaho and Utah about $8,000.

district where she hopes she can make enough to live on. If this doesn't work out, she is considering leaving teaching completely. Despite her meager salary, like many teachers in most states she needs to use her own money to buy supplies like paper, pencils, staples, decorations for the room, and books for the classroom bookshelf.

Upon entering, the substitute realizes that the class contains a few children who are not "class ready," meaning in this case that they seem completely incapable of doing schoolwork. Frankie is withdrawn, at times almost catatonic; PJ has anger issues, can't stay in his seat, talks out of turn and to himself, and if others are allowed to goad him, will fly into a rage. Melissa is very bright and does all the work to perfection but appears to be on the autism spectrum and could benefit from individualized assignments if the sub had the time. Because of confidentiality regulations, the overworked principal has not briefed the sub on these special cases or strategies to deal with them, nor is it clear why the disruptive ones are not in a special needs class. The lesson proceeds, with students reading in turn and some new words being put on the board and discussed. Next comes math. For the sub, and the person she is replacing, the teacher has little agency to depart from the learning objective for today, which is preparing for the high-stakes tests coming soon. By the end of the day some material has been covered for those who are ready to learn. Nevertheless, an inordinate amount of effort has gone into keeping order and maintaining some semblance of a learning environment. This happens even when the regular teacher is here.

Contrast this dire and all-too-common picture with a certified Whole Child School[2] in a different and not-so-stingy state when it comes to education funding. There we find classrooms in which children are fully engaged, not just their brains but hearts and hands as well. This is the second year the teacher has been with these students so she knows them well. This is called "looping," and it can create a bond of trust and affection that encourages learning. In this classroom, the teacher has a great deal of agency to determine both content and teaching strategy. Instead of sitting in rows of desks, these students gather around several tables on which they undertake projects, working in teams. One team is designing a building for use as an environmental center with a small chicken farm. Another team is figuring out how to break even selling vegetables the students grow in their student garden. The teacher moves among the projects, offering

---

2. See Educate the Whole Child, "Why Certify?"

advice, posing and answering questions. She coaches students to immediately apply geometry and math concepts to actual problems. Even though the school is not selective, with students admitted from the waiting list based on a lottery, for these engaged young people, discipline and concentration do not appear to be problems. All these students still have to take state-mandated tests, but the focus here is on project-based learning, not test scores. Because she knows them well, the teacher can individualize learning to some degree, building on students' individual strengths. For example, on the design team one student is doing an illustration of the finished design for the building; another is calculating building materials; another is writing up a description; a fourth is helping a slower student understand how it all comes together.

These are not actual classrooms or names, but the contrast highlights how importantly the learning climate of a school figures in academic success. And it dramatizes how limiting it is to define success in terms of test scores.

A Structure to Support Holistic Learning

What kind of structure and governance would afford teachers the optimum conditions for nurturing the whole child, for promoting creativity, community, love, and freedom? This seldom-raised question takes us into areas that demand particular openness because it is hard, but not impossible, to imagine that the mass of children can be educated without full-on involvement of government, with its tendency to become bureaucratic, standardize, and demand compliance. It may take more than a little upheaval for people to become open enough to consider a radically different model.

We can begin by listing the four major problems in the existing system for governing and funding K–12 public education in the United States:

1. **Funding inequities.** Most people will assume that the adage "He who pays the piper calls the tune" applies here. Whether it does or not, how well is the piper doing? The state average for annual spending per pupil is the highest in New York at $20,645, but in New York City it is currently $28,004. The affluent town of Sharon, Connecticut, clearly an outlier in that state, spends $41,996. At the other end of the spectrum, nine states spend less than $10,000 per pupil

per year, with Utah and Idaho at the bottom with roughly $8,000.[3] When I last visited Jackson, Mississippi, I was told the teachers had not received a raise in twenty years. This helps us see why resource inequity tops the list of problems with school funding and governance. When inequity is severe enough, it becomes injustice.

If you read the Fourteenth Amendment to the Constitution, it seems to provide unequivocal justification for equitable and just funding for all public schools. But in what may have been a tragically misguided decision in 1973, a narrow majority of the Supreme Court decided in *San Antonio v. Rodriguez* that the Equal Protection Clause did not apply and that equality in education was not an explicitly guaranteed right in the Constitution. Thus, an opportunity was missed to correct a situation even the language of the majority opinion admitted "can fairly be described as *chaotic and unjust.*"[4]

2. **One size fits all.** An overriding ideal for the government sphere is justice, which means treating everyone equally. Yet when that gets applied in the cultural sphere, where education resides and where the ideal is the flourishing of individuals in their individuality—their differentness—then we run into problems. A government bureaucracy does not lend itself to accommodating individual differences, interests, or talents. Standardization and rigidity become the pattern. This characteristic is deadly when dealing with the exuberant individualities of little people. Of course, everyone needs to learn certain basic skills. Of course, special education tries to individualize learning for those who cannot learn in conventional ways. But if Helen is a natural leader and will flourish if put in charge of a project team, and Oscar learns more using his hands to build things, our present system doesn't lend itself to letting the teacher adapt teaching to differences between students. Rather, an unimaginative pedagogy and a standardized curriculum, enforced with rubrics and tests, denies teachers the right to nurture individual strengths and differences (see the discussion of the three spheres and their respective ideals in chapter 2).

The case of Joyce Irvine, a principal in Vermont, illustrates what can result when government management—with its inflexible and

---

3. Teaching-Certification.com, "Education Spending by State."
4. Chaltain, "Most Important" (emphasis in original).

bureaucratic tendencies—imposes its will on an entity (a school in this case) in the cultural domain. As noted earlier (pp. 31), government can have a role in *funding* a creative enterprise like a school because that helps ensure equal access. In its role of advancing the ideal of equality, the political sphere should defend the *right* of every child to an education. But having political interests *managing* schools and dictating standards and procedures can result in scenarios like this one. Unfortunately, this is not an isolated case.

From 2004 until 2010, Principal Irvine led Wheeler Elementary School in Burlington. As reported in the *Washington Post*:

> Wheeler serves a highly disadvantaged population; in 2010 thirty-seven of the thirty-nine fifth-grade students were either refugees or special-education students. During her time at Wheeler, Irvine added a number of enrichment programs, including a summer school, and converted the school into an arts magnet. She worked very hard—often eighty hours per week—and both her hard work and her success were recognized by her colleagues and her superiors. Her final evaluation began, "Joyce has successfully completed a phenomenal year," and the superintendent called her "a leader" among her colleagues.
>
> In 2010 she was fired from her job as principal and assigned to a lower-paying administrative position. The reason: low test scores. Under one of [Secretary of Education] Arne Duncan's policies, to qualify for funds from the federal economic stimulus program, the district had to . . . remove the principal. . . . Irvine had to go. As she said, "Joyce Irvine versus millions. You can buy a lot of help for children with that money."[5]

3. **A compliance culture.** When you step inside a school, you can tell almost immediately the tone of the learning culture there. Some schools are full of life, with student artwork in the halls and a creative energy that welcomes kids. Others feel like prisons for young people. A compliance culture means teachers are expected to use scripted lessons, do as they are told, and forget about bringing much initiative or creativity to the classroom, precisely the qualities needed for dynamic learning to take place. Such a culture virtually shouts to teachers, "We don't trust you."

---

5. Strauss, "How a Fabulous Principal."

For a compliance culture to work, someone has to enforce the compliance. This results in a caste system in which the administration and the teachers exist in what unfortunately too often takes the shape of a them-us arrangement, embodied in unionized teachers and in some districts even unionized administrators. Thus, as opposed to optimizing learning, where everyone is on the same team with shared aims, schools are apt to have an adversarial climate. This can become especially evident where skilled leadership is absent.[6]

4. **Measuring the mind.** Materialistic thinking manifests in different ways and lies at the root of much that is wrong with public education. One sees it on a superficial level in the stinginess of many voters when it comes to funding schools. As parents age and no longer have children in school, and grandchildren are apt to be in another district, the taxpayers' sense of connection with local schools diminishes. But the more insidious and pervasive form of materialistic thinking lies with policy makers who conceive their main responsibility to be bringing up test scores. "If it can't be measured it doesn't count"[7] is the stultifying rule. Some testing can be valuable, particularly if the tests are designed to be learning experiences, not just evaluations. But what we currently have are elaborate systems of accountability and data management, sucking up time and energy that could be devoted to teaching. Built on distrust, these structures disempower teachers and miss the point of education.

The causes of these deficiencies are not so complex that we cannot identify them. Affluent communities tend to have good schools, but in many states and communities, voters simply do not value public education enough to pay for it. Poor communities simply lack the tax base to support decent schools. At the same time, public education consists of a multi-layered bureaucracy, with characteristic resistance to change, top-down management and at the same time unresponsive management, political interference, and a climate of distrust. Politicians on the

---

6. There is ample anecdotal evidence that inept principals and unresponsive school administrations cause teachers to quit. See Vouloumanos, "Teachers Who Quit." An inspired program with excellent results solves this problem with the Principal Residency Network. It prepares principals in actual schools through an internship arrangement. See CLEE, "Principal Residency Network."

7. In *Beyond Measure*, Vickie Abeles takes up test tyranny as well as the pressures created by excessive homework and the tendency to overschedule students to the point where they do not get enough sleep and their health becomes affected.

right tend to have a low regard for teachers and an antipathy to teachers' unions. Consequently, they want lessons to be "teacher-proof," which is degrading and disincentivizing to teachers. It robs teachers of their freedom to teach. For an underperforming school to become a good school, extraordinary leadership and incredible effort to overcome the obstacles are required.

Finland Again

Each of these four problems has been successfully addressed in Finland, which is widely considered to have the best schools in the world. The first problem of inequitable school resources has been tackled by having 40 percent of school funding come from the national government. It is distributed on a per-student basis.[8] This helps ensure that rich and poor neighborhoods get similar appropriations. Finnish parents have the freedom to choose the school they want for their children, subject to available space and certain equity guidelines. Since 2003, schools must register students on a first-come, first-served basis. All schools have common registration data, publicly communicated. Schools may not be selective, except to give preference to families where an applicant has a sibling in the school, or to favor children from a disadvantaged background. A similar system prevails in Sweden.[9] The concept of funding the student rather than the school allows a student to go to any of a wide range of public and private schools and bring their tuition with them.[10]

Finland's example also helps chart the way for dealing with a second major problem. Teachers in Finland can individualize learning more easily because average class sizes are below twenty students.[11] And the schools are smaller as well, which means that all the teachers can know all the students in a climate of nurture and support. No one slips through the cracks. Nurturing applies, not just to students but to teachers. A climate of trust prevails. This stems from the fact that though major funding comes from Finland's central government and a national curriculum exists, the standards are treated more as guidelines

---

8. National Center on Education and the Economy (NCEE), "Top-Performing Countries."

9. Musset, "School Choice," 21–22.

10. In the United States, Vermont has something similar. See the discussion of Compass School later in this chapter.

11. Finnish National Agency for Education, "Average Group Sizes."

than inflexible mandates. Less intrusive government control allows a culture that empowers teachers, and they can exercise their discretion. Furthermore, this encourages creativity and initiative. Administrators and teachers are respected and paid at a professional level.

As Tony Wagner explains in his film *The Finnish Phenomenon*, teachers in Finland all earn masters degrees. They are both well-prepared and well-supported. They get prep time, meaningful professional development, and coaching. A climate of trust engenders initiative. This contrasts with federal mandates in the United States to catch and dismiss teachers who, as measured by standardized tests, are underperforming. As one thoughtful commentator put it, education has been one of the last fields to realize that you cannot fire your way to excellence.[12] He goes on to cite a comprehensive national survey of the testing regimes that concludes, "We find that, on average, [test-based] teacher evaluation reforms had no detectable effect on student achievement or attainment."[13]

Apart from a test at the end of the senior year and the PISA test given throughout the world at age fifteen, Finland gives no standardized tests.[14] Time that might have been devoted to testing is instead devoted to learning. American tests focus heavily on literacy and math, yet PISA proficiency for Finnish students in these two areas typically places its students at or near the top of the list of nations. Reading levels in the United States come in at sixth place in PISA rankings, math at about thirty-second place. These figures vary from year to year but suggest the US system does not reflect America's real potential.[15]

Regarding these international tests like PISA and NAEP, on which Finland excels and the United States performs poorly, it should be noted that if only strong schools in affluent neighborhoods were considered, the American schools would fare much better.[16] This tells us that some American schools are doing a reasonable job, but it also suggests that the extent of child poverty in this resource-rich country needs to be addressed.

---

12. Greene, "This Decade-Long Experiment."

13. Bleiberg, et al., "Effect of Teacher Evaluation."

14. Hancock, "Why Are Finland's Schools?" The PISA is the Programme for International Student Assessment.

15. National Center for Education Statistics, "Fast Facts."

16. Caffeinated Rage, "Poverty Affects Schools." The NAEP is the National Assessment of Educational Progress.

Small Can Be Beautiful

For twenty-six years Compass School in Vermont provided an inspiring response to the third major problem, showing the *esprit* that is possible in a small school. It served fewer than one hundred students in grades seven through twelve. In a building that was formerly an Elks Club, the children enjoyed an education stressing personalized learning plans, deep connections and service in the community, assessment by exhibition, a very flexible and responsive schedule, and active learning that engaged not just the intellect but hearts and hands as well. Testimony of graduates confirms the lasting value of these features.[17]

Another feature of the school, one that could make it a model for replication in other settings, is that it was an independent school serving both private-pay and public school students. Vermont is one of three states that has no charter schools but instead allows high school students to attend public or independent schools in the state through a program called Public High School Choice.[18]

At Compass, 40 percent of students came from public schools. Open admission made it necessary to have a lottery when applications exceeded space available. The school's former director reports that there was a conscious effort to ensure that the students who came from public schools, some of whom were on free or reduced lunch, were treated exactly the same as students whose parents paid. The school's bus was used for field trips, but all parents needed to arrange for transporting children to and from school.

Other features at Compass besides small size make it an attractive model. As one of the instructors says, "When we have a good idea, we have the liberty to pursue it."[19] This freedom to teach conveys support for faculty and constitutes a formidable motivation for attracting and keeping talented teachers. When the school head said, "This place is about seeing each person as an individual," he meant instructors as well as students.[20]

Compass also had an answer to the problem of two castes in a school building—teaching staff and administrators. A much healthier climate can be created if this division of labor does not become a kind

---

17. Student testimonials appeared on the school's website—compassvt.org—before its closure and the website was altered to reflect the closure.
18. State of Vermont Agency of Education, "Public High School Choice."
19. Ron BosLun, personal communication with author, Oct. 19, 2021.
20. Ron BosLun, personal communication with author, Oct. 19, 2021.

of apartheid. For as long as it operated, there was no union at this school because everyone was on the same team. The director did some teaching, and teachers shouldered some administrating. In fact, in such a small school everyone had to wear more than one hat. Thus, for example, in describing his role at the school, teacher Ron BosLun stated that in addition to teaching Algebra 1 and middle school science, "I direct our school play, coach basketball, drive our bus, and coordinate our evolving health curriculum." He was also a class advisor.[21] This is a demanding but healthy mix, and it definitely makes for a "we're all in this together" view of the school.[22]

Although this runs counter to the drive to save money through economies of scale, I maintain that the trend toward consolidated schools, which involves closing all neighborhood schools and bussing even the youngest children to schools that are as big as factories, is a bad idea. Yes, some children, who make friends easily and are survivors, can thrive in such a setting. On the other hand, those who are more vulnerable or introverted are apt to get bullied, overlooked, or lost in a school where they are just one of many. Advocates for consolidated schools point to the possibilities for labs, libraries, and other amenities. Those advantages cannot be denied. But the quality of instruction and a truly nurturing environment in which to learn cannot be replaced by facilities.[23]

Turning Lemons into Lemonade

In mainstream schools, teachers who have the moral courage to take risks and buck the system are the heroes. In the process, they can turn student apathy into engagement. Here is an example of what is possible

---

21. Ron BosLun, personal communication with author, Oct. 19, 2021.

22. Former school director Eric Rhomberg, personal communication with author, Oct. 19, 2021. Even though financial difficulties forced Compass to close, I believe that the school's public-private model holds promise and continues to be worth consideration.

23. The Institute for Local Self-Reliance endorses small schools with the statement, "Hundreds of studies have found that students who attend small schools outperform those in large schools on every academic measure from grades to test scores. They are less likely to drop out and more likely to attend college. Small schools also build strong communities." See Institute for Local Self-Reliance. "Small Schools." A few years ago, a small schools movement, funded by the Gates Foundation, had disappointing results. This was largely due to failure to make downsizing schools part of a larger initiative that included, for example, a caring school culture and serious attention to individual students. For a valuable discussion of this see Schneider, "Small Schools."

if teachers are given the freedom to take initiative and color outside the lines: Meet Pablo Muriel, whose father and mother came from Puerto Rico with a third and eighth grade education respectively. They lived with their children in the South Bronx and never learned English. Growing up in the projects, Pablo had to be wary getting to and from school so that he didn't encounter crackheads who wanted to shake him down for his lunch money or that he didn't stray into a street where bullets were flying. After graduating from college, Pablo returned to the borough to teach at a public school much like the ones he attended as a boy. The school had a leaking roof, peeling paint, and some classrooms so unusable they had to be locked and abandoned. Moreover, there were not enough textbooks to go around. Taken together, these conditions communicated to students: "You are not worthy of a decent school." No surprise, then, that students responded with apathy about learning.

Pablo decided to turn the situation into an opportunity to energize his civics class. His first activist assignment was to tackle the textbook issue. Students were coached to analyze the source of the problem and identify the people who could correct it. They created petitions, wrote letters, visited officials, placed the problem in the context of the neighborhood, and learned how city government and school bureaucracies work. The result: $40,000 from the district for textbooks.

Next, they tackled the condition of the school. Students surveyed the damage and decay, wrote reports, and learned more about the workings of government and how the neglect came about. They even met with leaders in the state capital. The result this time was millions of dollars to fix up the school.[24] In his recent book about student activism in support of learning, Muriel says models exist to inspire civics classes—the students from Parkland, where a gun rampage ignited a national campaign; Greta Thunberg, who continues to call out adults, even at the United Nations, for failing to come to terms with the climate threat; Nobel laureate Malala Yousafzai, who survived being shot in Pakistan for advocating for girls' education.[25] We admire efforts by these young people and their teachers to turn a bad situation into an opportunity. They convert passive learning into active engagement. But at the same time we need to ask what is wrong in the realm of governance that allows these abusive or neglected situations to develop and persist.

---

24. Muriel and Singer, *Supporting Civics Education*, 37.
25. Muriel and Singer, *Supporting Civics Education*, 80.

Addressing the fourth major problem (p. 95), the pervasive materialistic thinking in education, may be the toughest challenge of all because we live in a very materialistic culture. Materialistic thinking is corrosive to human relationships, including education, because it reduces the whole person to a fraction of who and what they really are. Some businesses operate using Human Capital Theory,[26] which allows them to put a dollar value on an employee's experience and skills. In education, the same reduction of individuals to numbers obtains where we find an obsession with test scores and accountability monitored in quantitative terms. In prep schools, materialism manifests in the metrics of how many of the graduates get into prestigious colleges. "Materialism" in this school context means treating students with a business mindset, as if they were products with an expected return on investment.

I have heard European friends observe that Americans seem to have a love affair with material things. Those who can afford to are apt to acquire more and more "stuff," until they have to rent a storage unit to keep it all. More insidious, however, is materialistic thinking, which manifests when one thinks of a person not as an individual human with dreams and aspirations but as an evolved animal, a machine, or a data point. If you imagine yourself to be a fourth grader, laboring to get an education in a system shaped by this kind of thinking, you can see how undermining it would seem at a time when, in order to grow, you need to be seen and nourished *for who you are*, not as a reduced or abstracted version of yourself.

Some schools, particularly charters, have been able to minimize the use of standardized tests by switching to "authentic assessments." That means having students demonstrate what they know through portfolios, presentations, and projects. These require something more than proficiency with multiple-choice questions. Students must organize their learning, take initiative, and develop skills needed to convey what they know. Teachers, parents, community members, and peers often participate in these evaluative presentations and they afford a fine opportunity to build bridges to, and interest from, the surrounding community.

Unchaining the creativity of teachers, giving them agency, and encouraging personal, inner development as a prerequisite for professional development can foster a climate of dynamic change. If teachers themselves are growing and learning, their example impacts students.

---

26. Ross, "Human Capital Theory."

Three things can be particularly effective in conveying to students what Europeans call *bildung*,[27] close to what Americans call social and emotional learning—"a harmonious development of all human capacities."[28] This can be understood as everything education provides that is not curriculum content. These three things are: service to others and the community, experiences in nature, and arts integration. The more these activities can be integrated into the instruction, rather than being kept apart in different silos or in after-school programs, the better. Each of these three activities potentially intensifies the students' sense of *belonging*. This makes for a more supportive learning environment and at the same time strengthens individuals' inner resources and resilience.

Many brave teachers do their best to reach students and cover material, but it occurs in spite of the existing public school paradigm, not because of it. Let us return to the question: How should a school be run in order to deliver a whole-child education?

Preparing Teachers, Then Giving Them Agency

I have contended in this chapter that giving educators the freedom to teach can transform education. But for that to work you need teachers with deep preparation and continuing support that allows them to function both as teaching professionals and as administrative decision-makers. Finland has done this. Teachers there function with a measure of independence, and many teach with imagination and verve. They must complete at least a masters degree, but more is expected. When they enter the classroom, they need to be on a path of continuing personal and professional development in both teaching and *leading* young people. Arguably, teachers convey more of enduring value through who they are than through what they teach. When George Bernard Shaw snarkily pronounced, "Those who can, do. Those who can't, teach," he was implicitly referring to the difficulty in attracting top people in sufficient numbers to staff schools.[29] Finland has solved this problem. In the United States, even under disincentivizing conditions, of course,

---

27. Although the term may have little draw for Americans, the Bildung Movement in Europe has garnered much support from thoughtful educators and from some of the great figures in German culture—von Humboldt, Goethe, and Hegel to name just three. Learn more at the Global Bildung Network website: globalbildung.net.

28. Stoll, "Forming Humanity."

29. Ingram, "Teaching Profession in Decline?"

there are extraordinarily dedicated and gifted people in the profession. But by paying teachers more, insisting on deeper and more rigorous preparation, and restructuring how schools are run and how they relate to the community, I believe the United States could equal or surpass what has been accomplished in Finland.

The ideal of transforming teachers into leaders was advanced by the Principal Residency Network (PRN), established in 1998 by Dennis Littky and Elliot Washor. This program did far more than teach the mechanics of being a principal; it set a high bar and instilled "Distinguished Principal Qualities," including moral courage and love of learning and leading. Aspiring principals worked under an exemplary school leader for a year, supported by a seminar that delved into problem cases and topics that require instruction.[30] Unfortunately, this innovative program died when No Child Left Behind came in and priorities shifted from student-centered instruction to test-centered teaching and so-called "seat time."[31]

Really empowering teachers so they can be creative, take initiative, and have the freedom to teach presents a larger challenge because it involves giving teachers more agency, a radical change from current arrangements. I take it as axiomatic that unions come into existence when management has been unresponsive, stingy, or inept. What does the almost universal existence of teachers' unions in mainstream public schools tell us? It testifies to the fact that schools run by governments inevitably tend toward bureaucratic ineptitude and neglectful response to legitimate needs. A prime example: teachers having to use their own money to buy materials for their classrooms. At the same time, large sums get spent on testing and related data management. Some districts have an assistant superintendent for data. Were teachers in charge, these would not be the priorities.

Would it be possible to have the teachers run schools instead of having teachers in their classrooms, and then a separate caste of administrators in their offices? Unionization makes this difficult but not impossible. When administrators are scrupulously excluded from teachers' unions (even though virtually all of them have been teachers), you have an adversarial structure that undercuts efforts to move together as one

---

30. Mancini et al., "Principled Principal Development."

31. For information in this paragraph I am indebted to Thomas McGuire, former PRN coordinator and retired principal, then superintendent, who lived through the painful transition.

team. However, different arrangements can be negotiated. One measure would require all school leaders to do some teaching. At a small public school in New Marlborough, Massachusetts, teachers are unionized, but there is no principal in the building, only a lead teacher. This has worked well for years.

Schools can be liberated from management by officials who are at a physical and/or structural remove from classrooms. The key is to give thoroughly prepared teachers the freedom to teach, to exercise their initiative in order to release the talents of each young individual in their charge. The education establishment is full of people who mean well; many bring considerable experience, intelligence, talent, and creativity to bear on the problems of providing equal access and supporting democracy with an educated citizenry. But I submit that a new and robust educational paradigm requires, at a minimum, quality teacher preparation and adequate funding. Such newly minted professionals would have the agency to use their strong preparation to connect with students *in their individuality* and teach them with verve and dedication. Finland has already shown the way to do this, and over 95 percent of Finland's teachers are unionized. Unlike the United States, Finland is a small country with a relatively homogeneous population. That should not keep us from copying what succeeds there, starting with respecting and truly supporting teachers.

Politicians and government entities too often cannot resist the temptation to micromanage schools, even content being taught. In Texas and Florida, state government has actually prevented local school districts from requiring COVID-19 masks or vaccinations, thus putting the health of students at risk in order to score political points.[32] It does not have to be this way. Some countries support both public and private schools with government funding. In Belgium, for example, schools are given a large degree of autonomy. One can conclude that where appropriate safeguards are in place to ensure that school choice does not become an instrument of subtle or not-so-subtle segregation, it can work to the benefit of all. Advocates for this approach argue that it actually extends to all a benefit that had been available only to rich people, who could afford to move to an affluent school district or pay private school tuition.

---

32. Guardian Staff and Agencies, "Florida and Texas Schools."

Further Recommendations

Backing away from lockstep curriculum and giving teachers the freedom to teach can accomplish a diversity of approaches that are highly desirable. The more creativity and innovation in education, the more vital it becomes. Some guardrails are necessary, of course, so that the freedom does not go beyond what society has a right to expect. The ideal is to keep bureaucratic, legalistic, micromanaging at bay so that kids' natural appetite to learn can flourish. The funding and governance of schools should support a cultural and educational ideal that nurtures the whole child. Such a learning climate facilitates children maturing into rounded adults with a consciousness suited for a complex and challenging era. In the near term, nonprofit charter schools and school choice can move the needle in the right direction by providing more options for parents seeking an innovative setting that can meet a child's needs.

To combat the gross inequity in school funding, we should reconsider basing school support solely on the local tax base. A federalizing of school funding, but not governance, needs to be explored.

Rather than schools so big that they resemble mass-production factories, small schools, organically connected to neighborhoods, will get better results, bearing in mind that smallness alone cannot achieve the desired results. The Boggs School in Detroit provides an inspiring example of how this can happen and how schools can change communities.[33]

Good reasons exist for expecting schools to cover basic skills. There are two ways to make this happen and at the same time respect the agency of teachers: 1) create pared down national standards—Finland's are tiny compared to the United States; or 2) expectations could be framed in the form of guidelines rather than rigid requirements. When a government creates a climate of distrust and control, and when teachers are government employees, you will get very different results than under a learning environment that fosters bold innovation.

Charter schools have been controversial in the United States. For one thing, they typically are not unionized and unions have opposed them. They also are apt to siphon money away from the public system so that both unions and administrators oppose them. Finally, corporate charters, where the bottom line is return on investment rather than kids learning, evokes strong opposition from not-for-profit charters. The latter, often started by teachers and parents, typically afford teachers more freedom

---

33. See Boggs School, "About Us."

to teach. Schools certified by Educate the Whole Child—both charter and mainstream—have been able to strike a constructive balance between state standards and teacher agency.[34]

Such schools are places where children want to be. Several other measures can help this to happen. Integrating arts into the curriculum can change the whole tenor of a school. For example, Waldorf schools replace textbooks with books the students create themselves, writing about and illustrating the ideas they are studying. In the early grades, music, rhythm, and movement are used to teach math. This kind of instruction builds engagement and helps children learn, not just with their brains but with their bodies.[35] Getting students beyond school walls into nature and gardening gives them a connection to growing things. This should include service projects in the community where possible. Advocates of democratic schools try to involve children in an age-appropriate way in decisions that affect them and involve the school. This provides opportunities to reinforce caring for others and social and emotional faculties that will stay with them throughout life. The more open and imaginative and inspired that climate, the more children will relish learning and have the chance to become the adults their true and higher selves want them to be.

---

34. For a list of certified whole-child schools, see Educate the Whole Child, "Our Schools."

35. Learn more at Educate the Whole Child, "What Is Whole Child Education?"

Part Three—Indications for Two Other Fields

CHAPTER SEVEN: A HEALING AGRICULTURE

The ultimate goal of farming is not the growing of crops but the cultivation . . . of human beings.
—Masanobu Fukuoka

It all turns on affection.
—Wendell Berry

Love is a verb.
—Oprah Winfrey

As the last two chapters have shown, education is the key leverage point for moving toward a new civilization that is more caring, constructive, and healing. Through education people can take up questions like, "Who do I want to be?" and "What kind of society can help me become that person?" Moreover, through education, sustained through a lifetime, individuals can be empowered to reify the answers they develop for those two key questions. However, other areas of human endeavor also need transformation. As examples of how this could work, I next take up agriculture and the economy. Just as a head-heart-and-hands education brings a healing impulse to children, a holistic approach to agriculture can not only heal the soil but mend the frayed relationship between farm and community.

Each Friday afternoon in the growing season, my wife and I drive to our community farm and pick up salad greens and other produce harvested that morning. They contain no pesticides. And by supporting the farm we save the land from development. It feels right to be walking the land where our food is grown, to know the farmer who produced it, and to visit with friends and neighbors who are also picking up their shares in the barn.

In the new civilization this book helps you imagine, many will probably still live in cities and not have a Community Supported Agriculture (CSA) farm or family farm nearby. But one could very well see an increase in what exists already—rooftop beekeeping, urban gardens, and co-op and farmers' markets. The point is this: One need not go back to the nineteenth century to find examples of farming that do not subscribe to the industrial model for today's agriculture. A great deal more could be done with local and regional food production, even on a small scale; and it would pay dividends in terms of freshness for consumers and preservation of open space in communities.

A Blighted Paradigm

But that is not the prevailing paradigm today. "Get big or get out" was the advice to farmers from Secretary of Agriculture Earl Butz in the Nixon administration, and to a large extent that describes what has happened. Big Ag grows vast fields of corn or soybeans, with heavy reliance on chemicals for not only fertilizer but also pest and weed control. Powerful and complex machinery allows one person to cover many acres in a day. Each of these factors contributes to global warming. Increasingly, concentrated corporate power owns and orchestrates the operation.

This dominant agricultural model prompts one to ask: Are there better ways that heal instead of harm the earth, that produce nutritious food one need not be apprehensive to eat, and that allow farming to be both a business and an art (the culture part of agriculture)? Suppose principles drawn from the first three chapters of this book, namely freedom, community, and love, were to guide a rethinking of agriculture. It might be possible to break the corporate hegemonies that prevail in our entire food system today.[1]

---

1. Two pieces of media do a good job of revealing the problem: the documentary *Food Inc.* and the *New York Times* video series "Meet the People Getting Paid to Kill Our Planet."

CHAPTER SEVEN: A HEALING AGRICULTURE

Through the centuries, the phrase "eating the seed corn" has been an image of desperation. That is, people facing starvation eat the seeds that were reserved to plant next year's crop. Unfortunately, that image fits what industrial agriculture does to the land when it farms at such a scale and in such a manner that earth is poisoned and topsoil washes away. With the soil's natural fertility depleted or gone, large amounts of chemical fertilizer are required to get a crop. The current system is propped up by short term federal policy and subsidies, typically with a five-year farm bill; but this arrangement is completely unsustainable in the long term. Again and again, civilizations have died when they destroyed the soil that fed them.[2] The actual situation is more complex than that, but in the big picture "eating the seed corn" is an apt image.

Around 2012, two agricultural heretics, Wes Jackson and Wendell Berry, floated the idea of a "50-Year Farm Bill" to press the US Department of Agriculture (USDA) beyond its customary short-term, treat-the-symptoms-instead-of-the-problem thinking. Berry's indictment of the present system rings out with no apologies:

> This is agriculture determined entirely by the market, and limited only by the capacities of machines and chemicals. The entirely predictable ruination of land and people is the result of degenerate science and the collapse of local farming cultures.[3]

The collapse of farming cultures refers to large operations, often corporations, buying up land and depopulating rural areas so that small towns and their businesses can no longer survive, and at the same time the loss of a neighborly and cooperative social fabric where small farmers help each other to steward the land on what used to be more diversified farms. Everyone in the agricultural community knows about the problem of erosion, but the "50-Year Farm Bill" never got traction.[4]

It would be unfair to make that sprawling department, the USDA, the sole culprit here. It does worthwhile programs that provide food assistance; it does research; it educates consumers and farmers; and it manages fifteen nutrition programs. Among its many responsibilities and constituencies, the US Forest Service is itself a vast agency. I am concerned here only with its role in propping up an unsustainable form of agriculture. USDA crop insurance illustrates how too many of

---

2. Scholes and Scholes, "Dust Unto Dust," 565.
3. Berry, "50-Year Farm Bill."
4. Of course, erosion is only one of the problems with the existing paradigm.

the department's decisions are driven by political considerations. Crop insurance is popular with farmer-voters because it protects them to a degree against the capriciousness of the weather—hail, floods, and drought. But at the same time, it encourages farmers to overproduce and plant in areas prone to flooding that should be left alone as wetlands. An alternative system for decision-making, based on environmental and agricultural science, not politics, could yield better decisions.

You will recall that in Chapter 2 I identified a counterfeit form of freedom consists of simply "doing what I want." Too often, our food system tilts toward corporations doing what they want—profit maximization—and politicians doing what they want—currying votes by maintaining artificially low food prices. The consequences for farmers, however, have been disastrous because the farm economy today favors immense and specialized agribusinesses and drives out diversified family-sized farms.

Tyson

An example of how far modern agriculture has strayed from a wholesome model of sustainable family-scale operations can be found by looking at what happened in Arkansas as Tyson extended its control of the chicken broiler industry there. The word "farmer" hardly applies to those who raise birds for Tyson because they have been reduced to a form of peonage with their own destinies and stewardship of chickens strictly controlled by a complex contract only a lawyer could love. The chickens themselves are in prison, typically confined in tiny cages in a windowless, factory-like building. Birds in these concentrated animal feeding operations, or CAFOs, may never get to see the light of day. Aside from the inhumane crowding and the need to include antibiotics in the feed to prevent the spread of disease, a major problem such operations pose is the amount of manure they create. A CAFO of eighty-two thousand chickens will produce twenty-eight hundred tons of waste in a year, in either wet or dry form—a serious source of pollution.[5]

In the last four decades, Tyson has consolidated its control over the industry so that now it accounts for more than 67 percent of the broilers produced in the state. At the same time that chicken production has grown by 1,000 percent, the number of independent chicken farmers has been reduced by nearly half. A recent study by the Union of

5. Miller, "CAFOS," 7.

Concerned Scientists (UCS) called "Tyson Spells Trouble for Arkansas" details how, as the third largest employer in the state with immense political clout, Tyson can largely write its own ticket, securing tax breaks, flooding surrounding counties with chicken waste, weakening worker safety regulations, and getting away with exploiting undocumented and Native American workers.[6] The company's indifference to worker welfare during COVID became national news, and the BBC reported that supervisors at an Iowa plant were taking bets on how many workers would contract the disease.[7] A recent settlement with Tyson and other boiler operations required them to pay $180 million to settle worker claims and the charge that it colluded to keep wages down.[8] Unfortunately, CAFOs exist all over the country for poultry, pork, beef cattle, and dairy cows. In addition to the untold suffering caused to sentient beings, one cannot avoid the irony of how at the same time they are imprisoning the animals and birds, the farmers themselves become locked in the iron grip of soulless thinking and an inflexible industry that relentlessly pushes for efficiency and competitive advantage.

Monsanto's War on Bees

Consider *convivencia* or community from the point of view of bees. We depend on these little, hard-working, social creatures to pollinate about one third of the food we eat. They also serve as an indicator species on the health of the entire agricultural sector, and the indications are not good. In recent years, between 30 and 60 percent of hives were lost yearly to colony collapse disorder (CCD).[9] Not a disease in the conventional sense, CCD occurs when all but the young and the queen simply leave the hive and fail to return. It is believed, but has not been proven, that the presence of pesticides disrupts their delicate navigation faculties, so they cannnot find their way back. A bee can survive only about a day without returning to its hive.[10] Hives for bees exposed to fields and groves that have been sprayed, die out with CCD in large numbers. On the other hand, a bee sanctuary called Spikenard Farm in an isolated part of Virginia with no

---

6. Boehm, "Tyson Spells Trouble."
7. BBC, "Tyson Food Managers Bet."
8. Scarcella, "Tyson, Other Poultry Processors."
9. Aurell et al., "United States Honey Bee."
10. Langworthy, *Vanishing of the Bees.*

chemically treated crops nearby experiences no CCD, or, in a bad year, 13 percent. A relatively new class of insecticides called neonicotinoids was developed by Bayer, now Bayer/Monsanto, in the 1980s. They target insects' nervous systems with lethal efficiency and have come to replace older sprays and seed treatments.[11] The European Union has imposed a near-total ban on this class of insecticides is systemic, which means that it affects every part of each plant, including pollen and flowers. Monsanto also manufactures the world's most widely used herbicide—glyphosate (commercial name: Roundup). The *Guardian* reported in 2019 that this chemical reacts with the beneficial bacteria in the gut of honeybees and causes them to be more subject to deadly infections.[12]

But Monsanto's most egregious offense against *convivencia* occurs through the baleful combination of patented, engineered seeds that can survive being sprayed with Roundup. Thus, for example, a farmer who in the past might have saved and replanted his own seed, buys a patented corn seed because it produces well and can tolerate spraying of Roundup. Even at a premium price, this saves time and money. However, the corn produced under this regime contains the Roundup's active ingredient, glyphosate. In Germany, glyphosate is being phased out because it is a presumed carcinogen. In the United States, because of the immense power and influence of Monsanto (now part of Bayer), it is still widely used, and for years the company was able to avoid lawsuits for damages by legislation its critics call the Monsanto Protection Act, passed as part of the giant Agricultural Appropriations Bill of 2013. More recently, lawsuits against the company have been settled.

In India, where Monsanto has established a virtual monopoly by buying out other seed companies and then jacking up the price of seed as much as 8,000 percent, their predatory practices have led to widespread rural debt and a wave of farmer suicides. Between 1995 and 2013, in the state of Maharashtra in western India, these suicides approached fifty-four thousand people.[13] As in the United States, the company has been able to capture the regulatory process sufficiently to make it immune from prosecution.

11. Simon-Delso et al., "Systemic Insecticides."
12. Carrington, "Monsanto's Global Weedkiller."
13. Shiva, "Seeds of Suicide."

Organic Fraud

A third example of how corporate agriculture has defied human values of love and honesty is in the area of milk production. Aurora Organic Dairy uses the word "integrity" a lot, and it declares on its website, "We are proud of our work and deeply believe integrity and transparency go hand in hand";[14] but the company provides a stunning example of the co-opting of organic production. An investigative report by the *Washington Post* revealed that Aurora does indeed avoid pesticides, growth hormones, and GMOs. But it conveniently skirts the organic certification requirement that each cow have 120 days of grazing on pasture per year. Milk from grass-fed cows is different from conventional milk,[15] but most of Aurora's cows barely or never see a blade of fresh grass and are kept in barns or bare-ground feedlots for their entire milk-producing lives. During 2016 when the *Post* reporter visited Aurora's "farm" north of Greeley, Colorado, eight times (including one flyover with a drone) he saw only a few hundred cows out on pasture. In fact, with fifteen thousand cows in that one facility it would be logistically impossible to meet the pasture requirements.[16] Yet consumers of store brands at Walmart, Costco, Safeway, and other large retailers supplied by Aurora pay up to twice as much for what they believe meets USDA organic standards.

Why did the USDA, which is supposed to inspect farms for organic certification, not catch this omission? It allows producers like Aurora to hire its own inspectors. When an inspector from the department did come in 2016, he arrived in November, not in grazing season. A few years earlier, Aurora had received a Notice of Proposed Revocation from the USDA for "willful violation" of fourteen federal organic regulations.[17] But the company was able to generate enough political pressure on the department so that it was only hit with a toothless consent decree.

Such fraudulent organic milk can be produced at a volume that leads to lower prices, further undercutting authentic organic producers and driving them out of business. This happens particularly in the Northeast, where your typical organic family farm has sixty-six cows producing and is particularly vulnerable. Horizon, another industrial-scale "organic" label, notified eighty-nine small New England farmers in

14. See auroraorganic.com.
15. Organic Valley, "Organic Grass-fed Milk."
16. Whoriskey, "Why your 'organic' milk may not be."
17. Cornucopia Institute, "Aurora Farm's Certifier."

2022 that their milk contracts would end. Some of their output will be replaced by CAFOs in the Southwest.[18]

These three examples reveal an industry that clearly is not working for everybody. Inasmuch as it produces cheap food for many, it is democratic. But it does not pass the test of a just society because, though it reaps enormous profits for those at the top, workers, small farmers, and others are cheated, exploited, or used like so many disposable wipes. It especially disadvantages those organic farmers who work hard and play by the rules, but who lack the political clout to have the rules crafted to advantage them.

Rest assured that power wielded by these big firms, with the America Farm Bureau and other potent lobbying arms, will be used to fight furiously to retain their hegemony and block regulations that favor the environment over their profits. Cory Booker, until recently chair of the US Senate Agriculture Subcommittee on Food and Nutrition, admits being profoundly frustrated by the injustice inherent in the current system. "We've lost 90% of our hog farmers in just a matter of decades," he says. "Independent family farmers are being driven out at alarming rates. . . . The suicide rate among farmers and ranchers is three times higher than it is in the rest of America. . . . [This is] the hollowing out of rural America."[19]

In her essay "Whole Systems Change," Riane Eisler distinguishes between "hierarchies of domination" and "hierarchies of actualization." Some degree of hierarchy is necessary in any society—parents, teachers, managers, leaders. But in domination hierarchies, one finds "dog-eat-dog competition aimed at destroying competitors or putting them out of business." In an actualization setting (that no doubt would please Abraham Maslow), parties compete to spur excellence.[20] The three cases above exemplify a ruthless form of capitalism that places profits ahead of everything.

This tells us what we do *not* want. In a farm sector revisualized from the ground up for a new civilization, what is it we *do* want? In the rest of this chapter, I focus on steps that can heal the landscape and food supply now and that could be built into a re-envisioned agriculture in the future. Here are some possibilities.

18. Real Organic Project, "2022 Real Organic Symposium."
19. Litman, "Making Ends Meat."
20. Speth and Courrier, *New Systems Reader*, 75.

Restore Integrity to the USDA Organic Label

A relatively small measure and a place to begin would be to restore the integrity of the USDA organic designation, which has been so compromised that some independent organic farmers have instituted their own "Real Organic" label.[21] Realizing that organic could be profitable for them, giant companies have moved in, bought up organic brands, and come to control the National Organic Standards Board. Resulting changes have compromised the integrity of the USDA organic label, misled consumers, and placed small producers who grow according to true organic standards at a distinct price disadvantage.[22]

A core principle of organic farming is the long-term effort to restore and strengthen the soil. However, USDA now allows produce that has never seen soil but is grown in nutrient water to be labeled as organic. Other issues arise where there are rules but not enforcement, as with Aurora Dairy. The USDA does spend money to combat organic fraud, but the problem is complex, and results have been inconsistent. I believe much could be achieved with a different leadership at USDA, one that encourages cooperation in a collegial spirit between large and small producers and can resist the concentrated power and intense pressure of vested interests—gigantic producers, chemical and fertilizer companies.

But there is potentially an even greater concern than just keeping poisons out of food. Soil health affects human health. In the renewed civilization here envisioned this fact will be recognized and the USDA will have a role in promoting the kind of soil—rich in humus, teeming with microlife, enzymes, and trace minerals—that produces more nutritious crops. This contrasts with prevailing current practice in which the soil has been made largely inert through chemicalized agriculture and extractive monocropping. Studies in India have shown that, for example, the effect of growing rice in severely depleted soil can be detected in assays of human hair.[23] European peasants considered the connection between soil health and human health self-evident for centuries. The science on this is in its infancy, but the progression makes sense: soil vitality → edible plant vitality → human vitality. If the peasants were right, the health of the nation is at issue.[24]

21. Learn more about this initiative at the project's website: realorganicproject.org.
22. Kastel, "NGO Appeals to Biden."
23. Tata-Cornell Institute, "Study Reveals."
24. Soil Health Institute, "Connections Between Soil Health."

Make Farming Regenerative, Not Extractive

If you fly over Middle America and look down from the plane window, you will see mile after mile of corn and soybeans. This is conventional—sometimes called industrial—farming. Occasionally you will see a feedlot, with animals crowded into a space where they can be fattened up for slaughter. Farms of this sort do not operate like living organisms. Each is more like a mine, where the aim is to *take* all you can and *give* as little as possible to get it. Dowsing topsoil with chemicals has turned it into an inert medium, where it should be rich in nutrients and throbbing with microlife.

Regenerative agriculture, on the other hand, places emphasis on restoring soil health and the vitality of the whole-farm ecosystem. It minimizes chemical inputs. It promotes biodiversity, improves the water cycle, curbs erosion, and increases resilience to climate change. The older designation of *organic* goes further and pursues certifiable, chemical-free, and humane farming. If we take it a step beyond that, we come to *biodynamic farming*, a method that not only eschews chemicals but calls for the inner development of farmers so they can be a fully conscious healing influence on the land. For our purposes, we will focus on regenerative agriculture because it has the broadest appeal.

Some confusion arises when the term is applied to no-till farming. Because plowing and cultivating take time and a good deal of fossil fuel, no-till is sometimes promoted as climate-friendly. But if you don't till, the only way to control weeds is with a heavy reliance on chemicals. Calling that regenerative is really a stretch.

A conventional agricultural economist will likely tell you that regenerative or organic agriculture cannot feed the world. Small, diversified, old-fashioned farms are simply too inefficient to compete. They can't afford the technology and big equipment that makes large operations hum. On a modern farm, one man can plow many acres in a day, and self-driving tractors guided from satellites also can do the job. With a world population headed toward nine billion, we need all the benefits of engineered seeds and the Green Revolution, even though these innovations involve heavy demands for chemicals and irrigation.[25] So the logic goes.

Talk to a regenerative ag person, however, and you will hear a different story. The first thing they are apt to point out is how conventional agriculture contributes to the climate crisis. Farm animals, especially in

---

25. Lynas, "Organic Farming."

CAFOs, generate enormous amounts of methane through digestive gas and manure. The common forms of nitrogen used in chemical fertilizer degrade to nitrous oxide. Both are greenhouse gases many times more potent than CO_2. Thus, through its contribution to climate change, conventional agriculture is actually making more agricultural land unsuitable for farming, decreasing our ability to feed the world. Organic and regenerative advocates also claim categorically that their approaches are not only more sustainable but, if widely applied today, could feed the world.[26] Their research indicates that after a five-year conversion period, organic farms are just as productive as conventional ones, and more so in times of drought or flood, according to the same research.

Conventional farmers, backed by their own researchers, put their faith in horsepower and chemicals, and discount the skill and inventiveness of their organic peers. They believe the conventional wisdom that it is impossible to raise cotton without substantial chemical inputs. More than twenty-five insects attack the crop, the most notorious being the boll weevil. But biodynamic farmers associated with Sekem in Egypt have figured out how to raise their long-staple cotton in the Nile Delta with no chemicals. Yields are smaller, but the crop is more profitable because it can be sold at a premium as organic cotton.[27]

So what does a regenerative farm look like? Here are three examples—a dairy operation, a grain farm, and a CSA providing vegetables to two hundred member families.

Making Money on Milk

With politicians wanting to keep milk prices low, with the rise of monopolistic milk processors, and with the co-opting of USDA organic standards, noted above, few small dairy farmers can make it unless they can find a way to add value to their milk before it leaves the farm. One such operation exists in Vermont, where Strafford Organic Creamery makes and sells their own premium ice cream. A herd of 70 Guernsey cows, known for their rich, digestible milk, supplies the raw material for a small pasteurizing operation from which the milk goes into glass bottles for the niche market. A parallel operation produces different flavors of ice cream, sold locally and around the state. With a great deal of hard

---

26. Rodale Institute, "Can Organic Feed."
27. Hassan, "It's Cotton Harvest Time."

work and enterprise, farmer/owner Earl Ransom has built this business over a period of more than twenty years. But how many dairy farmers, just skating by, barely able to make tractor payments, are able to raise the capital, acquire the new skills, and embark on this kind of venture with ice cream, farm cheese, or yogurt? With the help of the USDA, the milk market has been skewed to favor the giant producers and squeeze out the small ones. A radical paradigm shift inspired by the burley tobacco co-op described below could change all this. The Northeast Organic Family Farms Partnership is an encouraging sign, as is a USDA program called Value-Added Producer Grants.[28]

Farming Grain the Organic Way

Fred Kirschenmann grew up on the family farm raising grain in Windsor, North Dakota. In 1976, when his father suffered a heart attack, he left a successful academic career and returned to the family farm. Fred offered to return home and take over the farm on the condition that he could convert it to organic. In a series of interviews sponsored by the USDA, he tells about the mistakes and eventual successes in making this shift and how he was able to convert a farm of over three thousand acres into a thriving, diverse, organic farm raising mainly cereal grains.[29] Instead of a monoculture of continuous wheat like his neighbors, Kirschenman developed a mixed rotation that included wheat, rye, oats, flax, and sunflowers, plus legumes like soybeans and clover to serve as cover crops that add nitrogen and organic matter to the soil. There were also times when portions of the land were allowed to lie fallow. The fallowing, soil building, and variety and rotation of crops prevented any pest from getting a hold and raging like a wildfire through the farm. By planting and then plowing under cover crops, he could control weeds without chemicals and add organic matter to nourish the soil.

Kirschenmann has become a sought-after speaker and spokesman for the organic movement because he was able to demonstrate that a regenerative or organic approach can work on a large farm if one is willing to bring a different kind of thinking to bear. As he explained it, conventional farmers tended to think in terms of inputs and outputs, or a "factory model." The output was the crop; the inputs were seed, chemical

28. USDA, "Value Added Producer Grant."
29. Kirschenmann, "Fred Kirschenmann Oral History."

fertilizer, and pesticides. Thinking differently, he called for a nutrient recycling system in which the fertility of a farm's soil is produced by the farm itself, with animal and green manures.

In a TEDx Talk in Manhattan in 2012, he eloquently gets an urban audience to understand that soil is not dirt. Rather it is "a very vibrant living community . . . in which there are more living organisms beneath the surface of the soil than there are above." This community of life—millions of microorganisms in a single teaspoon of soil—gives the ground its vitality and strength. He explains that a new generation of chefs in the farm-to-table movement have come to recognize that food grown in this kind of healthy, living soil actually tastes better. These chefs seek out relationships with local farmers in a symbiosis that assures organic farmers a market for their produce and assures restaurants that they can advertise and deliver absolutely fresh, local, and chemical-free food to diners.[30]

The CSA

A very different model, also regenerative, can be seen in Indian Line Farm in Massachusetts, which produces organic vegetables for over two hundred families through an approximately five-month growing season. This arrangement is called a CSA or Community Supported Agriculture. In 1986, Indian Line and another CSA in New Hampshire were the first such farms in the United States. There are now more than 2,500 in the country. Well before the growing season begins, farmer Elizabeth Keen invites local residents to become members by paying $760 if they want a full family share for the entire season. This represents approximately what one would pay for organic vegetables at the supermarket over this period. The advance payment allows Elizabeth to buy seeds, prepare the greenhouses, hire interns, and be ready for the growing season. It also spreads the risk so that it does not completely fall on the farmer. If one crop fails, there are many other vegetables, and each member family will get ample for their weekly share. Depending on the time of year, this will include salad greens, radishes, peas, beans, squash, tomatoes, potatoes, tomatillos, various delicious Japanese vegetables you may never have heard of, carrots, and other root vegetables. For an extra fee, people can buy a fruit share and get different berries and other fruit each week well into the fall. Organic eggs, grass-fed beef, and other farm items can also

---

30. Kirschenmann, "Soil" 1:45–1:56.

be purchased for cash at the farm on distribution days. A weekly emailed newsletter provides a list of vegetables for the week, an update on farm operations, and favorite recipes for one or two items in season.

The farm is amazingly productive in a small space. "We are a 20-acre farm growing vegetables on only five acres," says Elizabeth Keen. "Miniscule in the eyes of the statisticians! And yet we produce so much food.... Because most of our work is done by hand or with simple machines we are able to capture more of the produce and leave little waste."[31]

CSAs serve several food needs of consumers. They get vegetables picked the very same day, typically chemical-free. Members develop a personal connection with the person growing their food. CSAs help the local farm economy and preserve open space otherwise threatened by development. This is truly a win-win situation. Farmers can earn a decent living and consumers get healthy food, which is why the CSA model has become so popular across the country.

In a CSA one sees in action a remarkable contrast to the beleaguered agricultural economy. CSAs reify the values covered in the initial chapters. The farmer has the freedom to prosper locally and by his or her own initiative. No subsidies subject to political machinations prop up this operation. The very diverse individual members take joy in their food and in the spirit of *convivencia* that prevails when we share a potluck meal or in the field picking peas or beans on pick-up day. Empathy is expressed by the caring and personal connection between the farmer's family and the land, and further in the sharing of surplus vegetables with those in need.

Empower Farmers to Set Farm Prices

On the economic front, an enormous problem and one where *convivencia* could have transformative impact would be bringing stability and fairness to farm prices. The inherent instability of commodity prices existed long before big ag became dominant. Due to unpredictable factors like weather and pests, crops may be abundant one year and negligible the next. In flush years, a commodity's abundant supply drives the price down. If this prompts some growers to switch out of that crop for the next year, prices rise in response to smaller supply. But this is usually not predictable because some growers have a heavy investment in crop-specific

---

31. Elizabeth Keen, personal interview with author, Sept. 10, 2025.

machinery. Faced with low prices for their crop, they may simply produce more to generate the needed income in order to operate; this makes matters worse, driving prices down further. The whole farm-price, yo-yo dynamic cries out for some form of rational control.

After the First World War, when European farmers returned to full production and the American farm sector found itself with vast oversupply and plunging prices, one of the first measures of the New Deal was the Agricultural Adjustment Act of 1933. It resurrected the idea of *parity*. Parity means farm prices are set at a level that maintains the farmer's purchasing power on an equal basis with that of the rest of the economy. Various measures have been used by government to set fair prices and control supply. Free-marketeers have tended to oppose them even though without any controls farm prices can fluctuate wildly, and some years are so low as to not even cover the cost of production. Since the Agricultural Adjustment Act of 1948, parity has been whittled away, and by the 1980s the concept was largely considered obsolete and was phased out.[32] In this country and others all sorts of farm price controls and subsidies have been tried without consistent success. In the United States, subsidies have favored large, corporate producers.[33]

The problem with having the federal government control farm prices is that the economic objective of achieving fair or parity prices for farmers collides with the political objective of keeping consumer food prices low in order to win favor at the polls. Voters are many; farmers are relatively few; political concerns win out. That creates enormous pressure on farmers to go for efficiency, to "get big or get out," and to cut corners by abandoning ecological practices, relying on chemicals, and letting acres of topsoil escape into the Mississippi watershed and eventually the Gulf of Mexico.

One answer could be to take the setting of farm prices out of the hands of government as much as possible. It is rightly an economic matter, not a political one. A way to do this could be to take the idea of the farm cooperative and give it wings to fly.

Imagine a cooperative in which all producers of a single commodity are automatically enrolled. Give them the power through their democratically elected representatives to control production and set prices. Each

---

32. Teigen, "Agricultural Parity," 1–2.

33. "When it comes to agriculture, there is no such thing as a free market," said the head of giant food conglomerate Archer Daniels Midland in 1995. See Immerwahr, "Pitchfork History," 27.

grower would receive an allotment of how much he or she was allowed to produce in any one year. This would be based on the amount of land each devotes to a commodity on the one hand, and on the other, a calculation made by the super-co-op or association of how much of a market there would be for the commodity when the next crop came in. If there looked likely to be overproduction and depressed prices the next year, all producers' allotments might be reduced, for example, to 80 percent of their full production capacity. In spite of allotment adjustments, some years there would be an oversupply. In that case, the association would buy and store the excess, subsequently releasing it to the market when the demand and price picture improved.

The association would need to borrow money in order to pay farmers, in effect make loans, to cover the cost of the grain or commodity the association could not sell immediately. The loans would also cover storage, transport, and administration costs. Absent other options, the federal government could finance the loans, but on the condition that they be paid back with interest.

Thus, a stable, rational commodity price could be counted on, and farm income could be freed from the precariousness and sub-parity prices that now prevail. Not well-meaning federal bureaucrats but the farmers themselves would control the market. Government could step in if the association proceeded to set and enforce inflated or unreasonable prices. Otherwise the farmers would be left to their own devices.

At one time, a farm cooperative that managed supply to match demand actually existed in this country, not for food but for burley tobacco. The basic principle for the tobacco co-op was simple and brilliant—manage price by adjusting supply to match demand. What was most appealing at the time, even to advocates of small government, was that it operated at no cost to taxpayers and had limited involvement from the USDA. In that instance, farmers elected to join the co-op. They had the opportunity to elect their own leadership and to accept or reject, by vote, quota restrictions. In short, the growers determined their own destiny.

Making joining the co-op voluntary was necessary to make it acceptable to farmers at the time. This, however, also eventually proved its undoing. Buoyed by relative success and good prices, enough farmers ultimately decided not to pay the membership fees and thereby to circumvent the cooperative. When a critical mass was lost, the co-op lacked market leverage to adjust prices and failed. A more complete description of the Burley Tobacco Growers Cooperative Association appears in Appendix B.

But in the future, why should producers not be able to sustain a predictable and fair price, not subject to speculation and uncontrollable fluctuations? They could do this by forming superco-ops or associations that they control. Applied to food rather than tobacco, this would mean higher prices, but when people realize that the true cost of producing a food needs to be reflected in its retail price, this should be doable. It will mean divesting government of a job it does not do well—spending enormous sums for subsidies to cover its clumsy efforts to control prices and production. In each commodity, a crop-wide cooperative would assume these functions.

Such a system could be eased in, beginning with non-essential crops such as honey and cranberries. For cranberries, a strong, well-run cooperative, Ocean Spray, already exists. Limiting the arrangement initially to organic producers could be a good way to get started. Once the bugs are worked out, the system could be expanded to other crops and conventional farmers. As with all social and economic improvements, no single individual but a group working together in a constructive spirit can devise the best approach. To be sure, it will take time to implement.

Missing from my proposal is a way to prevent low-cost imports from crashing in and wrecking the balance of supply and demand. This *will* require government participation and some strenuous work because World Trade Organization (WTO) rules and foreign trade agreements aim to remove trade barriers. Given what has become a global economy, this could be challenging. A Price Stabilization Import Board could be established to liaise between the commodity associations and the State Department; together, they would need to debunk the dogma that unrestricted free trade is always the best policy.[34]

So a way forward does exist to make farm subsidies a thing of the past, *unless* politicians decided that for political or other reasons they wanted to subsidize low food prices. There could be justification for this under certain circumstances. What makes no sense, however, is making farmers shoulder the cost of these subsidies, which is what happens now.

In the spirit of *convivencia*, some education will be necessary for the public to appreciate the value of allowing farmers to compete on a level playing field. This will be particularly important when higher food prices are part of the new arrangement, as they inevitably will be. How

---

34. Naomi Klein, in a section called "Trade Trumps Climate," provides an illuminating discussion of this issue as it impacts climate change. See Klein, *This Changes Everything*, 68–72.

the conscious cultivation of a caring economy might be achieved will be discussed in the following chapter.

The kind of thinking that went into the Burley Co-op is being incorporated into an initiative, new at the time of this writing, to save 135 dairy farms in the Northeast threatened with extinction when they learned they would lose their milk contracts. If it succeeds, this will set an example of how farmers can empower themselves to control their own destiny instead of being at the mercy of government handouts and corporate aggregators.[35]

Design Farms to Grow People

As long as we are blue-skying farms of the future, let us go a step further and imagine the best way to grow people along with crops. This could have many benefits, ranging from the quality of life of farm families, to the husbanding of their birds and animals, to the nutritional value of the food they produce. It also could promote the growth of human consciousness (see p. 24f., 37) as people evolve toward greater degrees of freedom.

In *An Everyone Culture: Becoming a Deliberately Developmental Organization*, Robert Kegan and Lisa Laskow Lahey present a way to transform a business from a money-making machine into a cultural force that grows people. Instead of just asking, "How can we efficiently get this job done and make money?" businesses should ask, "What is the most powerful way to develop the capabilities of people at work?"[36] Profit would be a by-product of this central concern. As the authors describe it, continuous attention to this question would change not only the individuals but organizations themselves. The culture of the place would change for every employee, not just the high-potential ones, "immersively sweep[ing] every member of the organization into an ongoing developmental journey in the course of every working day."[37] In such an organization, everyone comes out of hiding.

If this idea were applied to farming, what would such a farm look like? It would not be a CAFO or a chemically saturated monoculture, planted fencerow to fencerow with, say, continuous corn with no natural spaces for birds or other wild creatures. It would definitely not be an

---

35. See the partnership's website: saveorganicfamilyfarms.org.
36. Kegan and Laskow Lahey, *Everyone Culture*, 4.
37. Kegan and Laskow Lahey, *Everyone Culture*, 5.

industrial-scale operation organized to achieve the greatest efficiency and maximize profit. Rather, the guiding principle could be earth-healing—and not just at the soil level. As the climate crisis heats up, this factor looms large. Food and agriculture account for 31 percent of global climate change emissions.[38] The ideal for the farm would go beyond doing no environmental harm; it would be to create a harmonious, holistic organism consisting of people, animals, plants, and a living soil.

On the people level, the deliberately developmental farm would be a somewhat self-sufficient, diversified operation providing numerous growth opportunities for the farm's children and adults. They would acquire skills in husbandry; learn to integrate and recycle various elements the farm produces, and create a culture that would embrace horizon-expanding skills, such as creating value-added farm products. Family members and the farm team could learn to think differently, applying mantras from the Kegan and Laskow Lahey book: "Most problems are potential improvements screaming at you" and "An error is an opportunity to learn."[39] Children might participate in an intensified 4-H, that one-hundred-year-old movement for farm youth, whose original "H" values of thought (head), compassion (heart), service (hands), and healthy living (health) would be amended with the organization's updated values of promoting personal development in the areas of *belonging, generosity, independence,* and *mastery*.[40] Together, these qualities would build the social and emotional intelligence needed to be a responsible farmer, citizen, spouse, parent, or coworker. In other words, participants could grow into free and fulfilled lives.

The depopulation of the rural landscape works against this expanded vision of what constitutes farming. The advent of giant operations that consolidate formerly independent farms, the relentless drive for efficiency through substituting chemicals and machinery for manpower and frequently corporate control of the mega-farms, all lead to rural communities that no longer have enough people to support a doctor, a school, or a hardware store. One means of repopulating farm country would involve encouraging locally-produced food.[41]

As for animals, rather than regarding them as units of production, livestock would be accorded a standard of care that stems from gratitude

---

38. Douglas, "How Food and Agriculture."
39. Kegan and Laskow Lahey, *Everyone Culture* 43, 86.
40. See Kleinath, "Essential Elements of 4-H." See also 4-H, "About."
41. Farmer and consultant Brian Donahue explores this in Johnson, *What If,* 49.

for their gifts, including, for most, the ultimate sacrifice made in their prime of life. Organic farmers already know how to do this. Think of free-range chickens and grass-fed beef. Research has shown that stressing animals affects the quality of their meat.[42]

Similarly with planted crops, cared for and cultivated out of an appreciation of the marvels involved. The cultural climate of the farm, especially for children, can be completely different when, instead of a laser focus on profitability, attention can focus as well on such things as the miracle of a single kernel of corn giving rise to a plant eight feet tall full of sugars and nutrients, reproducing and sustaining life with its own seeds.

Children who retain a sense of wonder remain open and appreciative. As Valerie Kaur says in her remarkable book *See No Stranger*, "Wonder is an admission that you don't know everything about another. . . . Wonder is where love begins."[43]

Soil and Soul

It is hard for people who have never farmed or gotten dirt under their fingernails to understand the depth of connection and respect that can develop between an individual and the soil underfoot. But a well-balanced farm growing people as well as crops sustains a level of caring that in turn generates productivity and profit.

The various religions have teachings that support this view. Thus, in the Qur'an we read, "We have made you trustees of the land . . . see how you would act" (Q 10:14). A farmer friend sees the soil of the earth as the medium that received Christ's body and that is consequently blessed. In the decades of work it took my friend to heal land exhausted by tobacco cultivation and sod farming, he stayed motivated by seeing this effort as "redeeming the Redeemer." However one chooses to regard it, soil needs to be a living presence for the farmer. With the build-up of sufficient organic matter, it will become that—rich in microlife and nutrients and those miracle workers, the worms. Charles Darwin had such a high regard for earthworms that, not long before he died, he wrote a whole book on the subject. When vegetable matter or manure passes through the gut of an earthworm, the resulting castings are near-perfect, slow-release

---

42. Xian et al., "Stress Effects on Meat."
43. Kaur, *See No Stranger*, 11, 19.

plant food that provides not only nitrogen, phosphorus, and potassium but also iron, sulfur, calcium, and micronutrients.[44]

Shakers, Amish, and Mennonites demonstrate how a respectful relationship with the soil serves them well as farmers. Respect and gratitude for what a healthy soil can give need not have a religious basis, but it provides a foundation for a harmonized relationship between a family and its land.

Regenerative agriculture restores land instead of depleting it, and various regenerative models that exist today provide an alternative to industrial farms. This can mean capturing carbon instead of dumping it into the atmosphere. It can mean the use of cover crops to prevent erosion. It often means incorporating animals into a healthy nutrient cycle so their manure takes the place of purchased chemical fertilizer.[45] A deep tradition and other quality-of-life factors typically underlie the successful models. In Switzerland, farmers have raised cows that produce rich milk for cheese on small, diversified farms that have operated for a thousand years without degrading the soil, even when on steep hillsides. There are still family-sized operations in the United States, but often they are designated by the USDA and IRS as "hobby farms" because owners can only afford to operate by holding a full-time, off-farm job. Many do it out of love for the land and farm life, and the realization that a small diversified farm can be a wonderful place to raise children.

There are also therapeutic, educational, and intentional communities that use farming to help people become centered—"grounded" is a good word—to throw off addictions or to heal past trauma. Some urban farms help ex-offenders to thrive.[46] Corporate ag, on the other hand, emphasizes other priorities, like driving out or buying up small competitors, and vertical integration. Unfortunately, it has the resources, attorneys, and lobbying money to write the rules by which the game is played. As Wendell Berry has repeatedly pointed out, this corporate colonization of rural America has had a devastating effect on rural towns and life.[47]

I have already hinted at what happens when love, gratitude, and respect are applied to farming. In part, it involves bringing *conscience* to bear on farm decisions. There is nothing sentimental about this. If you

---

44. University of California Agriculture and Natural Resources, "About Worm Castings."
45. Newton et al., "Regenerative Agriculture."
46. For example, see Brown, "Kale, Not Jail."
47. Berry, "Liberal Elites."

have a dairy herd, you don't need to give every cow a name. But with love or empathy present, would you consider keeping each cow in a barn, neck clamped in a stanchion for her entire lifetime, never having the opportunity to graze with her herd in the open air? Would you countenance keeping a steer confined to a crowded, unhealthy feedlot, knee-deep in manure? Would you allow at the time of slaughter for an animal to begin being cut up while still conscious?[48] Sikh writer Valerie Kaur says that "love is labor."[49] When shaped and inoculated by love, labor in farming becomes not a means to an end but an end in itself.[50] In the sense intended here, love is not something one passively falls into. It is propelled by conscious, active volition. All three epigraphs for this chapter allude to love. Seeing farms and farming through that lens, thoughtfully, even prayerfully, changes the way we treat animals, plants, the soil; it affects daily acts and decisions; it changes the whole landscape.

All these measures are worth pursuing. And, as suggested in the section above on CSAs, *presencing* has a place here. For a problem as vast as the one before us in this chapter, an arsenal of problem-solving tools is needed. Otto Scharmer might have us ask ourselves, "What better world is trying to be born?" Pursuing this line of thought could lead in several different directions. On one of them we might come to the conclusion that a great deal more empathy—for one another, for the earth, for our brothers and sisters in feathers and fur—wants to emerge. This would transform farming, and it already has to a limited degree where authentic biodynamic, organic, and regenerative practices are allowed to flourish.

The empathy and love referred to in the epigraphs for this chapter are not coextensive, but they overlap. If one reasons backward from symptom to reality, views the treatment of animals in factory farms, for example, and asks, "Of what is this a symptom?" then a complete breakdown of empathy becomes obvious, and also of love. Many of the destructive practices institutionalized in mainstream agriculture are just that—symptoms of inner deficiencies that could be remedied. Over the long term, a different kind of education of the sort discussed in Chapter 5 could be very helpful. For adults, an awakening can come in different forms, often prompted by suffering, for example, when the health or life of one's child is taken by pesticide load in the body.

48. Warrick, "'They Die.'"
49. Kaur, *See No Stranger*, 139.
50. Smith, "Revolutionary Love."

A different line of thought emerges if one asks, "What kind of farming could occur if farmers were to apply the traditional Native American assumption that nature is literally sacred?" Fertile soil is a gift. The animals hunted or slaughtered get thanked for allowing people to eat. The Native way meets this sacrifice with gratitude, even humility. It's hard for me to see a mammoth tractor, unmanned and guided by satellites, and not think *hubris*. Perhaps I am just being old-fashioned.

People living in the United States take a lot for granted—that the eggs, milk, cheese, and meat will be in the supermarket when we shop for it, that fuel to heat the house will be delivered before the tank is empty. Yet barreling toward us from the future are climate catastrophes and other trials that shatter our indifference to the planet's travail. Instead of waiting until our too-little-too-late approach to climate change crashes upon us, folks can begin right now with farming and their food choices to bring a healing impulse. To get there, people will need to muster the will to change their inner landscape so that there will be a livable outer landscape for our children and others unto the seventh generation.

Before concluding this chapter, I invite readers to review the chart on page 14 with Scharmer's four levels of problem-solving. I find it an incredibly useful thinking tool. See if you can apply it.

If we take the problem of toxic chemicals in our food and tackle it at the *symptoms* level, we would simply buy organic produce, free range eggs, and the like. To get more serious and try to address the problem at the *structures* level, we might try to get legislation passed that would provide incentives for producers of safer, more wholesome food. To pursue more fundamental change, we could go to the third problem-solving level, changing our *thinking*. To consider farming as a form of incredibly powerful global healing, rather than its present industrial form, global harming, would open the way for real traction and fundamental change. To carry this further and apply *presencing* to the problem of widespread soil poisoning and pesticide residues in food, one could ask, "In the future, how could farms become not only regenerative in terms of soil health and natural resources but how could they become an opportunity to address the urgent need to build human communities the way we seek to build soil?" One answer could be the CSA model, as well as other forms of cooperation that draw people together in creative ways.

You could pick another food- or farm-related problem and see how you might address it at all four levels. And there are plenty of problems. Farming in an era of climate deterioration delivers enough hardship and heartbreak, especially for the small operation, to make one sink into victimhood. But the thirteenth-century poet Rumi offers an original perspective, not only for farmers but for anyone being tested by life:

The Guest House
This being human is a guest house.
Every morning a new arrival.

A joy, a depression, a meanness,
some momentary awareness comes
As an unexpected visitor.

Welcome and entertain them all!
Even if they're a crowd of sorrows,
who violently sweep your house
empty of its furniture,
still treat each guest honorably.
He may be clearing you out
for some new delight.

The dark thought, the shame, the malice,
meet them at the door laughing,
and invite them in.

Be grateful for whoever comes,
because each has been sent
as a guide from beyond.

CHAPTER EIGHT: A COOPERATIVE ECONOMY

> *We face an "apocalyptic" future.... We're going to need new ideas ... a new conceptual understanding of reality....Over and against capitalism, we need a new way of thinking about our collective existence.*
> —Roy Scranton

> *Our current economic system is killing us and the planet.*
> —Emily Kawano

> *It is clearly time for ... a new environmentalism that seeks a new economy.*
> —James Gustave Speth

I RECEIVED A THANK-YOU card for a donation to the local humane society. It showed a little boy reading from a picture book to a very attentive cat. Seeing an adopted cat being welcomed into a family and attended by a generous little person as he learned to read, was, I thought, both touching and brilliant. The cat's face is in the foreground, the boy in the background. And the expression on the cat's face seems to signal both attention and contentment.

Many human communications and exchanges are non-monetary like this one. We fall in love. We raise our children. We laugh. We cry. We don't put a price on these things. Yet we exist in an economic system that exerts enormous influence on who we think we are and what we believe we are worth. "Net worth" conveys a very narrow sense of a person's value. I submit economics could benefit from a much broader perspective, one that connects meaningfully with humans' responsibility to each other and the earth. In this chapter I try to invoke a broader context, like the monk who asks a question. Speaking out of a tradition that sees life on earth as coming from distant realms, dipping into physical existence for a time, and then returning to the Source, he asks, "What did you come here to do?"

In addition to looking far forward toward a possible future, this chapter will look at three alternatives to the prevailing version of capitalism. Two of these exist into the present. There are other alternatives that could be explored, but these three open up a process of breaking free from assumptions and taken-for-granted patterns of thought. The cat, the little boy, and the monk begin a process of finding a new perspective.

Others are pushing at this frontier as well. For example, in her 2024 book *The Serviceberry*, Robin Wall Kimmerer calls for an economics that stresses abundance not scarcity, giving not taking, and reciprocity of the sort found in nature in the carbon cycle. She points to the obvious unsustainability of an economy that gobbles up resources faster than they can be replenished. Acknowledging the entrenched power of the existing economy and its value system, she calls for starting a parallel gift economy based on the principal that "all flourishing is mutual."[1] Important perspectives that could be included would be those of John Fullerton and Hunter Lovins,[2] but to do justice to their "regenerative economics" would require a book not a chapter.

If Capitalism Were Satisfactory . . .

If capitalism were achieving satisfactory results, we would not need to change it. Instead, it has promoted profit maximization as the preeminent objective, caused ever more extreme economic inequality, and cynically rationalized profiteering with a trickle-down theory of taxation

---

1. Kimmerer, *Serviceberry*, 72.
2. Fullerton, *Regenerative Capitalism*; and Lovins et al., *Finer Future*.

favoring the haves at the expense of the have-nots. Capitalism has fueled consumption and squandered energy to the point of destroying the global climate. Under capitalism democracy has been eroded to the point where corporations can buy the laws and politicians they need in order to continue reaping revenue, ignoring social and environmental consequences.[3] Businesses have promoted the legal fiction that corporations are people and launched campaigns of misinformation, especially by fossil fuel companies, that make them look like good citizens, even as they continue to destroy the climate. In the current workings of capitalism, one sees a great deal of ego, of selfishness, of me-first.[4]

At the same time capitalism lifted millions out of grinding poverty; the wealth it generated built schools and universities. It can plausibly be claimed that it was the engine behind the world as we know it, engendering incredible inventiveness and growth. Yes, the forces working *through* capitalism have done great harm, but lying, greed, hubris, a thirst for power and control all existed before capitalism came on the scene. Perhaps without them it could be relatively benign. Not according to John Fullerton, who speaks extensively about "regenerative capitalism," and claims that the fundamentals of finance and perpetual growth are inconsistent with a finite planet.[5] Nevertheless, replacing capitalism completely could mean throwing the baby out with the bathwater. To sort this out and discern what forces and motivations can work through capitalism, I turn first to a book about GE CEO Jack Welch called *The Man Who Broke Capitalism* by David Gelles.

Welch took capitalism to new levels of heartless avarice. When he became CEO in 1981, GE had been treating employees so well it was known by some as "Generous Electric." Welch went full bore in the opposite direction. Cost cutting and layoffs were so extreme that he earned the nickname "Neutron Jack" (the neutron bomb was designed in part to kill people and leave buildings intact). Welch redirected this respected and innovative firm away from creating a team devoted to engineering a better world. He focused it instead on profit and growth, as

---

3. Robert Reich, in *The System: Who Rigged It, How to Fix It*, does not attack capitalism but charges wealthy business leaders like Jamie Dimon of J. P. Morgan/Chase with creating an oligarchy that is ruining democracy while making themselves fabulously rich.

4. For a perceptive book looking at how capitalism lost its way, see Kelly, *Wealth Supremacy*.

5. Fullerton, "Introduction to Regenerative Economics."

reflected in quarterly earnings. To do this he combined three strategies: downsizing, dealmaking (mainly acquisitions), and financializing the company. One of his favorite strategies for pleasing Wall Street in what author Gelles calls his "war on loyalty" was "rank and yank." Employees were pitted against each other and in the competition for rankings the lowest 10 percent each year was fired.

At the same time, Welch aggressively acquired all sorts of companies from around the globe so that for a time GE was the largest corporation in the world. To make sure these numbers continued to please investors, there was also some creative accounting. Realizing that more money could be made in finance than in manufacturing, Welch turned the company into a financial powerhouse that operated essentially as an unregulated bank. For two decades, Welch ran GE this way and was the darling of investors, business schools, and the media. *Fortune* dubbed him "Manager of the Century." Employees, who saw years of innovation, a focus on quality, and employee loyalty thrown in the toilet, and who lived in fear of the next round of layoffs, had a different view.

According to Gelles, because Welch was an evangelist for his views, and as his acolytes and imitators assumed leadership of major companies, he had tremendous influence. The relentless focus on earnings trumped sound engineering, safety, product reliability, and company morale. This was nowhere more tragically apparent than at Boeing with the 737 Max, where a former GE executive made the decisions to cut corners and rush development of the plane. Gelles makes a compelling case that the Welch model of management and profitability led to tragedy.[6]

Welch's remarkable success in growing the company and producing profits gave him an outsized influence among corporate titans. They chose to overlook what drove him—naked ambition and inordinate greed. The motives led to so much overreach that they ultimately destroyed everything he had built. After Welch retired, the feverish pursuit of profit could not be sustained. A downturn in the economy, COVID-19, and other factors contributed to a collapsing stock price. GE had to sell off divisions until only aircraft engines remained.[7]

Not all CEOs are driven by greed. Like Welch, Jeffrey Brown of Brown's Super Stores is a consummate problem-solver. But at the same time, he aims to heal communities by bringing supermarkets to

---

6. Gelles, *Man Who Broke Capitalism*, 186–94.
7. Gelles, *Man Who Broke Capitalism*, 226.

impoverished neighborhoods. Coming from a family of independent grocers, Brown breaks with tradition and treats community members as partners in enterprise, not merely customers. Brown's approach is described by Cheryl Heller, a consultant on social design for nonprofits and corporations:

> Simply by asking them, Jeffrey Brown has discovered that poor people want to buy the things they want to buy: the brands they recognize, the ingredients their favorite family recipes call for, with uncompromised selections of quality and sizes. They want to shop in stores that are clean and attractive, staffed by people who treat them with respect. He's also discovered that when customers are listened to and provided with what they want, a superstore can help address structural poverty and poor health as well as hunger, it can offer second chances to former inmates who've been taught by experience they will never get a break.[8]

Brown is omnivorous, tackling issues as disparate as obesity, guns in the neighborhood, and employment for ex-offenders. He is willing to make neighborhood problems his own and has even established a nonprofit consulting arm of Brown's Stores called Uplift Solutions to support others who want to make healthy food available in "food deserts."[9] When Brown wants to undertake a new initiative, he calls a local town meeting, tells people what he has planned, and seeks guidance on moving ahead. Giving agency to his customers makes these meetings popular and builds momentum for success. Putting a supermarket in a poor neighborhood is risky and costs more. A Clinton-era initiative called the New Markets Tax Credit Program, intended to encourage businesses in depressed areas, helps cover the additional work and expense involved in places where poverty and crime create additional challenges.

Like his friend Trump, Welch was a *taker*. You see this in his astronomical compensation and retirement package. Brown is a *giver*. That is why his employees and customers love him. His many initiatives stem from a motive of wanting to help. This may mean promoting fire-roasted chickens, as opposed to less healthy fried ones. Or it could mean an initiative to buy guns in exchange for groceries, or an ex-offender training program with a guaranteed job at the end. As Cheryl Heller points out, "With the right opportunities, the same skills required to be a successful drug dealer can be applied to management of a profitable

8. Heller, *Intergalactic Design Guide*, 72.
9. Brown's Chefs Market, "Uplift Solutions."

dairy department." Now 15 percent of the stores' workforce has been "touched by the criminal justice system."[10]

How would Otto Scharmer look upon these two different ways to make money? I keep returning to him because I think his approach to visioning the future using presencing is so valuable in efforts to imagine what will want to emerge as a new civilization. I believe he would first point out the obvious, that the Welch approach, even though still widely emulated in corporate America, has proved itself a failure for the long run. It weakens the stature and sustainability of the business that employs it, and it weakens the society and broader economy. For one thing, treating employees as a cost rather than an asset, while the leader becomes fabulously rich, has contributed to absurd levels of inequality. According to a RAND study, in the past forty-seven years the top 1 percent has successfully redistributed $50 trillion in wealth from the bottom 90 percent to themselves.[11] No wonder people in the heartland feel the American Dream has been ripped away from them.[12]

If one imagines a motivation continuum, with narcissism on one end and altruism on the other, the Welch brand of capitalism lies near the me-first extreme. Seeking to discern the economic future that wants to be born, Otto Scharmer would embrace a society that sought to encourage motives like Jeff Brown's, or any others that move people closer to a heartfelt concern for others. Such a shift could take place either within an existing capitalistic system, allowing for initiatives like CSA farms, or eventually a completely new economic system that wants to evolve and is neither capitalist nor socialist.

Bernie Sanders sees capitalism as definitely unsatisfactory. In his book *It's OK to Be Angry about Capitalism* he lists questions that mainstream politicians and the corporate media today scrupulously avoid. They include the following:

- "Why do we accept childhood poverty in a land of plenty?"
- "Why do we spend twice as much per capita on health care as other nations and have so little to show for it?"

---

10. Heller, *Intergalactic Design Guide*, 78.
11. Cited in Sanders, *It's OK*, 263.
12. As far back as 1968, Robert F. Kennedy remarked in a speech that GDP "measures everything . . . except that which makes life worthwhile." See Kennedy, "Remarks."

- "What kind of "democracy" are we when billionaires are allowed to buy elections?"[13]

Welchism and the capitalism Sanders disdains show a consistent *failure to care*. Jeff Brown proves that this need not always be the case within capitalism.

Steward Ownership

In Europe, particularly in Denmark, a model has taken hold that effectively addresses the alienating and dysfunctional arrangement whereby control and ownership of a company resides, not with the stakeholders most concerned with it but rather with distant investors who are only interested in profits. Promoted by the Purpose Foundation,[14] steward ownership typically has ownership reside in a foundation, and it dedicates profits to strengthening the company, compensating stakeholders, or philanthropy in the community. Legal and governmental structures have not yet really adapted to this alternative so obstacles exist but are not insurmountable.[15]

Companies that have embraced steward ownership include IKEA, Rolex, Bosch, Zeiss, and in the United States Mozilla and the Equal Exchange Cooperative. Carl Zeiss pioneered this concept when he founded his optical company in Germany in 1846.[16]

Can Capitalism and Cooperation Coexist?

In an important essay called "A Pluralistic Commonwealth," Gar Alperovitz makes a case for working within the existing capitalist system to offer "system-altering alternatives." A giant in the field of economic alternatives, Alperovitz calls for a variety of ownership forms and control of enterprise. This can include worker-owned businesses, state-owned banks, municipal internet systems, community land trusts, community-owned utilities, credit unions, employee stock ownership plans (ESOPs), and various kinds of cooperatives. Each of these alternative

13. Sanders, *It's OK*, 260.
14. Learn more about the Purpose Foundation at their website: purpose-economy.org/en.
15. See Impact Terms, "Steward Ownership."
16. Markonnen, "Steward-Ownership Is Capitalism 2.0."

economic options already exists to a limited extent. Enabling legislation could encourage them. Most of the changes in this direction would need to take place on a local or regional level, but he also suggests national ones such as Medicare for All and the Green New Deal. He proposes having the US government buy out the top twenty-five fossil fuel corporations in order to remove them as obstacles to climate change mitigation and green infrastructure. We know this kind of buyout is possible because it has happened in countries that nationalized their railroads and in some cases utilities.[17]

The thrust of Alperovitz's proposals would move the economy away from individual or corporate control to something more political, what he calls a democratic economy. No question, in many cases this could be an improvement. Whether or not it is the ideal model for a new civilization is open to question because ordinary citizens, who would be using their votes to control businesses in a democratic economy, lack the technical knowledge and special skills in the planning, financing, management, marketing, etc. needed to run an enterprise. Capitalism and cooperation already coexist, so there is room in the Alperovitz universe for capitalism, but clearly the most predatory forms need to change.

A heartfelt concern for others needs to be part of this change. The Shakers, Mondragón, and the Sekem communities provide food for thought on how this can be achieved. As I have shown in Chapter 4, this heartfelt concern can be taught. Some individuals and communities illustrate to differing degrees how people can work selflessly toward a greater good.

In the balance of this chapter, I take up three communities that incorporate this feeling of solidarity as a defining element of an evolved economy. They are: the Shakers in the United States, the Mondragón Cooperatives that originated in the Basque region of Spain, and Sekem in Egypt. In each we see how our highest and best selves can find economic expression, and how self-change and education can prepare for the work of caring.

Not one of these presents a perfect model, but they share this important characteristic: each has been able to replace "Every man for himself" with "We are each other's harvest." These two alternatives speak not to action but to motive. The latter carries a soul force that involves caring for others and not putting one's own interests first. It

---

17. Gar Alperovitz, personal conversation with author, Dec. 9–10, 2017.

challenges us to find ways to want more cooperation, mutuality, and *convivencia* in economic affairs.[18]

The Shakers

While the name "Shakers" was a pejorative one applied by their critics, (it is a contraction of "Shaking Quakers"), the community's decision to embrace and use it was actually an economic one.[19] It became their distinctive brand. They were able to build respect for their honesty and the quality of their meticulously-made rocking chairs, their seeds in packets, flat brooms, clothes pins, washing machines, and many other inventions. But theirs was a craft economy, and a reason contributing to their dying out was that they were unable to adapt and compete with goods that could be made and sold for less through industrial production. At the same time, their young men often were lured away to jobs in industry, which they preferred over arduous rural life.

From a modern perspective, Shakers may seem quaint and anachronistic. But the fact is they grew to a total of nineteen communities and flourished for generations before a gradual diminishment began. It is hard to make your economic model work sustainably if you are in the process of going extinct. The other major reason each of their communities shrank until they were no longer viable was their celibacy. Let me digress briefly on that subject.

Thomas Merton, monk, mystic, and scholar, developed a profound appreciation of the Shakers living near his monastery in Kentucky. Is it possible he realized that they achieved what the Catholic church had not been able to achieve in two thousand years—a coed monastic order? Arguably, strict celibacy made this possible. Moreover, at a time before contraception, when marriage meant a woman devoting years of her life—like it or not—to household drudgery and child-bearing, celibacy could be seen as a form of liberation. Shaker women were treated as equals and from the outset held leadership positions in the order.

Picking up the discussion of the Shakers in Chapter 3, let us take a look at what they were able to achieve in the economic sphere. While

---

18. For additional perspectives and possibilities consisting of incremental changes to our existing system, I recommend a report of the American Academy of Arts and Sciences' (AMACAD) Commission on Reimagining Our Economy. See AMACAD, *Advancing a People-First Economy*.

19. Morse, *Shakers*, 132.

most utopian communities in this country were single settlements and relatively short-lived, the Shakers established nineteen different villages from Maine to Indiana and endured for more than two hundred years. They were the most successful communitarian society in American history. The values that governed how they worked and supported one another were very different from the rambunctious capitalism in the society all around them and with which they did business.

On a superficial level, they adhered to the same idea—"From each according to his ability, to each according to his need"—popularized by Karl Marx. But the Shakers added a dimension that made a critical difference and, for them, was able to make this core socialist principle work.

The key factor in Shaker economy and productivity was that they strove for everything they did to be spirit-guided. They began and ended each day with prayer and held fervent services of a Pentecostal nature more than once a week. Unlike outside society, which regarded labor as a commodity, they explicitly affirmed that *work was prayer*. As if to reinforce this prayerful perspective, Shakers were enjoined, "Do all your work as if you had a thousand years to live and as if you knew you must die tomorrow."[20]

This decommodification of work has profound implications. It means that work gets done for its inherent worth rather than its cash value. Shakers clearly recognized that egotism pulls people and communities apart.

To add a personal note, as a retired person living off my pension and some investments, I do the work I consider most important, as the Shakers did, without pay. For most people, if you were to ask them why they work, they would not hesitate to answer "for the money," or words to that effect. Some might be lucky enough to add that their labor contributed to a truly worthwhile objective. Upon retirement, the yoke is lifted. And it feels like a yoke or a chain, unless along the way individuals learn how to appreciate their work for its own sake. To me, this disconnecting of labor from the expectation of compensation feels tremendously liberating. It also intensifies my focus on the job to be done.

Making labor sacred conferred a certain dignity to even menial tasks for Shakers. Their motto was "Hands to Work and Hearts to God." The quality of their furniture and other work was so admired because it was measured by a different standard. Individuals in a Shaker

---

20. See the values in Canterbury Shaker Village, "Our Mission," and above, p. 45.

community would not get a guaranteed annual income, but all their earthly needs were taken care of until they died. They surrendered all their worldly assets when they joined the order, and all things, including clothing, were owned in common.

Once established, the Shakers prospered, and they shared the wealth by buying slaves, giving them their freedom, and accepting them as equal members into their communities.[21] Well ahead of the rest of the country, they affirmed that a person should not be a commodity. Neither was labor.

The larger vision into which work fit was the belief that they could create a heaven on earth. Their striving and sacrifice were keyed to a higher purpose, a Christ-centered evangelism paralleling religious enthusiasm of the day. The main point for this discussion of their economic life is not as much the content of their belief as the fervor with which they held it and their willingness to make it the driving force in their lives. They were able to sublimate their wanting, even sexual desire, to become instruments for God's will. For a collection of strong-minded farmers and craftsmen, rough-hewn in an age of rugged individualism, to be able to hold together at all was an achievement. To form disciplined communities that produced such quality work and to sustain their settlements for as long they did, is truly remarkable. This is the force of a unifying ideal. It need not be explicitly religious, though for the Shakers it was.

Intensely principled in dealings with the outer world and each other, the Shakers left a legacy, relevant to envisioning a new economy:

- Accepting all races, genders, abilities on an equal footing
- Community responsibility for each individual's earthly needs[22]
- Separation of work from money compensation
- Cultivating a community of caring, rather than of wanting
- Holding land, assets, and goods in common with no individual property
- Committing strongly to acting ethically in all matters[23]

21. Morse, Shakers, 179.

22. Not the same but worth mentioning is the idea of Universal Basic Income (UBI) managed and funded by government. The nation that has come closest to implementing UBI to date is Norway. See World Population Review, "Countries with Universal."

23. The Bruderhof is an existing intentional community movement that shares these values. Inspired by the early Christians, they view work as a form of worship and

The Shakers were hard workers, producing boxes and barns, dwellings and whole communities that were simple and beautiful. They could do this because their belief in higher purpose gave energy and direction to all labor. Not the details of their beliefs but the fact of their dedication can still sing to Americans in this century.

Mondragón—a Cooperative of Cooperatives

A very different kind of community sprang up in the Basque region of Northern Spain. In 1941, a young priest arrived in the industrial town of Mondragón, nestled in a valley between low mountains. José María Arizmendiarrieta was uninspiring in the pulpit, but he had other talents. He was able to connect with young people. He had an acute sense of social justice. And he could organize programs. The priest became concerned about high levels of unemployment among his flock. Focusing on jobs and training as a precondition to solving other problems in the community, he raised funds and established a polytechnic school where young workers could learn skills needed for manufacturing jobs. He also taught them the principles of worker democracy so that in 1956 he was able to take five of this best former students and establish the first Mondragón cooperative. They made kerosene stoves.

Over time, other cooperative enterprises followed, including an insurance company, retail operations, a sports club, and a credit union able to finance the co-ops. Manufacturing co-ops were established for furniture, machine tools, kitchen equipment, printing, metal smelting, and shipbuilding. Good-paying jobs, worker empowerment, and opportunities to be educated into more responsible positions, all contributed to the renewal of what had been a less-than-thriving community. Even as the co-ops prospered, José María continued to live simply, travel third class on the train, and ride his bicycle around town as the workers did.

The flourishing of the Mondragón initiatives illustrates the extraordinary potential of the cooperative movement. Mondragón is now the largest and best-known cooperative in the world. Before explaining what accounts for that, it would be good to understand more about cooperatives generally. The co-op movement began in Rochdale, England, in 1844 with a small group of weavers. They banded together to open a

---

hold all assets in common. There are more than twenty communities in six countries. Learn more at the movement's website: bruderhof.com.

shop and sell what they produced and to resist exploitation by industrial weavers. The original principles of the "Rochdale Pioneers," somewhat revised but enduring to this day, are the following:

- Voluntary and open membership
- Democratic member control
- Member economic participation
- Autonomy and independence
- Education, training, and information
- Cooperation among cooperatives
- Concern for the community[24]

Mondragón is primarily a producer cooperative.[25] The businesses run on democratic principles, with all producer-members able to vote and participate. Today there are a great many producer co-ops around the world, especially in farming.[26]

Consumer cooperatives, on the other hand, draw consumers together to gain advantages in buying goods and services. The most popular form of consumer cooperative today is probably the credit union. Mutual insurance companies, housing, and food co-ops are other forms.

I believe the core principle for co-ops, particularly producer co-ops, is the commitment that *we grow together*. The soul of a true co-op, if I may put it that way, is this attitude. It requires a willingness to learn, to work, and to share not just the benefits but the demands of the enterprise. Come together in the spirit of solidarity. This is *convivencia* in an economic application. Education and growth are part of the dynamic.

There are limits to how much can be achieved through education. Recognizing that in business, decisions have to be made by individuals with specialized knowledge, Mondragón does not have workers vote on everything. Instead, Mondragón workers own the co-ops and vote to hire managers, but then delegate to them and specialists the power to run the operations.

---

24. See International Cooperative Alliance, "Cooperative Identity."

25. Eroski, a chain of supermarkets throughout Spain, is a consumer co-op and part of Mondragón Corporación Cooperativa.

26. For an example of how regular businesses can cooperate in a purchasing cooperative see CCA Global Partners, "CCA in the Community."

Mondragón today is a worker cooperative federation, or a cooperative of cooperatives, with 95 participating cooperative businesses, employing 80,000 people. It includes 14 research and development facilities, and has sales in 150 countries.[27]

Skeptics who believe that cooperatives cannot compete and survive in the modern world would do well to study Mondragón. In William and Kathleen Whyte's definitive work, *Making Mondragon*, they write, "Mondragón has such a long and varied experience that it provides a rich body of ideas for potential adaptation and implementation elsewhere."[28] In addition to its pioneering work empowering workers and cooperatives, Mondragón cooperatives more recently have embraced the need to reduce their carbon footprint and make their operations sustainable.[29]

In 2013, the first factory that began with making kerosene heaters and went on to become very successful manufacturing and selling white goods went bankrupt. Assets were sold off to pay debts. This failure was brought on by the combined effects of a flood of cheaper Chinese appliances, the 2008 financial crisis, and an ill-timed expansion program.[30] Other cooperatives in the federation contributed €300 million, but the operation could not be saved. Of the many employees who had to be let go, most were accommodated either with transfers to other co-ops or with early retirement. More recently during the COVID-19 pandemic, when factories had to be shut down for a period, layoffs were averted by trimming paychecks by five percent and asking workers kept at home to agree to make up some of the hours missed when better times returned.[31]

This brings us to the principles and values baked into the Mondragón system. As might be expected in an organization founded by a priest in a Catholic country, the values align with Catholic social teaching—human dignity, social justice, solidarity or commitment to the common good, and economic justice, which would include a defensible wealth distribution.[32] Thus, for example, the highest paid managers in a Mondragón co-op receive no more than nine times the pay of the lowest paid worker. Each co-op sets its own ratio, with the average being six-to-one. This

---

27. Learn more at Mondragon Corporation, "About Us."
28. Whyte and Whyte, *Making Mondragon*, 5.
29. As affirmed in their 2023 annual report. See Mondragon Corporation, "Humanity at Work."
30. Fernández, "Mondragón's Cooperative Model."
31. Goodman, "Spain's Basque Region."
32. Herrera, "Mondragon," 1–2.

dramatically contrasts with the private sector, where in the United States CEOs of the largest 350 companies are paid about 320 times as much as the typical worker.[33] According to *New York Times* writer Peter Goodman, "If the Basque region of Spain were a country, it would have the second-lowest income inequality in the world."[34]

Mondragón has always been a cultural experiment as well as a business. From the first, José María taught workers about solidarity and the need for active participation in the purposeful work of their co-op. He incorporated and then built upon the Rochdale Principles. The Mondragón values he enunciated were: *cooperation*, i.e., all participants pulling together as owners and participants in an operation; *participation*, i.e., contributing the time necessary to make decisions such as selecting and hiring managers; *social responsibility*, i.e., sharing the proceeds of the cooperative business in the spirit of solidarity; and *innovation*, i.e., seeking to stay at the cutting edge in order to remain competitive because cooperatives still have to operate within a capitalistic system.[35] Consistent with cooperative values, the Mondragón code of ethics expects considerably more of participants than a typical corporate code.[36]

To appreciate how radical Mondragón principles are, compare them with this description by Univision reporter David Herrera of a traditional for-profit organization:

> It is characterized by top-down decision-making, [with] restricted participation of employees, a concentration of power at the top of the organization, and limited information about the organization available to employees. A traditional for-profit organization is further characterized by capital investors and employees usually being different people; maximization of economic benefits to primarily reward capital investors; objectives of investors, managers and workers often not being consistent with each other and voluntary economic participation in the community.[37]

The success of the Mondragón experiment proves several things. First, that the cooperative model can be both sustainable and can operate

---

33. Goodman, "Spain's Basque Region."
34. Hendersen, *Reimagining Capitalism*, 151.
35. See Mondragon Corporation, "About Us."
36. Mondragon Corporation, "Our Code of Ethics."
37. Herrera, "Mondragon," 2.

at scale. It contradicts Margaret Thatcher's famous assertion that "There is no alternative [to capitalism]."[38]

Second, worker ownership confers distinct advantages, provided it does not employ time-consuming and inefficient management by committee or use workers for day-to-day management tasks. Workers, who are owner-stakeholders in a firm, take a keen interest in its success, deriving not just money compensation but pride.

Third, Mondragón cooperatives prove that capable leaders will work for far less because they embrace the organization's ideals. Fourth, Mondragón illustrates how regional pride can support a value system of cooperation, solidarity, and identity. The Basque region has its own language, culture, and a historic sense of neglect by the Spanish central government. Intense feelings spawned a violent Basque separatist movement—the ETA—that only recently disbanded.

José María built on regional identity and pride to educate workers about cooperative principles, instill in them the ideals of cooperation and solidarity, and ensure that their hearts would be invested in what at that time was a radically original movement. His faith in workers, educated into a culture of cooperation, casts a long shadow down to present times. He wrote in his journal:

> Participation in a creative process confers on the worker the dignity of being part of something bigger. The worker becomes more of a person by actualizing inner potentials. As a person, the worker has not only mechanical abilities but intellectual and moral capacities.[39]

The culture that still nourishes Mondragón depends on this very impulse—an affirmation of inner growth and self-improvement that feeds the fires of creativity and enthusiasm for the shared work.

The importance of education in preparing people to understand and advance the innovative system in which they work cannot be overestimated. José Maria spent countless hours not just in establishing the polytechnic school but in teaching workers the principles of the Rochdale pioneers and the skills needed to assume the responsibilities of a

---

38. A living refutation of Thatcher's remark exists in the stewardship model of corporate ownership and governance, as seen in the Zeiss Company in Germany and Armin Steuernagel's TED Talk "Transforming Ownership to Create a Better Economy." See Steuernagel, "Transforming Ownership."

39. Arizmendiarrieta, *Reflections*, 16–63.

cooperative worker/owner. Solidarity does not just happen. It needs to be built on a foundation of understanding and shared vision.

In contrast to relatively meaningless factory work, Mondragón employees learn how their tasks fit into the larger picture of their firm's production. Moreover, because the cooperative model depends on informed, democratic participation, their interest must be constantly tended and encouraged to achieve what the founder called "dynamic equilibrium." "The cooperative must be reconstituted and renewed constantly," he wrote.[40] *Making Mondragon* expresses it this way: "The social vision of Don José María and the dedication of his followers to systematic and objective analysis of hard technical and economic realities have combined to build a movement of impressive dynamism."[41] All this was achieved by a cleric who was not charismatic, whose public speaking was lame. He pushed himself and others to levels regarded as beyond reach, and in so doing surprised everyone when he realized his ultimate ideal. "Our cooperative commitment cannot lose sight of the goal of a new social order,"[42] he said.

The key elements of Mondragón relevant to the new economy I envision are the following:

- Stress cooperation in as many forms as make sense
- Empower workers in several ways, such as the following:[43]
    - Provide opportunities for personal and professional growth
    - Be transparent as to how the firm works and achieves its aims
    - Encourage ownership stakes in the co-op
    - Encourage workers to participate in key strategies and decisions, but without allowing micromanagement

---

40. Arizmendiarrieta, quoted in Whyte and Whyte, *Making Mondragon*, 262. A more recent version of economic democracy that could comprise another whole chapter is the Evergreen Cooperative in Cleveland, Ohio. Unlike Mondragón, its aim is to promote economic revitalization in a defined area of six neighborhoods, persuading anchor institutions (a hospital and two universities) to source goods and services from local cooperative businesses rather than import from outside. For a comparison of Mondragón and Evergreen, see Iuviene et al, *Sustainable Economic Democracy*.

41. Whyte and Whyte, *Making Mondragon*, 87.

42. Arizmendiarrieta, quoted in Whyte and Whyte, *Making Mondragon*, 266.

43. An initiative in the United States to empower workers using Mondragón principles can be found at 1worker1vote.org.

- Facilitate group problem-solving that elicits insights of as many participants as possible, rather than coming to workers with a take-it-or-leave-it solution
• Build a culture of solidarity and caring for one another
• Cultivate a sense of shared purpose

Sekem and the Economy of Love

My final example of a successful alternative economic model exists in the inhospitable environment of the Egyptian desert northeast of Cairo introduced in chapter 3. Based on Muslim principles, the intentional community of Sekem thrives. Muslims and Christians live, work, and study together harmoniously, while calls for *jihad* and signs of a general restlessness swirl in the society at large.

European-educated chemist Ibrahim Abouleish visited his home country of Egypt in 1975 and saw overpopulation, poverty, unemployment, and environmental pollution, among other problems. This prompted him to formulate what he called the "Sekem Vision," which he described as:

> Sustainable Development towards a future where every human being can unfold his or her individual potential; where mankind is living together in social forms reflecting human dignity; and where all economic activity is conducted in accordance with ecological and ethical principles.[44]

Two years later, he returned and bought seventy hectares of desert and proceeded to implement his vision. He died in 2017 after receiving the Right Livelihood Award (sometimes called the Alternative Nobel Prize) and numerous other awards. What he accomplished in his lifetime was remarkable. Starting with a single building and a handful of people, he used organic/biodynamic methods, at first to grow only culinary and medicinal herbs for export to Europe. As this proved profitable, he added fruits, dates, vegetables, cotton, and other crops. Over time, Abouleish educated more farmers in chemical-free production and created a kind of federation for marketing and distribution and for educating producers and consumers. He started cooperatives, built a

---

44. See Sekem, "Dr. Ibrahim Abouleish."

clinic, set up a foundation, and founded what became Heliopolis University for Sustainable Development.[45]

Abouleish was a natural leader—visionary but practical—with deeply spiritual roots. "SEKEM is an impulse, a kind of swing, a power, which puts the I of the human being into action," he wrote in his notebook. "The I sets particular conditions of growth. It nourishes itself through movements which are self-induced."[46] Building from this conception of the human individual that puts freedom as an ultimate objective, Abouleish established a culture that today supports a thriving farm community.

This was no simple achievement. In 1928, when Egypt was a British colony, the Muslim Brotherhood was formed with the aim of kicking out the British and establishing a Muslim state. The fundamentalist Brotherhood is still a force to be reckoned with in the country. In 1981, just four years after Abouleish began his initiative, Egyptian president and Nobel Peace Prize laureate Anwar Sadat was assassinated by Muslim fundamentalists. Even today, Egypt, where a majority still favor Sharia law, is viewed by many as too restless for democracy.[47]

Indeed, Sekem is not a democracy but a holding company. This arrangement, operating within a larger capitalist economy, has allowed the community to prosper. However, the designation of a holding company is misleading because it implies a purely fiscal and transactional arrangement, whereas Sekem deliberately cultivates values for individual and social transformation that move in the direction of democracy. Its cooperatives are run democratically. Sekem provides a unique modern example of a community that explicitly embraces inner freedom of the sort explored in Chapter 2. The community articulates its core beliefs this way:

> Humanity creates the world from ideas. All learning, researching, inventing, and artistic activities are ideally free and not influenced by material benefits. It is only through holistic thinking and acting that a materialistic society can be transformed into a cultural society guided by meaningful values. Therefore, free education and spiritual development of all human beings must be the highest priority.
>
> The advancement of every individual is a continuous challenge in the fields of education, science, art, religion, and spirituality.

45. Learn more at Sekem, "History."
46. See Sekem, "SEKEM Inspirations."
47. Harris-Perry, "Is Egypt Ready."

Without a sound understanding of the world around them, people will not be able to live in unity with nature and fellow human beings. Lifelong learning enables the individual to improve living conditions and contribute to the development of the community and country. Children who have been given the opportunity to receive a holistic education are likely to become free-spirited and responsible individuals.[48]

Fair Trade

Before proceeding to how Sekem implements its Economy of Love, let me briefly digress to say something about fair trade. The existence of fair trade coffee and other products, typically from the Third World, signals that there is something unfair about the present price system. In fact, often price does not equal value, even though we assume that it does. Supply and demand, while bringing a certain discipline to price, are blunt instruments to ascertain true value. When you drink your OJ in the morning, doesn't it taste just as good when oranges are abundant, as when a blight practically wipes out the crop, sending the price of juice sky high? This value anomaly is not just true with agricultural products. The melt value of a Lincoln copper penny is actually 2.4 cents, and that does not include the cost of producing it. A painting by Picasso that art critics regard as an experiment that failed is worth more than a really magnificent one by an unknown artist, in terms of price. But here price is driven up by people who see art as investment and other factors.

Moreover, price in our present system typically ignores the externalities, as Kate Raworth has pointed out and attempted to remedy with *Doughnut Economics: Seven Ways to Think Like a 21st-Century Economist*. The price paid by the printer for the paper of the book you are reading almost certainly did not reflect the loss of trees needed to make pulp, the damage to the environment in terms of what the trees had been doing to absorb CO_2, downstream effects of poisoning the river at the paper mill, the inequity of pay and benefits in the plant, etc. From this point of view, price can be arbitrary and capricious.

Fair trade systems get around that by basing price on the cost to produce say, an avocado, plus a markup to compensate the farmer equitably so he can have a decent life and support his family. The fairness factor also typically includes taking into account the treatment of soil

---

48. See Sekem, "Cultural Life."

and environment by the farmers. A fair trade coffee co-op, for example, can encourage shade-grown coffee bushes, with shade provided by nut or fruit trees, and possibly chickens foraging about on the ground below. Agricultural products from a diversified operation like this are far more earth-healing than a scorched-earth monocrop typical of industrial agriculture, and price should recognize this.

The Founder's Focus

Ibrahim Abouleish's conception of the cultural life, the world of ideas, as a counterbalance to the materialism of modern existence lies at the heart of what shapes the economic arrangements at Sekem. Leadership encourages community participants to free their self-worth from being determined by material values. The alternative comes to economic expression in what Sekem calls the "Economy of Love" (EoL). It works like this:

Instead of having an economy and financial arrangements that are purely transactional, Sekem expands a central teaching of the Qur'an—to be fair in trade—to an ideal that encompasses the entire life cycle of a commodity or product. The retail price of a product produced in this system is not determined by sometimes arbitrary dynamics of supply and demand, but rather by the entire value chain. Thus, in an EoL the farmer who grows cotton in the Nile Delta, treats the soil with respect, uses no poisons, and receives a fair price for what he produces. The ginning, spinning, and manufacturing of cloth and then clothing are also done ethically, and any worker involved in the production gets treated respectfully and is compensated fairly. Distribution, sales, and customer service are all carried out in an earth-friendly manner, without losing the goal of making a profit.[49] Sekem has a number of businesses that operate this way.

Recently, carbon credits became an important factor in Sekem farming operations. As Sustainable Development Lead, Max Abouleish observed in an interview, "We know that land farmed conventionally emits 5 tons of carbon per acre per year. With regenerative, the same

---

49. American farmer/activist Robert Karp proposes taking this one step farther, arriving at what he calls "True Price" by involving not only all who contribute to the production but also consumers in a negotiation that is also an education so that all parties can have their legitimate needs and wants reflected in the retail price. See Karp, *Toward Associative Economy*, 49.

land can sequester 10 tons per year."⁵⁰ By trading carbon credits on the global market, Sekem can make biodynamic farming more profitable than the conventional, chemical-intensive approach. This important carbon-credit dimension is factored into Sekem's Vision 2057, which calls for a continuing expansion of organic/biodynamic agriculture to forty thousand farms throughout Egypt. Already, more than two thousand farms are using chemical-free farming methods developed at Sekem and their Heliopolis University.⁵¹

Operating under the Sekem Holding umbrella, Isis produces foodstuffs, such as organically grown vegetables, honey, dates, herbs, spices, edible oils, fruits, and juice. Sekem Health produces herbal teas and healthcare products. Lotus grows and distributes culinary herbs and spices. NatureTex uses organic, long-staple, Egyptian cotton to make clothing for babies and the high-end market. Atos Pharma makes phytopharmaceuticals to treat cancer and other ailments. Each of these lines is profitable and sells both domestically and internationally.

All Sekem companies use EoL principles, and outside businesses can apply for EoL certification. The process assures consistent quality and a humane organizational culture for each company. The minimum standards in the areas of culture, society, environment, and economy are detailed at Sekem's EoL website.⁵²

Perhaps most remarkable is Sekem's emphasis on providing holistic opportunities for workers to grow, what they call their Core Program. In the short term this could seem impractical and unproductive. But in the long term it communicates that leadership is interested in workers' personal thriving; it encourages them to be brave and try new things; it builds confidence and versatility. This actually improves productivity, loyalty, and morale. Sekem aims to allow up to 10 percent of a worker's time each week to horizon-expanding activities, with an emphasis on creativity. With over two thousand employees, a lack of instructors constitutes a limiting factor, but the goal remains important. Workshops get employees acting, singing, and developing communication skills in art, movement, and dance.⁵³

50. Max Abouleish, personal interview with author, Oct. 22, 2022.
51. Abouleish et al, "SEKEM Report 2022," 33–35.
52. See Economy of Love, "Certification."
53. The approach aligns well with a management philosophy articulated by Harvard professor of developmental psychology Robert Kegan and explained in his book *An Everyone Culture: Becoming a Deliberately Developmental Organization*.

Unlike Mondragón, management of Sekem firms is hierarchical, but there are two kinds of hierarchy—domineering and nurturing. Sekem's is caring. Intensely so. And it could be that hierarchy is the more appropriate form for this time in the prevailing culture where Sekem operates. Only a few companies outside the immediate Sekem orbit have signed on for the EoL, and they tend to be high-markup, boutique firms. However, the model can become more attractive and viable in the future.[54]

The EoL incorporates a level of transparency that anticipates a future when more consciousness and conscience enter into consumer purchases. For example, one can go online and trace the complete life cycle of a duvet cover, from cotton farm to retail sale. This life cycle story factors in not only how labor is treated but such things as CO_2 emission and water conservation.[55]

As success followed success, Sekem set up a holding company structure to secure funding and appropriate management for an expanding network of companies. This new entity, designed to "supervise, evaluate, and support all subsidiary ventures, and to . . . act as investor and lender to them,"[56] was in turn able to borrow funds when necessary from a financial co-op in the Netherlands, the Oikocredit Ecumenical Development Society,[57] and sympathetic banks, mainly in Germany. Thus, Sekem achieves the rare goal of operating within the larger capitalist international economy, while infusing its ideals into the capitalist infrastructure. Specifically mentioned commitments for Sekem Holding and its subsidiaries are the following: "A marketing strategy sensitive to human values, truthfulness, sensibility, and . . . promotion of biodynamic agriculture, and the principles of associative economics."[58]

Key elements of Sekem's efforts to affirm human dignity through a new economy are:

54. For a parallel initiative, begun in Austria in 2010, see Economy for the Common Good, "Common Good Matrix 5.0"; and see Felber, "Common Good."

55. Trace the life cycle at Economy of Love, "Barton Duvet Cover Sateen."

56. Sekem, "Sekem Companies."

57. Oikocredit describes itself as "a social impact investor and worldwide cooperative, with five decades of experience. It's our mission to ensure access to opportunities by investing in the empowerment of people with low incomes across the world, thorugh trusted local organisations." See Oikocredit, "About Oikocredit."

58. See Sekem, "Sekem Companies." Associative economics means having the economic sector and prices managed by industry associations on the one hand and consumer associations on the other, instead of through business competition (capitalist system) or government fiat (socialist system). Rudolf Steiner's *Rethinking Economics* elaborates the idea.

- Strong and purposeful leadership that provides an inspiring vision for the organization and a better world
- An organizational culture that stresses creative and inner growth for individual workers
- Lifelong learning for all
- Support for workers to see the value of their work and how it fits into the larger community
- Gratitude and environmental responsibility
- Everything belongs to Allah—we are his stewards
- Fair wages and benefits
- Full-cost accounting (triple bottom line)

In each of these three communitarian examples, a consciously cultivated sense of higher purpose enables participants to act less for personal gain and more toward including others in their conception of the good. As groups and economic entities, they move the needle away from ego and toward cooperation. This orientation allowed them to succeed and prosper.

Motives Make a Difference

The chapter now turns to see how three contemporary writers not living or working in intentional communities see possibilities for constructive economic alternatives. It turns out that all of them are women.

As becomes apparent in the contrast between Jack Welch and Jeffrey Brown, as well as in each of these three models, the motives people bring to economic endeavors shape the results. At the same time, another fact comes into focus—the importance of culturing a climate of caring. I like the idea of *culture* as a verb for something like this because it emphasizes that the process is not economic or political. Moreover, when you make cheese or yogurt, you normally use a culture, a living cluster of micro-organisms, that totally transforms and improves what otherwise would become spoiled milk.

In *Reimagining Capitalism in a World on Fire*, Rebecca Henderson envisions a transformation by which businesses can evolve from being part of the problem to becoming part of the solution. She lays out the problem this way:

We are destroying the world and the social fabric in the service of the quick buck, and we need to move beyond simple maximization of shareholder value before we bring the whole system crashing down around our heads.[59]

Businesses can become more socially conscious, she writes, by cooperating with government to tackle tough issues or by becoming public benefit or B corporations. She also endorses the triple bottom line, which measures a company's success not just in terms of profit, but also by development of people and preservation of the planet. All this is commendable, but in this chapter I want to push readers to think more radically, beyond rejiggering capitalism. Today—modify if possible. Ultimately—replace.

In 2022, Hazel Henderson called for a "Love and Caring Economy," asserting, "Everything in this country is about incentivizing behavior with money, and that game is over."[60] There are indications that this goal of pushing beyond money motivation can be reached. As we shall see, pieces of it have already been achieved. Striving toward a more humanized and cooperative system, less purely transactional and predatory, can advance human evolution beyond our current rudimentary moral development and limited awareness.

A precondition for finding and implementing solutions of this sort is a willingness to think differently. Yet there is inertia; actually a tremendous resistance to doing this. For corporate leaders earning in the top 1 percent, the preferred solution to inequity is likely to be less government and fewer tax burdens. For the education policy planner, the solution for a public school system producing poor levels of achievement is precisely what is being done now—more testing and accountability. Unimaginative, more-of-the-same thinking often perpetuates what we are already doing that is not working.

The Doughnut

In her important book *Doughnut Economics*, British economist Kate Raworth provides valuable fresh perspectives about the kind of thought that has dominated her discipline. Subtitled *Seven Ways to Think Like a*

---

59. Hendersen, *Reimagining Capitalism*, 44.
60. Houston and Smitsman, "Love and Caring Economy."

21st-Century Economist, her book breaks out of the mold by thinking in pictures, the principal one being the doughnut.

The diagram below shows how she has revolutionized the boundaries of economics by addressing what economists have traditionally deemed "externalities" and largely excluded from consideration. Looking at economic activity with fresh eyes, she sees that too much of it operates without guardrails and actually does damage. It lacks a social conscience. In effect, she asks: How can we justify ignoring concern for people and planet when so many live in deprivation and the planet's climate stability is under threat? She gives this reconceptualization visual form with the doughnut.

The safe and productive zone for human economic activity is bounded on the inner side by the Social Foundation and shows in lighter green. The safe zone is bounded on the outer side by the ring labeled Ecological Ceiling. Beyond this point, economic activity damages the environment (overshoot). Ways this can happen show in salmon, outside the doughnut. The boundary below which stingy levels of economic activity cause harm, gets represented with a ring labeled Social Foundation. Too little economic activity (shortfall) in this direction causes human deprivation in areas like food, water, health, and housing.

As an example, housing developments in Arizona splay out across the desert at an alarming speed, as if water to sustain them were unlimited. But Lake Mead, which supplies the region from the Colorado River, is at dangerously low levels. The overshoot takes the form of freshwater withdrawals, land conversion, and biodiversity loss, among other things, all outside the doughnut. In the same state, we see shortfalls where state administrations underinvest in infrastructure and schools in order to curry favor with companies and voters who want lower taxes, ignoring people living hand-to-mouth.

Living within the viable and stable zone of the doughnut, Raworth says, will be impossible unless we overcome our addiction to growth.[61] She has many other valuable things to say about how traditional academic economists fail to account for the big picture, including preserving the planet and attending to human welfare. Raworth's heterodox thinking about "externalities" and other assumptions of her profession has been embraced by Amsterdam, Philadelphia, and Portland,

---

61. Raworth credits Herman Daly (1938–2022) with pioneering ecological economics and the steady state. He said criticizing economic growth was like poking "a big hornets' nest with a short stick." See Shanahan, "Herman Daly."

Oregon, and other municipalities that have incorporated the Doughnut into their planning.[62]

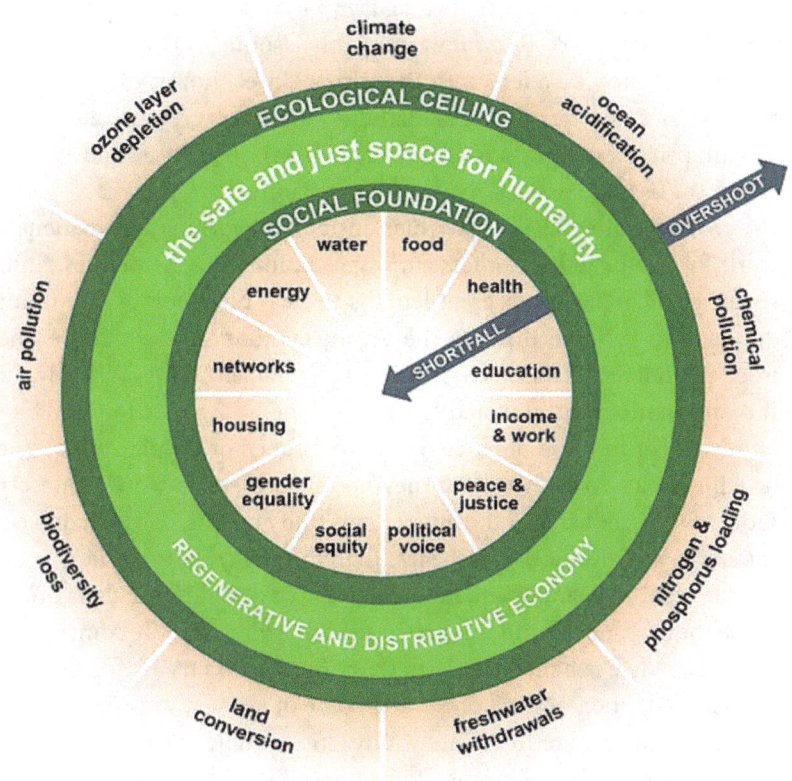

Figure 4. THE DOUGHNUT. Courtesy of Kate Raworth and the Creative Commons.

A New Lens

Raworth provides a valuable new lens for seeing the economy. To frame and implement new economic arrangements, a new lens or lenses for viewing the world will also be required. They may be discovered in unexpected places—a poem by Rumi, a personal tragedy, a near-death

62. Raworth, "Doughnut Economics."

experience. If you visit the home of a Native American and admire something there, chances are they will give it to you. Generosity, one could say, is the lens through which they see the abundance of creation. Where the dominant culture values accumulation, they feel a kinship with all life and cultivate gratitude. It is part of their identity and worldview.[63] In her book *Braiding Sweetgrass*, Robin Wall Kimmerer tells stories that provide a lens into the tribe's gift economy, of picking wild strawberries for her father's birthday strawberry shortcake, and of learning that sweetgrass itself must be given, for if it is sold it cannot retain the essence needed for sacred ceremony.[64]

Systems already exist in which instead of working for my benefit, I work for the benefit of others. In organizations like Alcoholics Anonymous, participants go to great lengths to help one another. We find the altruistic impulse all through the volunteer nonprofit sector. We find it in open-source software, Wikipedia, and Mozilla. Jimmy Carter was not the only senior who donated time, swinging a hammer for Habitat for Humanity or in some other capacity. Thousands of people with pensions or with enough money so that they no longer need to work volunteer at food pantries, housing authorities, community boards, conservation commissions, and the like. It may be less than full-time, but they pitch in, often despite waning strength and failing health. They contribute their time because they see a need and want to be useful. As a result, the community in which they live is better, stronger, more livable, less trying for those who are disabled, poor, or hard pressed in some other way.

In addition to retirees, many fully employed people belong to service organizations such as Kiwanis, Rotary, and Elks. Others find time to contribute one night or more a week to help out with a youth team or scout troop, a community agency, or some other local need. Think of the volunteer fire departments and ambulance squads in rural towns. In my little town, when the siren sounds in the middle of the night, these men and women rush to the rescue, even if their political views are diametrically opposed to the people in need. At the high school or college level, growing numbers of students do what is called service learning—taking what they learn in class and applying it in a constructive and uncompensated way in the community. These and other reservoirs of goodwill and donated

---

63. See Topa (Four Arrows) and Narvaez, *Restoring the Kinship Worldview* for further development of these ideas.

64. Kimmerer, "Gift of Strawberries," 22–38.

time help society to function day to day yet operate independent of the conventional capitalistic "I only do what I'm paid for."[65]

Crises often activate the altruistic response, as Rebecca Solnit documents in *A Paradise Built in Hell*. A disaster can be a course in the School of Unselfishness.[66] The spirit of cooperation, *fraternité*, brother- or sisterhood, comes to the fore when people feel stirred by something higher than self-interest. The dormant human capacity for heroism and sacrifice is like the stars. We see them only at night, but they are up there shining all day long. We have a culture that doesn't do discomfort. We prefer fun, fast, and easy, which makes sacrifice, when it occurs, all the more moving and impressive.

Plenty of evidence exists that capitalism's one-sided assumptions about human nature are simply wrong. In her article, "Solidarity Economy: Building an Economy for People and Planet," Emily Kawano states, "Our real-world economy builds on assumptions about *homo economicus*—namely, that he is rational, calculating, self-interested, and competitive and has little concern for the community, common good, or the environment."[67] Examples in this chapter show that this need not be the case.

Taking Innovative Models to Scale

How can the three radical models featured in this chapter, or others, have any significant impact on the colossus of a global corporatist economy? First, it should be noted that the perfecting of small scale initiatives advances in parallel with their expansion. Thus, Mondragón began as a technical school and one co-op but grew to the largest cooperative network in the world. We need to walk before we run. Every cooperative enterprise, no matter how small, trains participants so that their wanting and their sense of belonging expand to include others. As time passes, problems become more acute and attitudes change; that which now seems unthinkable becomes possible. I am old enough to remember when practically everyone smoked. We never would have guessed

---

65. For a fresh perspective on work motivation, see Jordan, "Welcome Back to Work."

66. See p. 74.

67. Kawano, "Solidarity Economy," 289–90.

that in a couple of decades the cultural acceptance of smoking would shift to such an extent that practically no one would smoke.

Education has an important role to play in changing outlooks and instilling a culture of caring. With *deeply transformative learning*, a term we use in the gap year movement, the personal attributes of resilience, agency, belonging, and creativity are explicitly named and addressed.[68] Participants in the three communities profiled in this chapter all understood that for the living and working arrangements to succeed, everyone had to be personally committed to cultivating qualities like these and becoming a better person.[69] A holistic education can generate this kind of momentum.

Some businesses and nonprofits are already carrying the torch forward—with the example of Brown's Super Stores, with B corporations, and with initiatives like Community Wealth Building (CWB),[70] which offers alternatives to an extractive economy that benefits the elite few while exploiting people and planet. CWB, a division of the Democracy Collaborative, promotes strategies that encourage local control and money recirculating in the community. This includes collective ownership of land and farms, credit unions, co-ops, green space, employee ownership of businesses, municipal power systems, and social enterprise such as the Evergreen Cooperatives in Cleveland.[71]

For a major advance toward economic cooperation on a national scale, probably another country like Denmark or Norway would have to try it and chart the way. But that would not be sufficient to prompt fundamental change. The piling up of catastrophes, however, holds the potential to teach people that capitalism is not the only route to a better life, and that their primitive notion of freedom does not serve. A further learning component that would have to start at the preschool level and work up through the grades involves developing a social conscience. This development can be reinforced through art.

---

68. To learn more about this, go to the website for Springboard Foundation for Whole Person Learning: springboardlife.org.

69. This was the bedrock assumption of a powerful international conference in Sweden in 2022 springing from the work of Tomas Björkman and the Ekskäret Foundation. It holds that the United Nation's Sustainable Development Goals can only be achieved if people commit to changing themselves. Accordingly, their Inner Development Goals organization seeks to promote exactly that. Learn more about this at the organization's website: innerdevelopmentgoals.org. And see the next chapter, pp. 190–93.

70. Democracy Collaborative. "Community Wealth Building?"

71. See Evergreen Cooperatives, "About."

It has seemed to me that forms of art—truly significant and enduring ones—help prepare the consciousness of the future. This can be quite subtle; for example, wanting to care can be stimulated through music, art, and drama. A film like *Pay It Forward* shows one way. The International Teaching Artist Collaborative has pioneered using various forms of art to spur social change.[72] One such form is Forum Theater, also known as Participatory Theater.[73] It involves the audience in acting out a story in which oppressor and oppressed seek ways to dialog and reverse their customary antagonistic roles. This has met with some success in promoting understanding between Palestinians and Israelis.

The transition to a caring and cooperative economy is likely to happen one sector at a time, with possibly agriculture in the lead because farmers, despite their conservatism, have a history of co-op membership. Appendix B has some thoughts on how this could proceed.

Putting It All Together

An economic system is a fiendishly complicated arrangement, which is why I can only indicate points of departure for discussion, not a blueprint. However, some concluding and summarizing thoughts may prove helpful.

To achieve a more socially responsible and caring economic system, one that embraces rather than denies non-monetary values such as those intimated in the first paragraphs of this chapter, it will be necessary to educate people's wanting and help them become more consciously self-directing in their behavior. The qualities explored in the early chapters can indeed be cultivated through an enlightened whole-child education, starting with preschool. As Emerson pointed out, the more people self-regulate, the less government will be necessary. This will take some time to bear fruit. It reinforces the idea which runs through the book and is explored in the concluding chapter, that the future needs an education-centric society, consciously focused on growing its citizens but especially its children.

---

72. Learn more about the International Teaching Artist Collaborative at their website: itac-collaborative.com.

73. Gakhal et al. "Forum Theatre."

Even imagining success on this front, a government of laws will still be necessary to set boundaries and manage consequences for those who will not or cannot change and who pose a danger to society.

But even if people change in the direction of caring more for one another, and a humane but firm governmental system deals with those who do not evolve to the next stage of human consciousness, is there still a need to get to the root of the problem? Some will argue that people and their attitudes and primitive level of development *are* the problem. However, there is a structural issue with capitalism that cries out to be addressed. The existing system pits people against each other; it makes a virtue out of competing and winning, even at others' expense, much like Jack Welch's "rank and yank" policy at GE. This could have been more appropriate in the rough and tumble of the nineteenth century, a time of more rugged individualism when the United States was still taming the frontier. Even though there were plenty of casualties, a tremendous amount was accomplished as capitalism jerked people into the modern world. But society and human consciousness have changed since then. People now expect and deserve a more equitable and just arrangement than one where the winners amass incredible wealth, and the mass of workers have to scramble for their sliver of the pie after the CEOs and investors have gobbled down the rest. A new system will need to find ways to rebalance society so that the sectors that appear in the doughnut diagram on p. 222 no longer have a hypertrophied economy dictating to government and culture how they shall function. A new system will need to value cooperation and sharing, will accord more agency to ordinary citizens, and will educate them up to their responsibilities.

You may ask what ordinary citizens can do today to move the economy in a more cooperative direction. Opportunities include the following:

- Consider using a credit union instead of a bank.
- Buy your food through a co-op.
- Support Wikipedia and other open-source entities.
- Explore ways to pool resources or work together on a local basis.
- If you live near one, support your land trust.
- Join a CSA; they exist even in cities.
- Donate money, time, and/or expertise to a nonprofit.
- Use your buying power to support non-monopolistic businesses.

- If you have money to invest, be sure you are not underwriting destruction.
- Teach your children to share.
- Learn presencing, so that you can recognize creative opportunities and help them happen.
- Explore other successful cooperative models.[74]

To help readers think through how change can happen, how to get from the unsatisfactory present to the desired future, I would like to share one more tool called Three Horizons Thinking. As explained by Kate Raworth in a short video, three lines on a graph mark the likely progression of H1—Business as Usual; H3—the Emerging Desired Future; and between them H2—Disruptive Innovation.

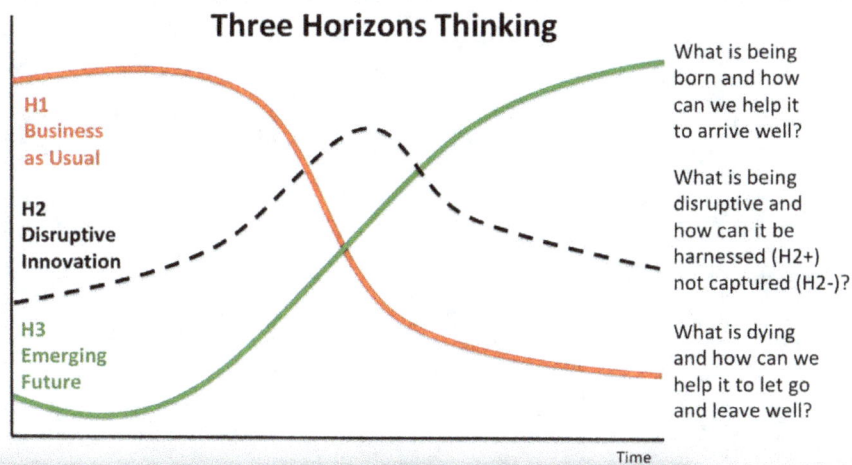

Figure 5. Courtesy of Bill Sharpe

H1 tracks current business and economic practice and shows decline because it contains the seeds of its own destruction as it destroys the environment on which it depends. H3 will become more or less

---

74. For example, the Rojava people in the Kurdish region of Syria have developed a highly cooperative social model for peaceful, multi-ethic coexistence—peaceful that is, except for the wanton bombing by the Turks. In their "democratic confederalism," women are equals and participate in leadership, and decisions are made by local councils. Their economy runs largely through cooperatives. See Winiecki, "Unremitting Turkish Attacks" and Trainer, "Kurdist Rojava."

ascendant, depending on the kind and amount of disruption. H2 can take two forms: H2+ harnesses benefits from positive changes such as the plummeting cost of solar panels; H2- represents net negative disruptions that result in no fundamental change. They simply prolong the life of H1. Carbon capture or Uber ride service would be examples. The three horizons allow discussion groups or individuals to delve into how changes in technology, business, or a shift in habits and attitudes can affect ultimate outcomes.[75]

For any of these suggestions or tools to work, people will need to overcome their immunity to change. We need to get off the well-worn paths into new territory. In the words of Robert Massie, "We can replace the dead totem of money that constricts our hearts with a living commitment to each other and our world."[76]

---

75. Raworth, "Three Horizons Framework."
76. Massie, *Handbook*, 123.

Other Considerations

CHAPTER NINE: SEEKING A BALANCE

Life is like riding a bicycle. To keep your balance, you must keep moving.
—Albert Einstein

A place for everything, and everything in its place.
—Benjamin Franklin

It always seems impossible until it's done.
—Nelson Mandela

IN 2002 A FOR-PROFIT prison corporation wanted to build a new facility on remote Gravina Island off the coast of Alaska. The fifty residents had been served by a ferry for years, but the prison people wanted a bridge and a connection, not even to the mainland but to another island and the community of Ketchikan. The project was expected to cost $398 million. Some political contributions were made, and, lo and behold, Senator Ted Stevens and Representative Don Young of Alaska became energetic advocates in Washington for the initiative; that is, until it came to be labeled the "Bridge to Nowhere" by Senator John McCain and others who pounced on it as a flagrant example of government pork. An FBI investigation of this and other abuses involving Alaskan oil and fishing interests was called the "Corrupt Bastards Club."[1]

---

1. Siegel, "Origins of Bridge," and Alaska Report, "Alaska's Corrupt Bastards Club."

This is but one instance of a system profoundly out of balance, in which businesses or the wealthy pay and lobby to have their economic interests advanced in the political arena, and at the expense of ordinary taxpayers. In this case, public money did not in the end pour into this venture, but in many cases ongoing subsidies, tax breaks, and other advantages go on for decades. Misalignments like this can be particularly flagrant when involving the fossil fuel industry, which gets subsidies from one government agency while other branches of government are trying to curtail the nation's dependence on those very fuels.

The absurdly high costs of pharmaceuticals and of health insurance provide other examples of a too-powerful economic sphere dictating to a submissive political one. Now, with the US Supreme Court's ill-advised Citizens United decision that opened the floodgates to billions in special-interest campaign spending, government is even more for sale to the highest bidder.

A Basis for Moving Forward

In this chapter, I intend to outline a conceptual framework that can provide for balance and avoid misalignments like this, where priorities from one sphere spill over into another sphere. To explain this vision of society in which the three spheres of society drive in their own lanes, so to speak, I will dig deeper into the framework introduced in Chapter 2. There, I propose imagining society as consisting of three broad and distinctive spheres—the cultural, the political/legal, and the economic. Grasping this framework, with its ideals of individual freedom, equality, and mutuality respectively, can bring a whole new meaning to aligning individual human potential, aims, and attitudes with what striving human beings need collectively in order to prosper. I say "striving human beings" because not everyone wants to become their best self and work hard to realize it. Many are probably content to just coast through life and avoid pain. In presenting this threefold framework, I make a stab at answering the question: What does a civilization need in order to promote human flourishing, achieve greatness, and ensure sustainability?

Please refer to the diagram on p. 31 and note that it presents an *ideal* relationship among the three spheres rather than a representation of current conditions. It is not just with money in politics where we see how important it is for one of the spheres not to dominate another.

Chapter 6 shows how government dictating curriculum and pedagogy in schools (political sphere interfering with the cultural) has not worked out well. Chapter 7 shows how government management of the farm economy, including the North American Free Trade Agreement (NAFTA), has driven small farmers out of business and depopulated many rural towns.

In theocratic Iran, the cultural-spiritual element mismanages the economy and co-opts government, sending morality police to patrol streets and enforce dress codes. Meanwhile, in communist China, the political machinery seeks to control and surveil all elements of culture, throttling the ideal of freedom. Among its many prohibitions, China's government banned the movie *Seven Years in Tibet* for acknowledging that Tibet exists. The government also dominates the economic sphere to such an extent that when an economic leader like Jack Ma becomes too powerful, he suddenly disappears.[2]

In the diagram on p. 31 the cultural sphere provides values, ideas, and a creative impetus for change to the other two spheres. Culture can provide "vision" for the political and "enrichment" (i.e., depth and ideas, not money) for the economic. Art feeds the soul. Ibrahim Abouleish, founder of Sekem, understood this from the start. Once water flowed from the well he had drilled and he was ready to begin farming, the first two major purchases for the community were a tractor and a grand piano.[3] A vibrant and healthy cultural sphere can function like a rudder to steer the other spheres in constructive directions; it can be the heart of the operation. Any human endeavor invites us to address the question "Why am I doing this?" and answer it not just at a superficial level. Doing so confers grit, purpose, and staying power to whatever one undertakes. The perspective offered by the culture can equip one to grapple with such questions. But the cultural sphere has to be healthy and strong. If its values have been co-opted by monetary concerns, as happens when balance is lost and the economic sphere has hypertrophied—think

---

2. Some of the most interesting and provocative writing about alternative economies pushes for a more democratic economy. Thus, Gar Alperovitz in "A Pluralist Commonwealth" praises worker ownership, co-ops, municipal ownership of utilities, and other forms that involve challenging the capitalistic way of doing things. These options deserve serious attention and should be explored, particularly if ways can be found not to kill the initiative of enterprisers who are willing to take risks and infuse the economy with bold innovations. In my experience, co-ops are far more reluctant to take risks than bold businesses. See Alperovitz, "Pluralist Commonwealth."

3. Van Seijen, "Helmy Abouleish."

entertainment filled with sex and violence—then the culture is apt to lose the stature needed to inspire and shape the working values of citizens. In *The Sekem Effect*, Helmy Abouleish, Sekem's current leader and son of the founder, captures how the cultural sphere can infuse all spheres with vision and purpose. He begins with an evocative quote from the Muslim poet Rumi (1207-1273):

> Beyond ideas of right and wrong, there lies a field. I'll meet you there.

And goes on,

> Sekem sees itself bringing new impulses into the world, that in practical application heal people and the earth. This requires a place, i.e. a patch of earth, and people who come together to form a working and learning community; people who form a social organism in which the spheres of life, ecology, culture, and economy can thrive. It is in people's encounters during work and learning that social life takes place, creating a community that can also be defined and lived in different ways, according to the different consciousness of its individual members. Thus, there are family communities, age communities, religious communities, communities of interest, communities of values and many more. We want to take into account and include such different forms of community, but at the same time model and promote a community of vision. Ibrahim Abouleish called it a community of spirit. This community seeks to help people see themselves as part of a larger world community that is constantly evolving in a vibrant way.[4]

The inspiration that quickens Sekem comes from Islam but also from Rudolf Steiner. Writing in the early twentieth century, Steiner invited readers to consider even more radical measures to apply the threefold ideas. Even today, one hundred years after he proposed them, they still seem revolutionary. For that very reason they can prompt lively discussion and generate fresh thinking. They include:

- The decommodification of labor, as the Shakers did (see p. 142.)
- Separate work and income; labor comes to be regarded more as gift than transaction

---

4. Abouleish et al., *Sekem Effect*, 129.

- Eliminating land ownership as we know it—use of land would be accorded to those with the capacities to use it wisely; a farmer who abused land would lose the right to farm it
- Breaking the economic sphere away from government and having it self-govern, but with rights of labor, the community, and the environment vigorously protected by the state
- Industries and commodities organized by associations (somewhat akin to co-ops), and the economy as a whole governed by associative principles or an association of associations (comparable to Mondragón on pp. 144–50)
- Prices determined not strictly by supply and demand but by actual value or "True Price"; that means cost of production and distribution, plus a reasonable markup that allows the producer to have a decent life and hopefully is affordable for the consumer[5]

Today these measures are non-starters. But in the future, who knows? Civilizations lurch forward, sometimes on many fronts simultaneously, as during the Renaissance. We no longer settle personal disputes with duels. If one studies the history of ideas and the evolution of human consciousness, it is like seeing one door open after another. These changes became reflected in music and art. Think of the difference between drumming and simple flute music and later a Bach "Toccata and Fugue." What an immense change in human consciousness this reflects. This leads one to ask what consciousness can be cultivated that would make forward-looking changes possible.

Can Art Contribute?

I believe that enduring art, art of high quality, holds potential to shape the future by affecting consciousness and changing values. Consider Anthony Doerr's award-winning book *All the Light We Cannot See*, and the subsequent film. In this work, a young French girl, who is blind, risks her life to broadcast a radio program during the Nazi occupation of France in World War II. The work shows grit and courage, an uncompromising adherence to truth, and occasional beauty in the midst of brutality and

---

5. Seth Jordan, personal communication with author, Nov. 14, 2023. See also Jordan's Substack site on threefolding: thewholesocial.substack.com. For a concise presentation of Steiner's ideas for social renewal, see Udell, *Agent of Social Transformation*.

destruction. In affirming these values, embedded in a dramatic and memorable story, Doerr contributes to the future by allowing overwhelmed young people, readers, or viewers a reason not to give up. And that is only one of the ways this beautifully-written story could have impact.

A few years ago, I saw a movie called *Pay It Forward* about a boy in Las Vegas. His waitress mother is barely making it on her own, but the boy's teacher inspires him to develop a system of sharing, where one good deed inspires two more and this spreads until society is transformed, or that's the idea. As a result of seeing this, I stopped giving Christmas presents. Instead, I make a gift in the person's name to a suitable charity. Finding just the right nonprofit for the individual gives a lot of pleasure, and in some cases it inspires people to reciprocate in kind.

Not all art contributes to expanding consciousness, or affecting us at all. Some art does not really touch the feeling life or soul of individuals. It may be just a poet spilling his guts out, or a composer showing off, or a painter contriving to produce something novel. But when art has substance of the kind that moves people—think of the soul-stirring, great choral pieces like Bach's *Mass in B minor* or Beethoven's *Ninth Symphony*—these creations have great power to arouse our better selves. Even the single poem or a story artfully told can be a lesson in the school of unselfishness, or can open a vista to the nature behind nature, or can make a hardened heart more able to experience compassion. The different forms of art can communicate with brutal force or great subtlety. Likewise, audiences vary enormously in their abilities to apprehend and appreciate—some relatively dense, others receptive. For those with the ability to be changed by its power and subtlety, art operates at the boundary between hard reality and the ineffable.

Art can also be destructive. When Goethe's *Sorrows of Young Werther* was published in 1774, it set off a wave of suicides. So many young people identified with the lovelorn protagonist and took their lives that the book was banned in Italy and Denmark.[6] Works with positive impact are more significant. Think of *The Diary of Anne Frank*, *King Lear*, and many poems. Even a single song can have impact—"Amazing Grace" or Sam Cooke's "A Change Is Gonna Come."

The effect of a painting is apt to be less easy to identify, unless it is something like Picasso's *Guernica*, a stridently anti-war creation. However, if one is open to it, a painting can reach one's feeling life or soul.

---

6. Kardaras, "How Goethe's *Sorrows*."

For example, the great canvases of the Hudson River School showed nature in remarkable ways—grand and beautiful. They opened people to an appreciation of the natural world at a time when industrialization was wrecking landscapes that had been pastoral. Some depicted natural treasures in the West and are recognized for their role in creating national parks and wildernesses.[7]

Other Components of the Cultural Sphere

This sphere includes much more than the arts. It is the arena of ideas—so science, religion, education, political theory, history, anthropology can all be part of the mix, influencing the values and direction a civilization takes. Will it follow the declining trajectory outlined by Margaret Wheatley (p. 58) or will the culture produce a renaissance? That will depend on whether or not it can achieve a creative balance. A key to accomplishing that will be the most important sector within this sphere—education.

As discussed elsewhere in this book, today in American public schools it is, for the most part, a story of lost opportunity. On the other hand, by allowing the arts in all forms to flourish in schools, they could become engines of creativity and initiative, and leverage points for a healed civilization. Think preschool through university. Therein lies the power to envision and shape a vibrant future.

A Healthy Balance

How can society be moved in the direction of a healthy balance among the different spheres?

At the national level today, the obstacles appear daunting. But locally, there are models that offer hope, especially for the future. Examples include Sekem (already discussed), Transition Towns (a movement initiated in England of purposeful communities),[8] and Richmond, California (a multi-ethnic, Bay Area community that seized control of its own destiny after years of domination by its Chevron refinery).[9] One thing all these instances share is successful opposition to an instance where the

---

7. Ferber, "Nature's Nation."
8. To learn more, see the Transition Town Totnes website: transitiontowntotnes.org.
9. McLaughlin, "Local Community," 187–196.

economic sphere (in the case of Richmond, an oil company) exercises hegemonic control of the community. There will need to be measures to keep capitalism from running rampant.

In chapter 2, where I introduced the three spheres of society, I pointed out that the ideals of freedom, equality, and mutuality, *in their proper spheres*, can help heal a broken world and counter the fractiousness of human nature. The ideal of freedom pervades a healthy cultural sphere, where creativity and individual growth can flourish and energize an entire community. The ideal of equality shapes the political/legal sphere. True equity, justice, and opportunity are guaranteed by this sphere. Mutuality, or the old term brotherhood, informs economic transactions that will take place in a spirit of cooperation; opposing parties craft win-win settlements. Having in mind the three ideals of freedom, equality, and mutuality can help, even today, in discerning where in each of the three areas a heightened clarity of purpose could led to improvements.

When government and economic interests align, these two spheres can coordinate, and much good work can be accomplished. This is different from the kind of unholy alliance represented, for example, by the 2010 Citizens United decision that opened the floodgates for billions of special-interest dollars to flow into influencing elections. Arguably, a relatively healthy balance existed in the foreign relations of the North Atlantic nations during the period after World War II, sometimes referred to as the "Placid Decade."[10] The 1950s brought to fruition almost a golden age of ideals applied to international cooperation. Peace and prosperity advanced together. The United Nations was formed in 1945. The United States provided extraordinary moral leadership in offering the Marshall Plan to rebuild its vanquished enemies in Germany and Japan. In response to an expansive communism, NATO was established in 1949. Democracies proliferated around the world. The European Union came along in 1957. How this balance was subsequently lost is detailed in Kagan's *The Jungle Grows Back*.[11] Egotism, nationalism, and predatory capitalism reasserted themselves, pushing nations away from idealism and cooperation and toward seeking advantage, often at the expense of others.

As noted in chapter 4, civilizations tend to cycle. The Chinese Dynastic Cycle describes one most people in the West know nothing about. However, the decline portion of the rhythm is not inexorable. Sometimes

---

10. Satin, ed., *1950s*.
11. See also Putnam and Garrett, *Upswing*.

after great suffering and disruption, constructive transformation takes place, when inspired leaders in the arts or statecraft are present. After the Black Death killed half the population of Europe (1346–1353), along came the Renaissance. After the bloodbath of World War II, there were remarkable breakthroughs, noted above. After the self-inflicted climate disaster that likely lies ahead, we can hope that a rebound will exceed our expectations. Long after I am gone, this book may become a bestseller.

The graphic on p. 31 shows how three spheres in a healthy relationship interact with each other. Author Martin Large, in a book called *Free, Equal, and Mutual*, has worked out in more detail how the threefold concept can work, with people participating in society in three different ways—as individuals in the culture or what he calls civil society, as citizens in the political and legal sphere, and as consumers and/or producers in the economic sphere. Each sphere is distinct, but they have to work together so that dialog is necessary.[12]

---

12. Large, *Free, Equal, and Mutual*, 115.

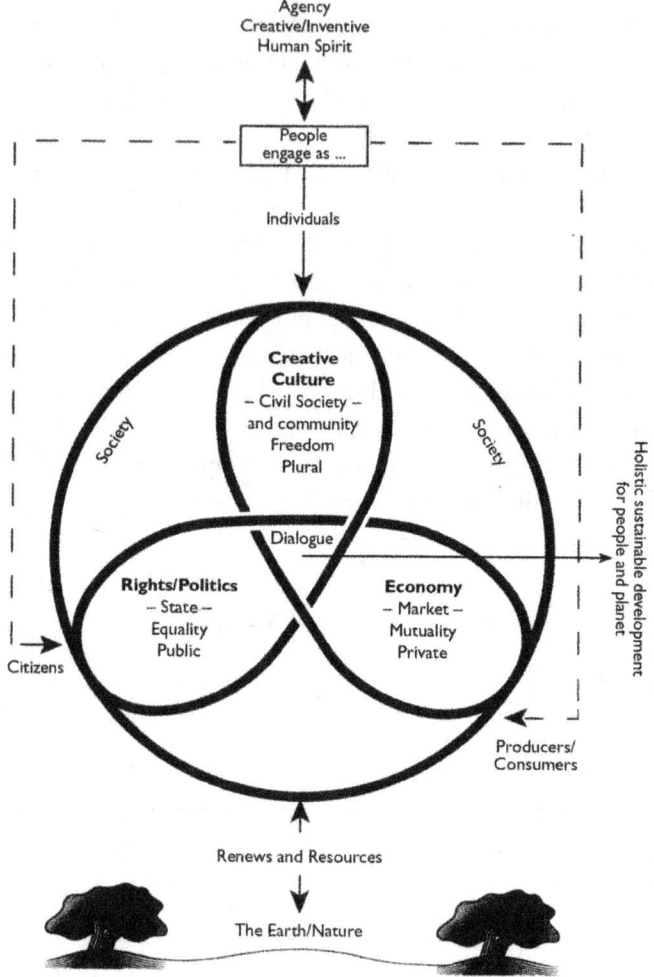

Rebalancing Society for the Common Good

Figure 6. By Martin Large and Steve Briault in *Free, Equal, and Mutual*. Hawthorne Press, 2018, with permission.

The basic threefold concept invites variations and amplifications. One noteworthy variant was developed by Sekem's founder, who was familiar with Steiner's foundational work.[13] Ibrahim Abouleish added a fourth sphere to accommodate the fact that environmental considerations

---

13. See Steiner, *Towards Social Renewal*; see also Masters, *Rudolf Steiner*.

have become so important in modern times. His fourfold diagram has been further amended so that it is now keyed to the Sekem Vision and Mission 2057.[14] I provide it here as an example of the possibilities threefold thinking can lead to, not as a model applied broadly or in the United States. One reason is that it is adapted for conditions at Sekem, and in Egypt, where the community needs to stay away from political engagement. Notice in the diagram below that the political/legal is absent as a distinct sphere. It is subsumed under the social sphere.

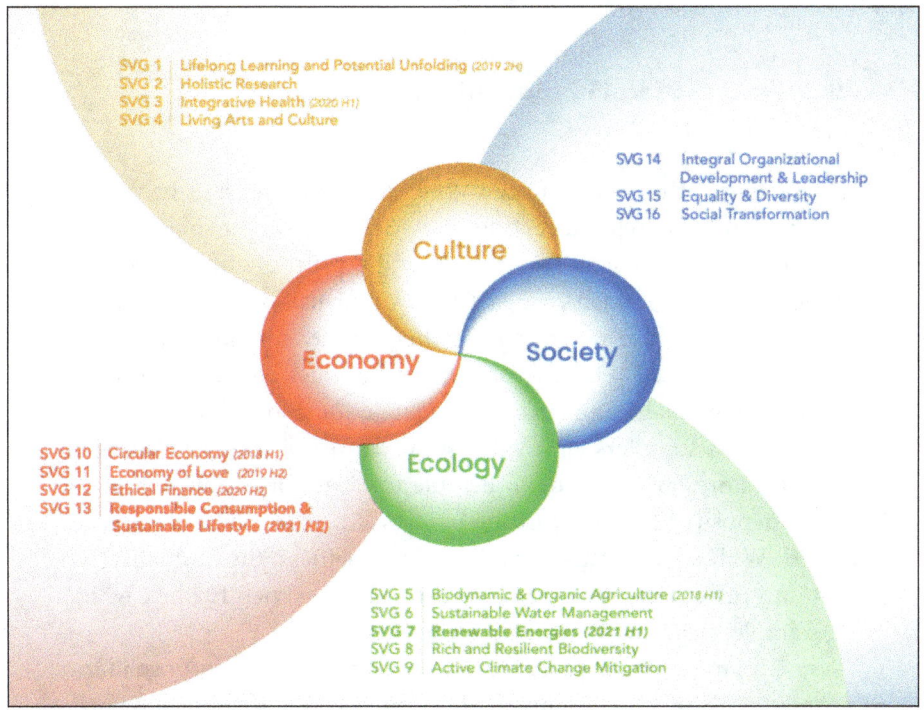

Figure 7. SEKEM'S FOUR SPHERES. Courtesy of Christine Arlt for Sekem.

In both the original and the variant conceptions, culture serves all of society with infusions of innovation, wisdom, purpose, ideals, and beauty. I saw this enacted at Sekem when I stood with two thousand workers in the great circle at the end of the work week, and I saw it in the emphasis accorded to personal growth and education throughout the community. In the culture sphere, education must remain true to its overriding ideal—individual development to the point where freedom is

14. Abouleish et al. "SEKEM Vision."

possible. It must be protected from overreach from the other spheres. In the United States, charter schools run by corporations violate this ideal by changing the primary purpose of education from individual development to making a profit. As discussed in Chapter 6, ideally government should actively protect the *equal rights* of children to a competent education, and the funding of the same, but not the content and management of schools. Politicians should not be telling teachers, for example, not to teach about racism, that they may not teach the extraordinary poem by Amanda Gorman, "The Hill We Climb."[15]

What Does the Ideal of Mutuality Look Like in the Economic Sphere?

I have devoted this much space to the cultural dimension because of its importance in giving direction and purpose to all of society. Many of the examples in chapter 8 show how the principle of mutuality or brotherhood manifests in co-ops, CSAs, land trusts, and any enterprise where the dynamic is a working together for the common good as opposed to individual profit. An ordinary business could not function without some measure of this. A store's relationships with its bank, its customers, its suppliers all involve some degree of trust and cooperation. The store owner needs to be able to trust, for instance, that the money deposited last week in the bank will be there next week when needed. With a cooperative or associative business, the mutuality gets built into the structure of the operation and is carried further, where, for example, the customers own the store.

With a multinational corporation, this kind of mutuality or solidarity becomes more difficult to achieve. For one thing, the size of the organization and its global reach create so much distance between top management and labor that any sense of personal connection with workers becomes unlikely. The pay differential between leaders and employees further divides them. However, wise management can do much to ameliorate this and create a measure of corporate *esprit*. At GE, before Jack Welch, workers were treated well, paid generously, and responded to that supportive climate with genuine loyalty. It was not unusual for a person to spend his or her entire working life at that one employer. Welch changed that culture and treated workers like expendable resources, pitted them against each

---

15. Chappell, "Amanda Gorman's Famous Poem."

other in a hyper-competitive climate, and used fear to drive ever greater efficiency. Workers hated him, and loyalty went to zero.

An enlightened corporate manager can go a considerable distance toward building a spirit of mutuality by providing leadership that embodies vision and moral courage. Thus, for example, at a Hewlitt Packard spin-off called Agilent Technologies, the three questions its human relations department worked energetically to ensure employees could answer "yes" to were the following:

1. Do you feel that your company creates authentic value in the world?
2. Do you see that your job contributes directly to creating that value?
3. Do you work with leaders and colleagues who recognize and motivate you?[16]

This working together to create value comes close to the kind of mutuality envisioned for a threefold economy.

What Does the Ideal of Equality Look Like in the Political/Legal Sphere?

The New England town meeting is often spoken of as the model for pure democracy, but for larger communities, states, or a whole country, obviously representative democracy must prevail. Suffice it to say here that everything the Civil Rights Movement fought for speaks to equality. And the ongoing efforts to include diverse voices in governance and various social and cultural institutions continues that goal into the present. In the legal arena, trial by a jury of one's peers and access to legal counsel represent the ideal of equality carried into practice. Favoritism in its many forms, subverting democratic processes, gerrymandering, creating obstacles to voting, buying political support—common sense tells us all these things subvert the ideal of equality.

The threefold conception of society with cultural, political, and economic spheres, together with the corresponding ideals, provide a framework that can guide thinking and discussion of what would ultimately work best. They take into account how human aspirations can be a unifying force when set forth by dedicated and inspiring leaders. This brings me back to the old monk (p. 134), who asks the young

---

16. Jean McClung Nye, personal interview with author, Dec. 15, 2023.

seeker, "What have you come here to do?" In other words, Why are you on Earth in this lifetime? Answering questions of this sort requires strength, love, and perseverance; but the answers on both the individual and social levels reside within each individual and out in society, waiting for people to find them.

The threefold conceptual framework clarifies the distinct roles of the different spheres. It facilitates balance and corrects misalignments where the ideals and purposes of one sphere spill over into others in unhelpful ways. With this in mind, I now turn to the thinking required for a new kind of constitution, one that can provide a basis for a healthy balance in society and a kind of renaissance when the time comes.

CHAPTER TEN: WHAT BEES CAN TEACH AND WHAT THEY CAN'T

> *Honey-bees . . . teach the art of order to a peopled kingdom.*
>
> —Shakespeare

> *If we change the lens with which we see the world, another future becomes possible.*
>
> —Jeremy Lent

> *We must transform ourselves to transform the world.*
>
> —Grace Lee Boggs

I HAVE TWO HIVES of bees. One is quite hospitable when I come with a quiet push-mower to cut the grass in the bee yard. The other is more excitable. I'm there to help, but they want to sting me anyway. I persevere because they have a hard time, what with loss of habitat, poisoned pollen in nearby corn fields, and something called colony collapse disorder. Both hives have things to teach.

As preposterous as it sounds, that we can learn anything from an insect with a brain the size of a pinhead, in fact, the bees—and more particularly the hive as a whole—are full of wisdom. A hive can serve as a beautiful metaphor or analog for human community, for bees have evolved to a point where they have a completely harmonious and complementary relationship with nature. There is nothing of the rapacious exploiter in the way they relate to the environment. Rather, they provide a kind of blessing to the flowers they visit, drinking nectar and at the same time pollinating so that the plants can produce fruit or seed. Without pollination, these flowers would die out and produce no fruit. Conversely, the flowers bless the bees in the sense that when a bee selflessly carries flower nectar back to the hive so it can be converted into honey, life-sustenance accumulates in the combs, without which the bees would die over winter.

Bee Teamwork

Honeybees offer valuable lessons in the way they organize and defend their complex societies. And they *are* complex. In addition to queen, drones, and workers, certain bees are assigned to make wax and build cells. Nurse bees groom, feed, and care for the queen and nurture the larvae, among other things. There are guard bees who police the hive entrance. Cleaners polish and prepare the cells. There are even undertakers, who remove dead bees from the hive and dispose of them. Most numerous, the foragers gather nectar for honey.[1] The process of converting nectar to honey begins in the foragers' gut, and continues after they pass what they have gathered to bees within the hive that continue the process and store the honey in their perfectly geometric cells.

At the same time the creative reciprocity exists between bees and nature beyond the colony, these industrious little creatures have a remarkable ability to cooperate and get along with each other. Unselfish in the sense that they operate without ego, bees seem to want to participate and to help each other out. Do they know something humankind does not?

When the early Mormons came to the Salt Lake Valley, they soon acquired bees and chose the beehive as their emblem, emphasizing the amount of cooperation and labor that would be necessary to establish a viable community in a land of little rain. To this day, the symbol persists, and Utah is called the "Beehive State." Brigham Young chose the name Deseret for the Latter Day Saints (LDS) community; it translates variously as "swarms of bees" or "land of the bee."[2]

---

1. For a more complete description of duties and roles of worker bees, see Williams, "Role."

2. Brinkerhoff, "Symbolism of the Beehive"; see also Scripture Central, "Where Does the Word."

CHAPTER TEN: WHAT BEES CAN TEACH AND WHAT THEY CAN'T

Another parallel emerges if you think of the whole Earth as an organism, with its unique coherence. Earth has a thin sheath of life covering its surface. Beneath that sheath lies inert rock, and beneath that the seething caldron of magma. Above lies the atmosphere and then an infinite cosmos. This remarkable organism goes hurtling through the heavens; it keeps to its customary course; it produces the seasons and the rhythms of day and night. Ice caps cover the poles. Trade winds blow. Despite incredible complexity, a remarkable balance is maintained. Similarly, a beehive functions as a single organism, even though it consists of as many members as a small city. In terms of balance, one can think of it as a microcosm of the macrocosm of the whole Earth, or alternatively of human society.

Over time, the beekeeper comes to admire the overriding intelligence that holds the bee colony together. The bees' system for getting through the winter provides another example of their teamwork. When it gets cold, they come together in a ball inside the hive; the muscles they use to move their wings adapt so that instead of being set up for flying, they shiver in a way that generates heat. The bees at the center of the ball are the warmest so they continually migrate to the outside of the ball, while the chilly outer bees migrate inward to warm up. This process goes on all winter until in the spring it is no longer necessary, and the wings revert to the flying configuration.

Bee Democracy

One of the most remarkable activities of bees occurs typically in May or June, when the hive divides and the queen departs with the majority of the workers to swarm and find a new home. After leaving their hive, ten thousand or more bees alight in a cluster on a nearby branch to decide where they will go. Next, a few hundred of the more senior forager bees set out to find and assess the real estate possibilities. These scouts return and report by means of a waggle dance they perform on the merits of the different options. There may be a dozen possibilities within a radius of five miles or more. The most desirable nesting sites evoke the most athletic and enthusiastic dances. More scouts fly out to examine further the leading site contenders. A process of deliberation takes place; sites are eliminated until there is a democratic consensus among the scouts on the best choice. The swarm flies off to occupy their new home. Often this is a hollow in a tree, fifteen feet or more above the ground.[3]

And then there is that most remarkable of substances—honey. What begins as a simple sugar solution in flower nectar is transformed into a substance unlike any other on Earth. It contains over 181 compounds, has healing properties, and can last indefinitely without spoiling. Some honey found in an Egyptian tomb, estimated to be three thousand years old, was still edible.

Honey has an affinity for another remarkable substance, human blood, and can be absorbed almost immediately. As honey is a mysterious substance, a product of transformation that confers healing powers, so blood does remarkable work in the human body, giving life to all parts and extremities. Karsten Massei, in *Gifts of the Honeybees*, gives an interesting interpretation of these two remarkable fluids of transformation. When he peers into spiritual dimensions of bees, colonies, and honey, Massei sees on one level the individual bees. He also sees them collectively as a remarkable organism with a kind of group intelligence. But beyond that, he identifies a spiritual presence, a kind of archetype, that confers wisdom and power to the hive and is the reason a beehive has "a deep connection to humankind." This "living force," he says, will be available to human beings in the future; it is Massei's perception of it that prompts him to offer this koan: "Through honeybees, human beings can look ahead into the future of their soul."[4] I am not smart enough to know just what this means, but it likely has to do with the fact that an individual bee is ready to die so that others can live. When a perceived threat approaches a hive, one or more workers will sting the intruder. A barbed stinger goes into the flesh, taking with it the sting gland and much of the bee's viscera. The bee dies. At the same time, from the base of the sting a banana-like odor emanates that signals to other bees to attack the intruder. Of course, this is an instinctive rather than a premeditated action, but that does not invalidate the fact that an individual sacrifices her life to protect the lives of other bees.[5] Massei seems to be saying that over time humans can transform to be more able to make major sacrifices, as indeed some citizens of Ukraine are doing today.

---

3. A book on this deliberative process provides details and scientific evidence about how and why this remarkable group decision-making occurs. See Seeley, *Honeybee Democracy*.

4. Massei, *Gifts of the Honeybees*, 124.

5. Miksha, "EO Wilson."

CHAPTER TEN: WHAT BEES CAN TEACH AND WHAT THEY CAN'T

The Shakers, the Mondragón cooperators, and the individuals in the Sekem community all have embraced personal transformation as an essential step in the way forward to make a better society. The original core of workers at Mondragón, for example, realized, with some prompting from José María, that they needed to grow and change themselves to be able to manage a cooperative enterprise. This impulse remains a core value within Mondragón to this day. Not in a scientific but in a poetic sense, honey can serve as an emblem of transformation, that indispensable quality without which individuals and communities are apt to remain stuck, unable to change.

Of course, bees lack intellect and ego, but the fact they do not make conscious choices but rather rely on finely-tuned instincts programmed into their genome does not mean we cannot learn from them. A summary of what bees can teach might look like the following:

- With regard to nature, rather than being locked in a transactional relationship, driven to extract as much profit as possible from nature, humans could learn from the creative reciprocity of bees with the nectar and pollen they depend on for their sustenance. This brings to mind the generosity and gratitude of traditional Native Americans who, though they could be warlike with each other, were reverential and restrained toward nature. Bees take, but they also give.
- Bees illustrate that elements of a complex society can work together harmoniously. They model bee *convivencia*. If an insect less than an inch long can summon this degree of teamwork and cooperation, they can inspire us into trying harder. They are amazing team players. Mondragón co-op members would agree: through cooperation the total impact can be greater than the sum of the parts.
- Bees are industrious, but their hard work is driven by something other than personal advantage. What these insects can accomplish through cooperation is prodigious.
- Bees live within natural limits. Unless assaulted by something beyond their control like pesticides, bee society maintains a balance or equilibrium that is sustainable indefinitely.
- Bees are neat and orderly. They clean up after themselves.
- Bees in a colony form an entity that is properly understood as a distinct organism and more than the sum of its parts. Similarly, some of the best thinking about regenerative farming views the farm as an

- Honey is a powerful symbol of transformation. Like human blood, with which it has a mysterious connection, honey can inspire us to undertake the transformations necessary to power a new civilization.
- The bees' selflessness can encourage people to be more mindful of what can be accomplished when effort flows, not toward one's own welfare but toward the welfare of all.

Perhaps we can combine some bee lessons and bee inspiration with qualities that are distinctly human. Bees can inspire us to see human society from a fresh perspective, but it would be easy to take the microcosm–macrocosm comparison too far. For one thing, bees lack any conscience and, for example, have no compunction about kicking the drones out of the hive and letting them die of starvation once winter comes. The workers will make new ones in spring.

Toward Freedom: Self-Transformation Through Inner Development

The examples from bee society can help us appreciate how distinctly different we are from those resourceful insects. Humans lack the bees' instinct of mutuality or cooperation, instilled in them over eons. In order to achieve anything like it, we humans must apply some inner effort to develop qualities like resilience, compassion, and tackling weaknesses like anger that undermine one's effectiveness in the world. Appendix A offers options for accomplishing this. In choosing a course of action, we can be guided by something no other animal or insect possesses—a conscience. If, as adults, we wanted to use our freedom, a capacity no bees possess, to transform ourselves to become fully human and contribute to a new civilization, this could bring us again to the question "What kind of person do I aspire to be?" Obviously, this is a highly individual quest. The last thing needed would be a set of one-size-fits-all qualities or even principles. Each person should be able to choose what to them constitutes forward movement, or, if they prefer, no movement. However, if global warming continues on its current trajectory, and, with it, democracies and societies unravel, the no-movement people are apt to be left swimming in a sea of their own indifference.

CHAPTER TEN: WHAT BEES CAN TEACH AND WHAT THEY CAN'T

Many today assume that after you grow up, you reach a stasis condition in which you age but for the most part cease to grow. They may even develop a kind of psycho-spiritual callous or immunity to change.[6] Let me propose instead that for a dynamic and evolving society, individuals need to be on a *growth trajectory*. Look around at older people you know. If they are still vibrant and creative, are they not on a growth trajectory? They are curious. They still manage to drink the honey of transformation. The sense of expanding horizons and the discovery of new capacities within oneself that occurs in a whole-child education can continue until you die. In fact, the process of dying, of disincarnating, is loaded with growth potential.[7] At least it seems so to me, a person who is within sight of the end. Whether or not I can continue to evolve, to own and cultivate a horizon-expanding education, depends on how I choose to use my freedom. At any stage of life one can ask the question: Do I wish to be a passenger or a driver in this body and mind I inhabit?

From what you have read in this book, especially the chapter on freedom, you can deduce that I believe human evolution wants you to be the driver. It is *your* life, after all. However, many people do not consciously take up this decision but default to the role of passenger, the stasis condition. It means going through life more or less taking things as they come, responding as seems appropriate, and not challenging social mores. The Higher Self of the passenger has other ideas and will throw challenges in the way that encourage a person to make decisions, change, and grow; but that is a topic for another book.

Guidance for tackling the question of how one intends to grow, of who one aspires to be, can be found in a new movement called the Inner Development Goals or IDGs. In 2022, a conference took place in Stockholm, with remote participants around the world. The first Inner Development Goals Summit worked from the premise that the United Nation's Sustainable Development Goals, or SDGs,[8] would be unattainable unless linked to and supported by IDGs, the inner development of citizens. The conference and the now global organization that grew out of it identified five areas of inner growth.

---

6. Harvard psychologist Robert Kegan has developed this idea and counters the notion of adult stasis by offering Immunity To Change workshops. See Minds at Work, "Facilitator's Workshop."

7. See the poem on p. 84.

8. Department of Economic and Social Affairs, "17 Goals."

The IDG movement breaks down these five broad categories into twenty-three skills or competencies that were deemed essential in individual citizens in a healthy society. These goals, enumerated, are available for study at the Inner Development Goals

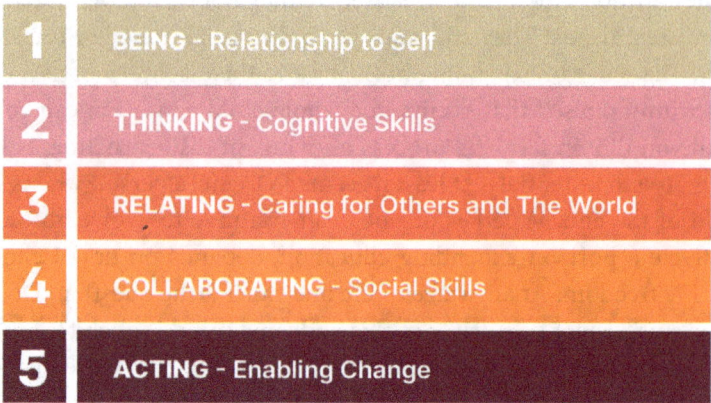

Figure 8. Courtesy of Inner Development Goals, Creative Commons.

website,[9] together with details and an explanation of the process.[10] In chart form they look like this.

Personal Competencies

Being – Relationship to Self	Thinking – Cognitive Skills	Relating – Caring for Others and the World	Collaborating – Social Skills	Acting – Driving Change
Inner compass	Critical thinking	Appreciation	Communication skills	Courage
Integrity and Authenticity	Complexity awareness	Connectedness		Creativity
		Humility	Co-creation skills	Optimism
Openness and Learning mindset	Perspective skills	Empathy and Compassion		Perseverance
	Sense-making		Inclusive mindset and Intercultural competence	
Self-awareness	Long-term orientation and visioning			
Presence			Trust	
			Mobilization skills	

Figure 9. Courtesy of Inner Development Goals, Creative Commons.

9. See Inner Development Goals, "Framework."
10. Jordan et al., "Inner Development Goals."

CHAPTER TEN: WHAT BEES CAN TEACH AND WHAT THEY CAN'T

As an advanced civilization, people in this country already have great resources for pursuing these goals, should they choose to do so. Work done at Sekem and shown in the chart on p. 181 can be useful.[11] The main point is that for humans, both the social change in the outer landscape and the very un-beelike interior landscape of self-change must work in concert. The example of the bees can take people partway to making both these landscapes lively and productive, but our own initiative, conscious thought, and moral courage will be needed to travel the rest of the way.

---

11. The Sekem website, sekem.com, provides current information, and the most recent annual report can be accessed there.

CHAPTER ELEVEN: CENTERING ON EDUCATION

We need to prototype . . . a deliberately developmental culture that brings out the best in people.

—Tomas Björkman

You will never know how much it has cost my generation to preserve your freedom. I hope you will make good use of it.

—John Adams

In this book I have tried to show how the path to a new civilization leads through education. I would go so far as to say that without an approach radically different from what currently prevails in our culture and public schools, a truly flourishing civilization will be impossible to create. In early chapters, we turned to what could be learned from the eternal verities of freedom, community, and love. The next chapters drilled down on the kind of education that can produce informed, centered, and strong individuals, and then how best to deliver it. The chapter on agriculture explored how a farm can safely grow, not just crops but people. And then in the alternative economics chapter, lessons from the Shakers, Mondragón, and Sekem came to light. Bees have things to teach, and we can learn from their limitations as well. The chapter titled "Seeking a Balance" provided a conceptual framework that I believe will be particularly useful to those seeking to process and learn from current complex conditions and plan a new civilization—to a certain extent from scratch.

What an audacious idea, to try imagining a new and better civilization! Of course. But that is what I'm interested in—how we break free from our familiar ruts and brainstorm beyond the boundaries of conventional thinking.

I want to explore further. What kind of *thinking* could produce the vision needed for a new civilization? In the first chapter I explained Otto Scharmer's important technique of presencing, and I stressed the value of intuition to supplement intellectual thinking. In this chapter I wish to mention other dimensions for the quality of thought needed for this task.

Instead of relying on established practices, the kind of thinking that comes into play here needs to focus on the future and the creation of a civilization that does not destroy the planet that is our only home. This different kind of thinking takes into account that the human individual is more than a highly developed animal with a computer-like brain moving about on two legs. The future citizens who need to envision new kinds of communities will have to know that they have the uniquely human potential to act out of conscience, make free and unselfish decisions, build caring into their institutions, and love one another. "Potential" is the operative word. By the time a new civilization becomes possible, these citizens likely will have been hammered on the anvil of very trying experience, and may well be ready to let go of a status quo that doesn't work and conventional thinking that fails to come up with answers that inspire.

Thought gets colored by the attitude one brings to it. Leading up to the Enlightenment in Europe, two philosophers' views contended for influence. Thomas Hobbes (d. 1679) held that human life was "solitary, poor, nasty, brutish, and short."[1] On the other hand, Jean-Jacques Rousseau (d. 1778) held that human existence was filled with potential, what he called "perfectablity." He opened his famous *Social Contract* with the words "Man is born free, and everywhere he is in chains."[2] Hobbes's vision went nowhere, while Rousseau's contributed to both the French and American revolutions. The latter attitude and vision may at times prove impractical; where it holds so much value, however, is that, forward-looking and optimistic, it opens up almost endless possibilities.

---

1. Hobbes, *Leviathan*, pt. 1, ch. 13.
2. Rousseau, *Social Contract*, 49.

These two contrasting visions of human nature crop up again in the domain of education. The gloomy one that stresses limits gets expressed in the academic model that makes learning comparable to pouring beans into a bucket. You pour facts, concepts, and skills into the students in a process that is finite, has no surprises, and is measurable. The contrasting and brighter vision sees learning akin to igniting a flame. Teachers still need to convey content, but their efforts aim to draw out innate talents, engage students with challenging projects, and unleash creativity. The results are unpredictable, difficult if not impossible to quantify, and potentially infinite.

One further note on attitude. When things go wrong, as inevitably they will, many people, including those of us who have spent time in graduate school sharpening our critical faculties, have a propensity to find someone to criticize and blame. This obviously can have practical value, but it also carries a certain freight for the blamer. It creates a psychological distance from the blamed, and this othering undercuts the impulse to come together to fix the problem. By contrast, an attitude of gratitude carries a healing emotion and closes the void created by everything we take for granted. Most importantly, gratitude opens one to constructive change. As Robin Wall Kimmerer points out in *Braiding Sweetgrass*, native stories, so important in the traditional raising of the tribe's children, are full of tough consequences when people neglect to be grateful.[3]

Aspirations

In August 1963, at the end of a long day for the March on Washington, it was so hot that the Red Cross was passing out ice cubes to help people cope with the heat. On the steps of the Lincoln Memorial, Martin Luther King Jr. was well into his address when singer Mahalia Jackson, who was nearby, called out "Tell 'em about the dream, Martin; tell 'em about the dream." King pushed aside his prepared remarks and launched into an improvisation that electrified the crowd. From the tens of thousands present, cries of "Amen" could be heard, as one might find in a rural church down South. Those four words—"I have a dream"—and the vision King conveyed of a people "free at last" inspired the Civil Rights

---

3. Center for Humans and Nature, "Questions."

Movement and decades later, influenced rights activists from Soweto to Tiananmen Square to Eastern Europe.[4]

Ideals and aspirations help raise people's sights so that instead of focusing on protecting the status quo, they envision possibilities that stretch beyond the known. An inspiring vision can confer motivation and courage, can pry one out of self-centeredness. King Solomon tapped into a timeless truth when he said, "Where there is no vision, the people perish" (Prov 29:18 KJV). Aspirations, well-expressed, can enliven any effort. In an earlier version of this chapter I called for a new kind of American Constitution, one that included, not just rights but aspirations and responsibilities as well. Should people choose to do so, everything in this book up to this point can be used to stimulate aspirations, and aspirations in turn stimulate learning.

I want to offer an overall vision of a society that sponsors individual growth and social transformation. Those who frame the vision for their new civilization will, of course, have their own ideas about what is appropriate at that historical moment. Elements of that vision could include the following aspirations:

- A universal right to early childhood education, conceived not as early preparation for testing but rather laying a social and emotional foundation for a mature adulthood
- Individual flourishing, growth, and education, prioritized ahead of defense and other budget demands
- A culture that celebrates diversity, but not in a way that compromises equality of opportunity
- A program of national service—everyone puts their shoulder to the wheel
- Replace the entire tax system, which is complex to the point of absurdity and exacerbates inequalities, with a simpler one such as the Automatic Payment Transaction Tax (APT);[5] this would assess a one percent or less tax on all transactions, including the billions of financial ones that currently go untaxed, and provide revenue for progressive measures such as affordable housing and free college tuition

---

4. Kakutani, "Lasting Power."
5. Feige, *Taxation*.

- Further tax reforms that encourage private philanthropy and in effect teach corporations to share and to grow beyond self-serving and image-oriented philanthropy
- A remade agriculture that, instead of favoring giant corporations that abuse animals and destroy topsoil, allows small farmers to once again make a living on the land; an economic system valuing cooperation over self-aggrandizement

Were these aspirations to be applied in the United States, it would mean enabling Americans to educate their way to a diverse and exuberant melting-pot nation. At the same time, it could rewrite the story of the country's possibilities.

In thinking about how high to aim for individual and social development, I find Maslow's pyramid of human needs helpful. It looks like this:

SELF-ACTUALIZATION
morality, creativity, spontaneity, acceptance, experience purpose, meaning and inner potential

SELF-ESTEEM
confidence, achievement, respect of others, the need to be a unique individual

LOVE AND BELONGING
friendship, family, intimacy, sense of connection

SAFETY AND SECURITY
health, employment, property, family and social abilty

PHYSIOLOGICAL NEEDS
breathing, food, water, shelter, clothing, sleep

Figure 10. MASLOW'S HIERARCHY.
This format was developed by simplypsychology.org.

Of course, the pyramid is a simplification of many possibilities and potentially infinite complexity, but it represents effectively the extent to which higher aspirations rest on safety, security, and other basic needs. It also offers an invitation to develop the possibilities for self-actualization, the apex of the graphic. The Inner Development Goals and the organization that encourages them, explained in the previous chapter, do a beautiful job of amplifying these possibilities.

The three chapters on freedom, community, and love also serve this function, and it is worth noting how these three qualities, *cultivated together*, strengthen a society and raise all boats. Inner freedom of the sort Nelson Mandela exhibited when in prison confers personal empowerment. It allows individuals to express their authentic selves, make choices aligned with their values, and pursue their aims and ideals without constraints imposed by social norms. This freedom goes beyond outer restrictions and expectations; it carries with it self-awareness and often the courage to act on one's convictions. When individuals have inner freedom, they are apt to have the confidence to form genuine connections with others, which in turn builds community or *convivencia*.

Convivencia, as embodied in eighth-century Granada, and more recently in the ideal of the Beloved Community promoted by Martin Luther King Jr.,[6] envisions a society based on justice, equity, and love, one in which individuals work together in mutual respect and solidarity. A Beloved Community is a growth environment; love and compassion guide citizens to create systems that uplift everyone. Inner freedom nourishes this vision because it empowers individuals to contribute authentically through acts of kindness and solidarity that strengthen communal ties. Love is the connective tissue that binds freedom and community, fostering empathy and a commitment to the well-being of others. Creatively exploring how these three concepts of freedom, community, and love can work together increases the chances that a new civilization will be able to see the arts, sciences, and social movements collaborate in shaping a flourishing future.

Responsibilities or Obligations

Aspirations or ideals provide a sense of where we are headed and why. Responsibilities and follow-through turn impetus into action. In a new

---

6. Pollak, "Idea of the Beloved."

civilization, citizens need to feel not just that they have rights but also that they are called upon to contribute, ideally to continue to grow and assume new roles. If at some distant time it becomes feasible to replace the American Constitution with a new kind of constitution, it should include not just rights, as at present, but aspirations and responsibilities. In this way it could be a source of inspiration and an instrument of constructive change. With the Electoral College, life terms in the Supreme Court, wildly disproportionate Senate representation for rural states, and other stipulations, the existing constitution serves as an obstacle to effective democracy, actually disenfranchising the electorate in significant ways.

To visualize how more explicit citizen obligations might work, imagine a new country where the founders want to promote in citizens not a *taking* mentality but a more *giving* one. Current trends are moving in the opposite direction, as autocratic leaders seem to get themselves elected based on promises to voters to let them keep more of what is theirs. Lower my taxes; keep out immigrants; stop subsidizing welfare queens; and so on. Isn't it common sense that a balance between rights (looking out for what is mine) and responsibilities (giving back where I can) makes for a better society than just rights alone? So why not state some visionary goals and back them up with responsibilities stated in the constitution?

Two kinds of responsibilities need to be considered by anyone imagining a new civilization or framing document: 1) those of the state for the populace; and 2) those of individual citizens for each other and the general good. One can imagine that in a properly functioning democracy the first form of responsibility will manifest as government assuring a safe and stable society. It will address needs on the bottom two tiers of Maslow's schema. It also needs to ensure that the mechanism of democracy actually works.

In addition to protecting the population and ensuring order and justice—the bedrock value, the one that can advance aspirations noted above—should be defending and supporting the development of individuals to their full potential. The constitution for this new entity needs to articulate its responsibility, along with parents and schools, for growing fully conscious citizens who in turn can make a dynamic community. This education-centric society will not be classroom-bound but will offer an open palette of every conceivable form of learning and growth, from birth through one's last breath.

CHAPTER ELEVEN: CENTERING ON EDUCATION

Can education really be transformative? Consider the story of Darren Walker. He was born in a charity hospital to a single mother in the little town of Lafayette, Louisiana. He was raised in a shotgun shack in rural East Texas and in 1965 was in the first class of a program designed to level the educational playing field for kids born in poverty—Head Start. He went on to public school. Admitted to the University of Texas, he was only able to attend with the help of Pell grants and private philanthropy. Growing up in the American South, he encountered bitter racism and, on top of that, discrimination because he is gay. He also said, however, that he encountered enormous generosity from people who believed in his potential and had his back. "My story is an American story . . . a story of what can happen when we the people live up to our ideals."[7] Until recently, Walker served as president of the Ford Foundation. They gave away $556 billion last year.

Walker's story is an updraft, not only because poor boy makes good but because he emphatically believes in the transformative power of education, especially when coupled with the goodwill of people who want to see the very best nurtured and encouraged in young people. Inspiration from examples like his needs to be built into the new civilization's aspirations and responsibilities.

The two chapters on education show how schools can do their part to nurture children to be resilient, creative, caring, and strong. In this way, they will be prepared to grow into effective change agents, and become builders of the good life for all. But this is only the beginning of a lifelong maturing process. Education and growth toward ever greater levels of maturity need to be the bedrock values for a reenvisioned society.

Because the overriding ideal for the political sphere is equality, to the state falls the responsibility to make sure it levels the playing field. Defense from outside invaders—military, microbial, or digital—has to be for everyone, not just those who live in gated communities and can afford private security. It means equal justice under the law and infrastructure such as a water supply that all can access. Here we see how responsibilities of the state pair with rights of individual citizens, almost two sides of the same coin.

The second form of responsibility, the one exercised by individual citizens, cannot always be codified in law. But there are ways that, over time, can encourage people to take up that sentiment so eloquently captured in

---

7. "UVM 2019 Commencement Address."

the Gwendolyn Brooks line "We are each other's harvest." The best hope probably lies with an enlightened and holistic education. For those who are too old to learn to share their toys in preschool, they can always form an intention to move away from the self-centered behavior of sometimes very rich individuals who act like spoiled children, blame others for their troubles, and think wielding wealth and power can bring happiness. Tax breaks, the example of committed leaders, and the work of service groups can contribute. The example comes to mind of Jimmy Carter who, into his nineties, was still swinging a hammer for Habitat for Humanity.[8]

Now to apply the framework for achieving a balance in society, outlined in chapter 9, I take up each of the three spheres and provide thoughts on aspirations, then responsibilities, and then rights for each one.

The Economic Sphere

In the imagined civilization, for the economic sphere's living ideal I have been using the term *mutuality*, but it lacks the punch of the earlier term *brotherhood*. *Solidarity* is not a perfect fit either. In any case, the term implies conscious cultivation of a climate of goodwill, you could say the antithesis of cutthroat competition. The mutuality assumes the form of a series of associations[9] for different economic interests. Think of them as cooperatives, expanded to include all producers for a given commodity, probably chartered by government but, like cooperatives, organized by the farmers themselves. There might be an association of cranberry producers (such a cooperative already exists),[10] another for grains, and still another for milk products. The members of each sector's association would coordinate with regard to production levels and prices, working conditions, compensation, and benefits. Legal considerations would still be handled by government—minimum working age, non-payment of wages, injustice of any kind in the workplace. A key aspiration here will be to eliminate the codependency of government and the economy, without precluding the chance to coordinate where this makes sense and can be done without undermining the sovereignty of either sphere.

---

8. O'Kane, "Jimmy Carter."
9. See p. 156, footnote 59.
10. Ocean Spray, "About Us."

Thus, the ideal, to be at least considered by those framing the new civilization and its constitution, would be establishing a framework that encourages the economic sphere to become more self-governing. This might happen in farming first. Imagine, for example, that the milk industry is caught in a cycle of overproduction and declining prices for milk. Instead of price supports, overt regulation, buying up excess, and turning it into cheese for storage or other government interventions, empower the industry to solve the problem itself by regulating supply and therefore price. An example of how this worked successfully in the past with tobacco can be found in appendix B.

Imagine another scenario where another country is dumping subsidized wheat on the American market and threatening to drive American wheat farmers out of business. Because this involves foreign relations and potentially treaties and tariffs, government would have to be involved. But their efforts to resolve the problem would be undertaken in concert with the wheat farmers' association.

It is fair to ask if anything this ambitious could be accomplished in a country as vast and complex as the United States. Would the divergence of views make cooperation impossible? This again is an education question. People may need to *learn* to cooperate and compromise. Further, I suggest that removing the political element from the associations as much as possible could allow an association to be highly effective. It would be democratic in the sense that representatives would have to be elected as they are in cooperatives, but measures could be set in place from the outset that controlled special-interest lobbying and prevented corporate capture. Association participants could step into their agency and assert their needs and interests.

Although it is not organized along associative lines, the Federal Reserve is an excellent example of how an organization, in this case within government but independent of political and business pressures, is able to operate very effectively. The "soft landing" engineered by the Fed to end the inflation that peaked in 2022 was only possible because it successfully resisted pressure brought to bear on it by economic and political interests.

In both the milk and wheat examples, the interest of the producers would be balanced by associations representing the consumers. The ideal would be to accomplish as much as possible without the machinery of government. One can imagine this in the area of pharmaceuticals, where if a company decided to jack up prices, as was done with insulin, the association of consumers could use the formidable power of its united members to bring the pharma company into line.

Other aspirations for the economic area could include having the idea of fair trade expand so that an Economy of Love (EoL) model, based on Sekem's pioneering work, could mean that price would equal or approximate value. While the citizens might not be ready for abolishing labor as a commodity and making it sacred as the Shakers did, there could be incentives to make more of that possible where it was felt desirable. This could begin with those who are retired and have plenty of free time while living off pensions and other forms of retirement income. If a further aspiration were to institute a guaranteed minimum annual income, this could help with homelessness and, combined with robust drug interventions, could have a significant impact on crime and the quality of life in cities.

In the guaranteed income and other measures, the economic sphere would aspire to implement the stated aim of the first article of the Universal Declaration of Human Rights (1948). It reads:

> All human beings are born free and equal in dignity and rights. They are endowed with reason and conscience and should act towards one another in a spirit of brotherhood.[11]

Each employer, whether a worker-owned cooperative or a conventional business, would have the opportunity to implement an EoL based on the Sekem model. These arrangements would be developed and implemented initially the same way fair trade has been implemented—through the initiative of leading individuals and small groups coming together. Then, as they were perfected and could demonstrate multiple benefits, they would grow. It seems to me, making this voluntary rather than mandatory makes sense. You can't command people to act out of love, but a society that builds caring, pro-social, dynamic institutions can create a favorable climate and promote community spirit, the *convivencia* outlined in Chapter 3.

The rights in the current constitution would carry over for the most part. Civic order would prevail. Citizens would have the right to a well-regulated economy that does not perpetuate injustice, that respects the separation of the spheres, and that operates using associations where doing so makes sense.

---

11. United Nations, "History of the Declaration."

The Political/Legal Sphere

Equality and fairness reign as ideals in this sphere. Thus the cleverly conceived separation of powers in the 1787 Constitution aptly advances this sphere's ideal and is completely compatible with a threefold conception of society. When applied, the aspirations in this area must reflect equality, interpreted as fair and equal opportunities, protections, and rights, not as any attempt to legislate that people must be culturally the same. In fact, diversity is seen as an asset rather than a liability. Thus, in education it would make sense to guarantee an uncompromising *right* to adequate and equitable funding and opportunity, made explicit in the constitution. But at the same time, let there be no effort to homogenize what is taught or dictate how it is delivered. Enterprising schools need to be free to move beyond the old paradigms that focus on content acquisition and memorization rather than creativity and skills needed for a complex and rapidly changing world.

As now, a core responsibility of government will be ensuring a just and civil public order. People need to feel safe in their homes and communities. They need to know that the country will be protected against invaders and that there will be avenues through which society can evolve and transform. As Goethe observed, order surpasses justice in importance because once chaos reigns, justice is impossible.[12]

With order assured, justice becomes a priority, and a particular kind of injustice can be addressed wherein those with money and influence seek to skew regulations and taxes to reward themselves, often at the expense of those who have the least to spare. In fact, taxation will be an important way these aspirations can be realized. Carrying the banner for this impulse today, and seeking to redistribute through fairer taxation on the ballooning wealth of the top 1 percent, an activist group of the wealthy calling themselves the Patriotic Millionaires conveys the message to an unresponsive government and corporate lobbyists: we have the money; tax us more.[13] The same message was conveyed at the 2024 National Democratic Convention by retired American Express CEO Ken Chenault: "[Kamala Harris] knows the way NOT to do it [build an

---

12. See Goethe, *From My Life*; and Montbrial, "Letter from Europe."
13. Learn more about the Patriotic Millionaires at their website: patrioticmillionaires.org.

advanced economy] is to give people like me a tax cut, when that money should be invested to grow the middle class."[14]

The other key aspiration for this sphere involves protecting the right to autonomy for each of the spheres unless injustice or illegality is involved. This may sound fanciful today, but think of a new game board with different rules than we are used to. Thus, in the future a radically new constitution could prohibit economic entities from buying influence and favors from government. At the same time, the principle of the separation of church and state could be taken one step further, and government itself would be prevented from dictating to the cultural sphere. A reimagined tax policy could make it advantageous for corporations, associations, and individuals to support all kinds of cultural events and activities. Were this the case, government support for the arts could possibly be phased out.

The responsibilities in this political sphere for individuals would be to observe the law, to serve on juries when called, and to vote. Those designing the new social order would need to seek ways to motivate citizens to become informed enough to vote judiciously at local, state and federal levels. But perhaps that is asking too much. The rights within this sphere are well developed in the existing constitution and constitutional law. Citizens need to do their part in upholding peace and order, which includes doing things commonly taken for granted, such as driving on the correct side of the road.

Another important consideration belongs in this sphere. If in the future, the United States continues to be the richest and most powerful nation on Earth, it also will have the responsibility to use its power, resources, and good offices to promote peace, justice, and sustainability throughout the world. To a certain extent this is already happening, as when our president and federal government go to great lengths to fund and preserve NATO, provide support for an invaded Ukraine, and advocate for the Paris Climate Accord. This responsibility will grow as the global threat of climate chaos looms.

Geographically isolated from most of the world, the United States has always experienced tensions between globalists and isolationists. But if one accepts as a moral fact that with gifts come responsibilities, then it follows that this resource-rich country has an important role to play in making the world a livable place. That role was implicitly recognized when

---

14. C-SPAN, "Democratic National Convention," 4:21.

it was time to establish the United Nations, and the decision was made to locate its headquarters in New York. Educating the general population up to a point where they expand their sense of belonging to include the entire world is a tall order but, as explained in the first chapter of this book, it can happen by degrees. First a sense of belonging extends beyond one's own skin, to the family, then to the community, then nature, and finally the world. Purely intellectual approaches cannot handle this task. It will take thoughtfully-attuned social and emotional learning. This change in values and orientation takes us into cultural territory.

The state has a responsibility to address poverty and not just with palliative measures. Citizens should have the right not to be ground down by poverty.[15] One of the famous paintings in Norman Rockwell's *Four Freedoms* series is *Freedom from Want*. This need not mean the turkey dinner Rockwell depicts, but at least a decent minimum and paths that lead to a place where people can thrive. Those of us who live comfortably and have plenty to eat often fail to feel the anguish of those who cannot provide for their children, or of the children themselves who go to bed hungry, or, in some cases, appear at school Monday morning not having eaten all weekend. Hunger blocks learning. Poverty undermines so many elements of society but especially hurts those children who grow up with stress and hopelessness. Commonly cited results of poverty include the following:

- Hunger and malnutrition, affecting physical and mental development
- Absence of a secure and safe home, rent stress, evictions
- Substandard education, stress-induced inability to learn
- Mental health issues
- Greatly increased likelihood of crime—as perpetrator or victim

---

15. Richard Shelton, who taught prison writing workshops for many years, observed that many of his students believed from childhood they would end up in prison. "Poverty results in the inability to make choices. Poor parents might choose to raise their children in a neighborhood without the friendly dope dealer on the corner, but that is not a choice they can afford to make. They might choose to send their children to a better school, but that is not a choice they can afford to make. They might choose to spend more time with their children, to teach them things they need to know, but scrambling to make a living takes up all their time and energy." See Shelton, "Prince Albert," 82.

- Poor self-image and demoralization, affecting one's ability to secure a job
- Likelihood of perpetuating a cycle of poverty

One way to address this would be some version of a universal basic income (UBI). While critics of the idea claim that it would subsidize young men who prefer staying home playing video games over working,[16] experience with pilot programs does not support the idea that such an arrangement would produce a generation of slackers.[17] Benefits included improved child health and nutrition, greater success in school, decreased use of alcohol and tobacco by parents, lessening of severe income inequalities, happier and less-stressed participants, and improved mental health.[18] There will perhaps always be people who argue that government need not protect people from the consequences of their own rotten decisions, choices that result in poverty. But an objective cost-benefit analysis could well show that even with a certain number of freeloaders, the benefits outweigh the costs. If UBI proves to be too costly or controversial, there are other options for dealing with poverty and homelessness. The principle that seems to apply here is that the moral worth of a society can be measured by how it treats its least fortunate. Conditions in Norway, where extreme poverty is almost nonexistent, prove that we can do better in addressing want.[19]

Closely allied to the above, shouldn't citizens have the right to at least basic health care? Having government-run hospitals has not worked very well for the Department of Veterans Affairs (VA) or in Britain, but having a single health insurance plan to replace the welter of competing private plans would streamline things. Something like Medicare-for-All holds promise.

The Cultural Sphere

One can think of the ideal in this sphere as individual flourishing, leading to true freedom of the type taken up in the chapter on that subject. The strengths and health of this sphere have everything to do with the

16. Nidess, "Universal Basic Income."
17. Hugill and Franklin, "Universal Basic Income."
18. Nyoike, "Countries That Have Tried."
19. Organisation for Economic Co-Operation and Development (OECD), "Better Life Initiative."

effective functioning of all spheres. In this one, new values emerge, such as those concerned with the rights of future generations. This is the eloquent message of *The Ministry for the Future*, a remarkable book by Kim Stanley Robinson that posits an agency tasked with protecting humans yet to be born[20] and "entities that can never speak for themselves, like animals and watersheds."[21] Creative people working in this area will encourage science research, the arts, and a general cultural flourishing. An education that prepares students in a holistic way to find their own path toward freedom will give an extraordinary vitality to the whole civilization over time. The aspiration of lifelong learning can become part of the DNA of this sphere.

A new value that will emanate from this sphere and will need to find its way into the constitution involves the rights of nature. Getting people used to this idea will involve a lot of education, but it holds the potential to completely change how we protect not just trees and rivers but all of creation. Current environmental protections fail because they were shaped by the very industries they were meant to regulate, and the thinking involved focuses on property and monetary values. Founders of the US-based Center for Democratic and Environmental Rights (CDER) have worked on the first rights of nature laws in the world. This includes pioneering work in Ecuador, which has changed its constitution to assert that Pachamama, or Mother Earth, has the right to exist and "maintain and regenerate its cycles, structure, functions, and evolutionary processes."[22] The clause in Ecuador's constitution enshrining the rights of nature has already been used to restrain flagrant destruction of Indigenous lands in the upper Amazon watershed. Other countries coping with inadequate environmental protection are pressing ahead to recognize legally enforceable rights of nature, including Panama, Bolivia, Uganda, and New Zealand. A court in India has granted the Ganges River the same legal rights as humans.[23] Colombia and Bangladesh have also recognized the rights of rivers and other

---

20. See also Our Children's Trust (ourchildrenstrust.org) and primarily a lawsuit, *Juliana v. United States*, in which twenty-one children from various states and different ages assert their right to essential public trust resources such as clean air and water. The complainants allege that in the face of overwhelming scientific evidence of climate change, the federal government has failed to provide basic protections and a healthy future for these young people who will grow up to deal with the consequences.

21. Robinson, *Ministry*, 98.

22. Echeverria, "Rights of Nature."

23. Safi and Agencies, "Ganges and Yamuna Rivers."

ecosystems. In the United States, tribal nations have been among the first to enact rights of nature mandates.[24]

A rejuvenated and rethought education will hold the potential to help young people discover their gifts, to learn at a deeper level, and thereby be in a position to recognize and take up their responsibilities as citizens, able to contribute to the community and help others. This more nurturing education will incorporate ecological literacy and a respect for the rights of nature and those who will be part of the human family in the future.

Accordingly, a core right for citizens is access to education of all kinds and all levels to support growth over the lifespan. The tax structure needs to indirectly support the arts, as noted; and the freedoms such as speech, assembly, etc. stated in the existing constitution of course continue.

Further Thoughts on Responsibilities

Two key documents can deepen any discussion of how citizens contribute to the social whole. Both present as rights declarations but have much explicit or implied about aspirations and responsibilities as well. These are the Universal Declaration of Human Rights[25] and the more recent and comprehensive Earth Charter.[26]

Rights and responsibilities often come paired. A child has the right to be raised without abuse and neglect, but parents have the responsibility for any child they bring into the world until that child is grown. Each individual citizen can carry both rights and responsibilities—I have the right to free speech but also the responsibility to allow others to speak their mind.

To prompt discussion and further thought I have listed below potential citizen responsibilities not already mentioned. I have not included all the possibilities. An alternate list has been developed by Robert Haass in his book *The Bill of Obligations*.[27] I intend my list to show the

---

24. To learn more, see both centerforenvironmentalrights.org and celdr.org.

25. The original text (1948), along with commentary, can be found at Peterson, *Universal Declaration*.

26. For the text of The Earth Charter (1982), see Earth Charter, "Earth Charter."

27. Haass, *Bill of Obligations*.

CHAPTER ELEVEN: CENTERING ON EDUCATION

kind of radical thinking that I believe will be necessary to prompt true societal change.

1. Twenty-two countries require citizens to vote. That should be considered as a new civilization is being visualized.

2. Government imposes the responsibility of citizens to pay taxes to support state functions. At the same time, citizens should expect the right of equitable taxation. This will mean an explicit constitutional requirement that taxes be aligned with wealth and ability to pay.

3. Citizens will have the responsibility to observe, not just the letter but the spirit of the constitution and derived laws.

4. Most parents want the best for their children and raise them accordingly. However, having a child involves a formidable responsibility and a commitment of eighteen years or more. When abuse and neglect occur, a child's right to be safe requires decisive intervention by the state.

5. Israel and some other countries have some form of universal national service. Usually one thinks of this in military terms, but a gap experience like VISTA (see appendix C) or almost any service after secondary school can have tremendous benefits to the young person finding her way in life, as well as addressing needs the country has.[28]

6. Individuals bear a responsibility for the community of which they are a part. Article 29 of the Universal Declaration of Human Rights states, "Everyone has duties to the community in which alone the free and full development of his personality is possible."[29] In a speech to the United Nations after the Declaration had been adopted, its principal author, Eleanor Roosevelt, said, "Where, after all, do universal human rights begin? In small places, close to home. . . . Without concerted citizen action to uphold them close to home, we shall look in vain for progress in the larger world."[30]

Acceptance of responsibilities like these will depend on what education can offer young people in the form of social and emotional learning.

---

28. A comprehensive report in 2020 by the American Academy of Arts and Sciences (AMACAD) calls for one year of national service for all. Find their justification at AMACAD, *Our Common Purpose*, 58–59.

29. United Nations, "Universal Declaration."

30. Quoted in United Nations Office of the High Commissioner, "Human Rights Indicators," 9.

One wants the motivation to embrace responsibility to come from within, rather than being enforced from without, to the extent that is possible. Doesn't everyone at some level want to become fully human? Ideally, yes, but this desire needs to be nurtured so that, in time, every citizen burns like a hot coal at exactly the intersection of his or her personal gifts with what civilization needs. From this intersection, people can expand their circle of belonging—from self to one's children and family, and eventually to all of creation. Whether one comes at stewardship of the natural world from the side of responsibilities or the side of rights does not matter as much as that we address how to preserve this Earth, the magnificent resource that has been so mistreated and taken for granted for so long.

# # #

The chapter on bees makes the point that the United Nations' far-reaching and ambitious Sustainable Development Goals (SDGs) will not be sustainable, or even possible, unless supported by a set of Inner Development Goals (IDGs). But I cannot conclude this chapter on foundations for a new civilization without pointing out the need to take this one step further. The IDGs cannot succeed if they are self-centered or superficial. In a sense, doing yoga to stay slim is inner development, but it lacks higher purpose. On the other hand, doing yoga or meditating or even staying in shape *in order to advance an ideal or to be of service to humanity* puts the activity in a whole different universe. See Appendix A for Inner Development Options.

I realize inner development is not something everyone will want to reach out and embrace. To those who struggle to make ends meet, who are bombarded with superficial information about where to find happiness, who live in a world dominated by consumerism and divorced from nature, inner development or self-change can seem like a luxury for those who have the time and resources. No problem. Circumstances of life will bring challenges that you have to grow through in order to meet. This can happen right up to when you draw your last breath.

For me, what gives thrust to my inner development and social-change work is the notion that if I can take ego out of the equation, it is possible to work in partnership with the spiritual. There are dear friends who have passed over, and indeed many higher beings, who want the best of human evolution and will help if they can and if we let them. I have had many instances where, for example, just the right person has shown up, just when they were needed, as if by coincidence. But there are no coincidences, rather levels of causality to which we are normally oblivious. The quotation about intention mistakenly attributed to Goethe, pertains here: form an intention, boldly commit to it, then Providence can move to help you. Wisely forming intentions—that's another thing we can learn.

EPILOGUE—DEVELOPING AN INNER COMPASS

> *The future can't be predicted, but it can be envisioned and brought lovingly into being.*
> —Donella Meadows

> *The one who plants trees knowing he will never sit in their shade has at least started to understand the meaning of life.*
> —Rabindranath Tagore

> *[May] the morning star [rise] in your hearts.*
> —2 Peter 1:19 NIV

This book airs various ideas, initiatives, and points of departure for remaking civilization once people become open to radical change. I posit that getting to that point will likely require upheaval on a scale few can even contemplate. That does not mean nothing can be done in the meantime. On the contrary.

Five important things invite action right away. Each offers a reasonable chance of progress.

1. **Fight hard for your child's education.** The compliance culture that prevails in public schools with their unimaginative, test-oriented

curricula, scripted lessons, and bureaucratic requirements has driven many of the most creative teachers from the profession. But concerned parents can push for whole-child approaches, get on school boards, and advocate for adequate funding for their schools. They can do what parents and allies in Baltimore did when they were dissatisfied with what the city was providing their kids—they secured funding and started a new school, City Neighbors, that could educate all children, even from very depressed neighborhoods. Inspired by the nurturing Reggio Emilia philosophy, the original City Neighbors school has been so successful that it has now grown to include three schools and a foundation.[1]

Good gap programs with their experience-rich and challenging content offer ways to mature that no classroom can convey. In the words of a recent alum, "The experience of . . . [this program] has shaped my way of living, thinking, eating, connecting with mind, body, spirit, and the way I approach relationships. This was probably the most impactful experience of my life" (see appendix C).

2. **Eat healthy food.** Buy as close to home as possible; lettuce shipped in a plastic box from California to the East Coast, even if it is truly organic, cannot be as fresh or as climate-friendly as a head picked the same day in a local field. Frequent farmers markets, join a CSA, grow some of your own vegetables if you can.

    Not all who would like to buy wholesome food have access to it, especially in poor and urban settings. But ostensibly organic food is now widely available. Consumers can educate themselves to spot produce and other foods that pretend to be organic. With the USDA Organic label significantly compromised, farmers have organized to make an authentic certification, and lists of farms are available, for example, by Real Organic.[2]

3. **Combat climate decline.** The opportunities for an individual to have an impact here defy counting. Buy electricity from a renewable energy supplier. Weatherize your house, get an electric car, avoid unnecessary flying, install solar panels, invest in ESG companies.[3]

---

1. See the foundation's website at cityneighborsfoundation.org.
2. See the Real Organic Project's website at realorganicproject.org.
3. Firms that apply environmental, social, and governance (ESG) standards to their conduct. See Capital Group, "ESG Global Study 2023."

It's impossible to avoid plastic completely, but one can "reduce, reuse, and recycle." As a consumer, one can simply acquire less stuff; get over affluenza;[4] live more simply.

When citizens of the United States travel to a developing nation, say Costa Rica, they are amazed to find that people manage to be happy with so much less. This points to a fact that the piling up of possessions does not create happiness. It is often just a form of egotism and therefore is no friend of mutuality.

Kim Stanley Robinson's *The Ministry for the Future* can serve as a companion to this book because it tackles the climate threat in an imaginative way. In the not-very-distant future a massive heat wave kills millions in India and is enough to get the world's attention and provoke decisive measures to deal with global warming. For example, a carbon coin called the *carboni* enables the ministry to regulate the carbon economy. This and various other bold steps, legal and extra-legal, make for entertaining reading and some serious strategies that could help at the national and international policy level. The book provides reason for guarded optimism.[5]

4. **Opt for mutuality, *convivencia*, cooperation.** Seek out ways of doing things that fall outside the capitalist paradigm. Community supported agriculture is a truly innovative form of cooperating. CSAs need to make a profit but are driven by a shared purpose that goes beyond that. Land trusts, co-op markets, service clubs, volunteer fire or ambulance departments, Meals on Wheels, interfaith dialogue, local currencies where they exist, and any initiative that places the needs of others or the environment above personal gain—all measures of this kind build a culture of mutuality for a post-capitalist system. When Kathleen Dean Moore's students ask "What can one person do to counter climate decline?" she responds, "Stop being just one person." There are many organizations formed or waiting to be formed that tackle aspects of this mega-problem.

5. **Consider inner development.** A strong inner compass positions a person for a purposeful life and service as a change agent for a troubled world. The leaders of the Inner Development Goals have

---

4. Affluenza—"the unhealthy and unwelcome psychological and social effects of affluence." See more at Graaf and Boe, *Affluenza*.

5. Robinson, *Ministry*, 173–76 et passim.

discovered that this is a great leverage point, and they share this insight with anyone willing to listen.

Inner development in the form of imagination can be tremendously productive. Conventional schooling tends to extinguish it, but the kind of early childhood education one finds in Waldorf or Reggio Emilia schools allows it to flourish. A dialogue between Iain McGilchrist and Phoebe Tickell titled "Imagination: A Way to Remake the World"[6] is full of insights on how imagination opens a world of possibilities. The most recent Scharmer book, *Presencing: 7 Practices for Transforming Self, Society, and Business*, is an amazing resource worthy of close study.[7]

The Two Questions

Threading throughout this book have been two questions I encourage readers to ask themselves, and beyond that, to create opportunities to discuss in groups. My wife thinks I should take a shot at answering them myself before signing off. I do this somewhat reluctantly because times will be so different in the future, and because I want to respect the freedom of those who come after to forge their own priorities. But here it goes.

What Kind of People Do We Aspire to Be?

I imagine myself sitting on a grassy knoll. I see some wildflowers, a blue sky, cottony clouds; a light breeze stirs the grass. The person I love sits beside me, unpacking a picnic basket. Two kids play farther down the hill. We are on vacation from demanding but purposeful work in a distant city. Life has a sustainable rhythm because we have been able to balance work and play, inner and outer, head and heart. There is still a way to go, but I am moving toward being free in a deeper sense. I have found my inner compass. At this moment here in the foothills, I feel nourished being outside in nature. Back at home, reaching out to friends and neighbors in a conscious way provides a different kind of

---

6. McGilchrist and Tickell, "Imagination."

7. Scharmer and Kaufer, *Presencing*, 140–71. I also recommend the last chapter of Christopher Schaefer's *Re-Imagining America: Finding Hope in Difficult Times*. He offers penetrating insights and practical suggestions that go beyond what there is space to include here. See Schaefer, *Re-Imagining America*.

nourishment. On the continuum that runs from narcissism on one end to selfless sacrifice on the other, I consciously choose to get away from self-centeredness and work in community, helping others when I can. My wife and I try to communicate this to the kids. Each one of us is on a growth curve; we expand our horizons. There are challenges, but on the whole we are happy campers.

What Kind of an Evolved Society Can Support This Personal Development?

Looking around today, we experience a fast-paced world of existential risk and bewildering complexity. Metacrisis manifests in a great deal of hopelessness, depression, and even a dramatic increase in suicides. It is easy to lose heart when you cannot see how to navigate what the world seems to be throwing at you. But it doesn't have to be that way.

In the envisioned civilization there is an energy encouraging people to move in positive directions, toward personal growth and purposeful work. Not all travel at the same speed. Not all are equally mindful of where they are headed. Some will favor comfort or security over the inner work that goes with freedom. But the constitution of this society articulates the ideals and aspirations that can help shape what citizens *want*. These aspirations get reinforced with popular entertainment. I envision my family going to a movie—perhaps one like *Casablanca*, *The Green Mile*, or *Pay It Forward*—that, in addition to telling a strong story, has some moral content that touches the heart, without preaching, without being obvious. In the new civilization, culture is not just decorative like wallpaper; it actually provides a positive impetus toward meaningful behavior. The Danish Folk Schools provided an inspiring example of how such a cultural impetus can change history. At a time when the existing schools focused on learning Latin, these students did a lot of singing and storytelling in addition to coursework. They took up questions like "What kind of a country would you like for yourself and eventually your children?" They learned crafts and skills like growing and preserving food. Thus, something for head, heart, and hands.

With a small foundation my wife and I have started, we intend to encourage a model similar to the Folk Schools but with gap year programs in the United States. The best of these programs for high school graduates holds the potential to deliver deeply transformative learning, often in an outdoor setting or even in wilderness, with meaningful intellectual content that takes up questions such as "What constitutes the good life?" and "How can the good life be shared by all?" Like the Folk Schools, the learning is holistic, involving head, heart, and hands; and it challenges young people to find their best selves and their inner compasses. We hope when a variety of prototypes have been developed that the movement can go national, perhaps as a program within Americorps.[8] This is just one way that the cultural sphere can become a generative force for renaissance and renewal.

It is easy to lose heart when you cannot see how to navigate what the world seems to be throwing at you. But hope is a plant that grows out of the ground of one's inner compass. After concluding her series "On Being," Krista Tippett spoke of hope as a muscle that people like John Lewis and Jane Goodall learned to exercise. "These are people who said: 'I refuse to accept that the world has to be this way. I am going to throw my life and my pragmatism and my intelligence at this insistence, that it could be different and put that into practice.'"[9]

The Greek root of the word *apocalypse* means "disclosure" or "revelation." But we do not need to wait for an apocalypse to open things up. We can begin visioning and planning right away, and let the morning star rise in our hearts. That visioning opens the way to hope. That rising star lights the way for us to fight for change in ourselves and our communities, starting now.

---

8. See the website for Springboard for Whole Person Learning: springboardlife.org.
9. Skipper, "Hope Is a Muscle."

APPENDIX A: INNER DEVELOPMENT OPTIONS

THERE ARE COUNTLESS APPROACHES to inner development, with discussions, events, and resources at the IDG website (innerdevelopmentgoals.org). My wife and I have found this one particularly useful.

1. THE SIX MONTH EXERCISES[1]

Franz Winkler often recommended these exercises for his patients with considerable success, and he emphasized that the results would be less obvious to the individual than to those around him or her. Although the exercises are simple, he called for a certain strictness in doing them—if one day was missed, the month should be started over from the beginning. What follows are my edited and extracted notes from his 1959 lecture "A Memorial for Rudolf Steiner":

> The first exercise is training in concentration. For the duration of a predetermined period—let us say four weeks—we devote five minutes daily to practicing self-induced thinking. During this exercise, not even our own fantasy must be allowed to determine the course of our thoughts. Thus, instead of choosing an exciting object, we pick some trifle like a pen, a pencil, or a sheet of paper, and concentrate on its properties and uses. At first it will be difficult to resist the distracting power of automatic associations. A black pencil, for instance, may remind us of that black suit we forgot at the cleaner's, a pen of a letter we neglected to mail. Every time we find ourselves straying

---

1. Gelder, "Six Basic Exercises."

on such detours, we must cut short our deviations and return to the subject. What matters here is the pursuit of thoughts generated by our own volition, not thoughts dictated by inner or outer influences that bypass our conscious attention. These voluntary thoughts need not be complicated and may even deal with such simple matters as description of the object, enumeration of its uses, speculation on the process of manufacture, and so on. When one line of thought has been exhausted, another one related to the same object must be chosen and pursued with complete concentration.

During the second month, we bring ourselves to perform a series of minor actions preferably of a kind that serves no intelligible purpose. To the seemingly meaningless act of the first day we add a second, similar act on the second, a third on the day following, and so on. It is obvious that any external advantage derived from such action would decrease its value. For example, if we know we *should* spend more time in the fresh air, and so force ourselves to take a walk, the willpower used here will serve a rational purpose; it becomes expedient. This may be useful enough, but it does not constitute an activity motivated exclusively by self-imposed will. On the other hand, if, for example, we walk around our bedroom once on the first day, twice on the second, and so on, we are performing a series of actions which originate in our brain and find their aim in pure motion which is an *intrinsic* rather than *extrinsic* objective. While this exercise may seem pointless to the materialist interested only in sensual perception and gain, it should be of interest to all those who seek an experience of the great mystery occurring in an individual whenever thoughts are translated into action.

The third, fourth, and fifth months' exercises are different from the first and second insofar as they do not consist of definite actions but rather in mental attitudes.

During the third month the student must try to retain an emotional equilibrium regardless of what may happen. It is helpful in such an effort to bear in mind the conviction familiar to [many] . . . that nothing happens to a human being unless it is for one's own good. Of course, it can take weeks, years, or a lifetime to understand why a certain event was necessary for one's own good or for the good of others. Yet, while it may be beyond human capacity to interpret the deeper meaning of an occurrence immediately, it is definitely possible to become intuitively aware of the fact that such a meaning exists. Such an attitude consciously adopted and maintained during a period of time can give to the student the invaluable gift of emotional stability.

The fourth month's exercise might be called *seeing holistically*. Time and again we are confronted with facts or events which seem repulsive to us. Moreover, although we may disclaim prejudices, being human, we are only too prone to judge people or events by first impressions. During this month we must keep in mind that wherever there is darkness, there must be light, hidden though it may be. It is hard indeed to find something positive in a depraved person, something beautiful in a repulsive scene, and yet, unless we have found it, we have not touched reality. This exercise differs from the previous one insofar as it is not concerned with what is good or bad for us, but with our judgment of the world around us.

An old Persian legend . . . [provides] an example for this exercise. Christ and his disciples come upon the decaying corpse of a dog. While his disciples turn from the sight in horror, Christ stops and draws their attention to the beauty of its gleaming teeth.

The fifth month's exercise is in reserved judgment. In our rapidly moving times immediate action is often required, which might be unduly delayed by too conscientious investigation. Thus we have all become accustomed to snap-judgments. During this one month, however, we should at least try to give any information, regardless how unlikely it may appear, the full benefit of doubt, until we have had a chance to check on its veracity.

During the sixth month the student alternates the exercises of the five preceding months. On the first day, one does the first month's exercise, on the second day the second, and so forth, until on the sixth day one starts the cycle again.

It is obvious that the benefit of the six month exercises would be small indeed, if each were done for one month only. However, this does not mean that we have to continue the first exercise all through the six months, or the second on through the following five months, since this would require more time than a modern person could reasonably spare. Yet, while we do only one exercise with absolute regularity, the others should be repeated occasionally, say every second or third day, lest we lose their benefit again.

Eventually the six month exercises must become a way of life and part of one's psychological nature. For who can meditate without learning to concentrate, who can do spiritual deeds without learning to act without external motivation, and who can find reality without learning to lift feelings above the narrow confines of subjective emotions?[2]

2. THE WALKING MEDITATION

This practice comes out of the Buddhist tradition. There are several ways to do it. One example is Greater Good in Action's "Walking Meditation."[3] Each involves making conscious what you would normally do unconsciously. A natural setting helps but is not essential.

3. CENTERING PRAYER

For those who seek a more prayerful approach to inner development, this technique developed by Thomas Keating at contemplativeoutreach.org has helped many, both those within established religion and others who describe themselves as "spiritual but not religious."

4. FIND A SPIRITUAL DIRECTOR

People who need professional psychological support should not avoid it by escaping into spirituality, but as Viktor Frankl shows conclusively in *Man's Search for Meaning*, developing a strong sense of purpose and a clearer connection to the whole of creation can be extremely helpful. Spiritual directors can facilitate growth in these areas. The profession has developed within the Christian tradition, but wise counselors can be found within every spiritual stream. One place to start is at the Transforming Center.[4]

---

2. Winkler, "Memorial for Rudolf Steiner."
3. For the website and guide, see Greater Good in Action, "Walking Meditation."
4. See Transforming Center, "Spiritual Direction."

APPENDIX B: BURLEY TOBACCO PRICE AND PRODUCTION MANAGEMENT

First established in the 1920s, the Burley Tobacco Growers Co-Operative Association helped farmers emerge from a chaotic market and depressed prices brought on by unregulated overproduction. One year, "Most growers failed to make the cost of production,"[1] according to the association.

In this first iteration of the association, which managed the market from 1922 to 1927, it got more than 75 percent of burley tobacco farmers to sign up for the cooperative. This enabled them to effectively control production and therefore the price. For those farmers who could not afford the cost of membership in cash, the public-spirited judge Robert W. Bingham advanced the money, to be repaid when the crop came in. Burley tobacco is a regional crop concentrated in Kentucky. This made it easier to organize, but not that easy. Over two hundred thousand farmers were involved in Kentucky alone, and organizing farmers has been compared to organizing frogs in a wheelbarrow. The system worked well for a few years until, perhaps confident that they could do as well without the association, growers started to trade outside the system, and it became impossible to get the critical mass to control supply. When the Great Depression came along, that disrupted the chances of reorganizing the association.

However, in 1941 a new association, the Burley Co-Op, was set up on a private-public basis. It relied on money borrowed from the Commodity Credit Corporation (CCC) of the USDA but was operated at no

---

1. Burley Tobacco Growers, *Producer's Program*, 25.

net cost to the government. A moving force in the new organization was John M. Berry Sr. (Wendell Berry's father).

The system worked like this. First the USDA, based on data it gathered, estimated demand for the next year and set a limit on how much tobacco could be produced. Then, in an annual referendum, the growers had a chance to approve or reject this restriction or quota. When the quota was approved, the government set support prices for the different grades of burley tobacco. These were based on 90 percent of parity. In theory, this sets a floor under the price of tobacco that protects the farmer from bankruptcy but makes no one rich.

When it came time to sell the crop to the association, if the farmer could get the parity price, he would collect the money and go home. If not, the association took the crop and advanced a loan using money from the CCC. It then held the crop in its warehouse until a more favorable market developed, at which time the inventory sold for a price that covered the loan principal, the interest due the CCC, and all processing and storage costs. This system operated successfully for years.[2] Not only did it not cost the taxpayers anything, the government actually made money from interest on the loans. Eventually a combination of declining demand for tobacco, cheap imports, and political opposition brought an end to the program, but the concept or a modification of it—preferably without reliance on government—could be made to work in many other commodities, particularly non-perishable ones. Today the principal advocate for this rational approach to farm prices is Mary Berry (daughter of Wendell Berry).[3]

---

2. Burley Tobacco Growers, *Producer's Program*, 14–15.
3. The Winter 2024 issue of *The Berry Center Journal* is devoted to this.

APPENDIX C: **GAP YEARS**

As gap year and gap semester programs become more popular, we find students who have seized one of these options saying things like the following:

> My semester at Seguinland Institute has been nothing short of spectacular. I found a passion for life here—the rich, full good life of reciprocity with the earth and others. The faculty and staff have been instrumental, and irreplaceable in finding my devotion to all life offers and all I can offer to life. The three courses themselves are life-changing and encourage the big thinker in everyone to come out of hiding. These courses will ask a lot of you at times, but what meaningful challenge wouldn't? I can't describe how enlivening The Creative Life Course was for me. Something clicked and I could finally see that I should commit myself to the study of sustainable design. I would not trade the experience in this program for anything (especially anything a traditional college could offer). This was my true education: how to smile more truthfully, laugh more fully, love deeply and unconditionally. This is how the good life should be taught.[1]

This student was at one of the best gap programs in the country, but most gap year experiences provide chances to mellow and mature and to find one's inner compass. Typically, they are positively transformational so that they prepare students to get far more out of subsequent college or work than would otherwise be the case. The best programs include actual service in a community; some college level coursework that provides opportunities for reflection; time in nature; an appreciation of the unique

---

1. A student in the Good Life program at Seguinland Institute, Georgetown Island, Maine. For more testimonials, see the Seguinland Institute, "Alumni Testimonials."

features of one's culture and country; opportunity to engage in something creative; activities that are physically engaging or challenging, such as gardening, boat building, or a wilderness experience.

VISTA, Peace Corps, and California Conservation Corps are examples of government-sponsored service options. Each offers great opportunities for growth and horizon-expanding work experience.

BIBLIOGRAPHY

4-H. "About." https://4-h.org/about/.
Abeles, Vicki. *Beyond Measure: Rescuing an Overscheduled, Overtested, Underestimated Generation.* New York: Simon & Schuster, 2015.
Abouleish, Helmy, et al. *The Sekem Effect: How a Sustainable Community Can Transform Egypt and the World.* Edinburgh: Floris, 2025.
———. "SEKEM Report 2022." *SEKEM Holding for Investments Company S.A.E.* 2023. https://drive.google.com/file/d/1los6lS7vRfIEelsdm2C_nGYpUCP-I3xD/view.
———. "SEKEM Vision and Mission 2057." SEKEM Foundation, 2018. https://sekem.com/wp-content/uploads/2018/10/SEKEM-Vision-2057_20180615-3.pdf.
Abouleish, Ibrahim. *Sekem—A Sustainable Community in the Egyptian Desert.* Edinburgh: Floris, 2005.
Alaska Report. "Alaska's Corrupt Bastards Club." http://www.alaskareport.com/news/z49999_corrupt_bastards.htm.
Alliance for Public Waldorf Education. "Core Principles." https://www.publicwaldorf.org/core-principles.
Alperovitz, Gar. "A Pluralist Commonwealth." Schumacher Center for a New Economics, 2019. https://centerforneweconomics.org/publications/a-pluralist-commonwealth/.
American Academy of Arts and Sciences (AMACAD). *Advancing a People-First Economy.* Cambridge, MA: American Academy of Arts and Sciences, 2023.
———. *Our Common Purpose: Reinventing American Democracy for the 21st Century.* Cambridge, MA: American Academy of Arts and Sciences, 2020. https://www.amacad.org/sites/default/files/publication/downloads/2020-Democratic-Citizenship_Our-Common-Purpose.pdf.
Andersen, Lene Rachael, and Tomas Björkman. *The Nordic Secret: A European Story of Beauty and Freedom.* Stockholm: Fri Tanke, 2017.
Arizmendiarrieta, José María. *Reflections: Insights from the Founder of the Mondragon Cooperatives.* Compiled by Joxe Azurmendi. Translated by Steve Herrick et al. Washington, DC: SolidarityHall, 2022.
Association of Waldorf Schools of North America (AWSNA). "AWSNA Principles for Waldorff Schools." https://www.waldorfeducation.org/about-waldorf-education/awsna-principles/.

Aurell, Dan, et al. "United States Honey Bee Colony Losses 2021–2022: Preliminary Results from the Bee Informed Partnership." Bee Informed Partnership, July 27, 2022. http://web.archive.org/web/20240708233855/http://beeinformed.org/wp-content/uploads/2022/07/BIP_2021_22_Losses_Abstract.pdf.

BBC. "Tyson Food Managers Bet on Workers Getting Covid-19, Lawsuit Says." BBC, Nov. 19, 2020. https://www.bbc.com/news/world-us-canada-55009228.

Bendell, Jem, and Rupert Read. *Deep Adaptation: Navigating the Realities of Climate Chaos.* Cambridge, UK: Polity, 2021.

Berry, Wendell. "The 50-Year Farm Bill." *Atlantic*, Nov. 13, 2012. https://www.theatlantic.com/national/archive/2012/11/the-50-year-farm-bill/265099/.

———. "The Peace of Wild Things." In *Selected Poems of Wendell Berry.* Brooklyn, NY: Counterpoint, 1999.

———. "What Liberal Elites Don't Know About Rural Americans Can Hurt Us." *Barn Raiser*, May 31, 2023. https://barnraisingmedia.com/wendell-berry-new-york-review-of-books-rural-america/.

Bittle, Jake. *The Great Displacement: Climate Change and the Next American Migration.* New York: Simon & Schuster, 2023.

Björkman, Tomas. "Peaceful Change." Singularity University. Filmed at the SingularityU Greece Summit 2018. Posted Jan. 15, 2019. YouTube video, 23:21. https://www.youtube.com/watch?v=FEsADtSCrTs.

———. "Tomas Björkman on Co-Creation, Consciousness, and 'The Nordic Secret': Part 2." This Is Not the Truth, Nov. 27, 2018. YouTube video, 10:18. https://www.youtube.com/watch?v=8PZ6j8-Zjbs.

Bleiberg, Joshua, et al. "The Effect of Teacher Evaluation on Achievement and Attainment: Evidence from Statewide Reforms." EdWorkingPaper 29-496. Brown University, 2021. https://files.eric.ed.gov/fulltext/ED616818.pdf.

Boehm, Rebecca. "Tyson Spells Trouble for Arkansas." Union of Concerned Scientists, Aug. 11, 2021. https://www.ucs.org/resources/tyson-spells-trouble.

Boggs School. "About Us." https://boggsschool.org/about-us#mission-and-core-ideology.

Brinkerhoff, Val. "The Symbolism of the Beehive in Latter-Day Saint Tradition." *BYU Studies Quarterly* 52 (2013) 140. https://byustudies.byu.edu/article/the-symbolism-of-the-beehive-in-latter-day-saint-tradition/.

Brooks, David. *The Second Mountain: The Quest for a Moral Life.* New York: Random House, 2019.

Brooks, Gwendolyn. "Paul Robeson." Poets. https://poets.org/poem/paul-robeson.

Brown, Patricia Leigh. "Kale, Not Jail: Urban Farming Nonprofit Helps Ex-Cons Re-Enter Society." *New York Times*, May 17, 2018. https://www.nytimes.com/2018/05/17/business/urban-farming-exconvicts-recidivism.html.

Brown's Chefs Market. "Uplift Solutions—Sustainable Food Systems." Apr. 29, 2021. https://brownschefsmarket.com/uplift-solutions-video/.

Buechner, Frederick. *Wishful Thinking: A Seeker's ABC.* San Francisco: HarperOne, 1993.

Burley Tobacco Growers Co-operative Association, Inc. *The Producer's Program: Fifty Golden Years and More.* Lexington, KY: BTGCA, 1992.

Burniske, R. W., and Lowell Monke. *Breaking Down the Digital Walls: Learning to Teach in a Post-Modem World.* Albany: State University of New York Press, 2001.

Caffeinated Rage. "Poverty Affects Schools, No Measurable Differences in 15 Years, And Reforms Have Not Worked: What The PISA Scores Show Us." Caffeinated Rage, Dec. 4, 2019. https://caffeinatedrage.com/2019/12/04/poverty-affects-schools-no-measurable-differences-in-15-years-and-reforms-have-not-worked-what-the-pisa-scores-show-us/.

Canterbury Shaker Village. "Our Mission." https://www.shakers.org/about-us/#our-mission.

Capital Group. "ESG Global Study 2023." https://www.capitalgroup.com/institutional/investments/esg/perspectives/esg-global-study.html.

Carrington, Damian. "Monsanto's Global Weedkiller Harms Honeybees, Research Finds." *The Guardian*, Sept. 24, 2018. https://www.theguardian.com/environment/2018/sep/24/monsanto-weedkiller-harms-bees-research-finds.

Carter, Jimmy. "President Carter Address on Crisis of Confidence." C-SPAN, July 15, 1979. Video, 32:57. https://www.c-span.org/program/american-history-tv/president-carter-address-on-crisis-of-confidence/154404.

CCA Global Partners. "CCA in the Community." https://www.ccaglobalpartners.com/cca-in-the-community/.

Center for Humans and Nature. "Questions for a Resilient Future." https://humansandnature.org/questions/.

Chaltain, Sam. "The Most Important Supreme Court Case You've Never Heard Of." Letters from the Future (of Learning), Mar. 22, 2023. https://samchaltain.substack.com/p/the-most-important-supreme-court.

Chappell, Bill. "1 Complaint Led a Florida School to Restrict Access to Amanda Gorman's Famous Poem." NPR, May 25, 2023. https://www.npr.org/2023/05/24/1177877340/amanda-gorman-poem-restricted-miami-school.

Chautauqua Institution. "About." https://www.chq.org/about/.

CLEE. "Principal Residency Network." https://www.clee.org/programs/principal-residency-network-prn/.

The Cornucopia Institute. "Aurora Farm's Certifier Found to Have Willfully Violated Orgainic Rules." Oct. 24, 2008. https://www.cornucopia.org/2007/09/aurora-farms-certifier-found-to-have-willfully-violated-nop-rules/.

C-SPAN. "Democratic National Convention (Day 2)." Aug. 20, 2024. YouTube video, 6:15:30. https://www.youtube.com/watch?v=2KWMYn7IpGo.

Davenport, Russell W. *The Dignity of Man*. New York: Harper & Brothers, 1955.

The Democracy Collaborative. "What Is Community Wealth Building?" https://www.democracycollaborative.org/community-wealth-building.

Department of Economic and Social Affairs, Sustainable Development. "The 17 Goals." United Nations. https://sdgs.un.org/goals.

Desilver, Drew. "U.S. Students' Academic Achievement Still Lags That of Their Peers in Many Other Countries." Pew Research Center, Feb. 15, 2017. https://www.pewresearch.org/short-reads/2017/02/15/u-s-students-internationally-math-science/.

Dewey, John. *Democracy and Education*. New York: Macmillan, 1916.

———. *Human Nature and Conduct: An Introduction to Social Psychology*. New York: Modern Library, 1930.

Doan, Sy, et al. "Teacher Well-Being and Intentions to Leave in 2024." Rand, Jun. 18, 2024. https://www.rand.org/pubs/research_reports/RRA1108-12.html.

Douglas, Leah. "How Food and Agriculture Contribute to Climate Change." *Reuters*, Dec. 2, 2023. https://www.reuters.com/business/environment/factbox-how-food-agriculture-contribute-climate-change-2023-12-02/.

Dungy, Camille. "Sanctuary." Emergence Magazine, Jun. 27, 2022. https://emergencemagazine.org/poem/sanctuary/.

Dyer, Wayne W. *The Power of Intention*. Carlsbad, CA: Hay House, 2004.

Earth Charter. "The Earth Charter." https://earthcharter.org/read-the-earth-charter/.

Echeverria, Hugo. "Rights of Nature in Ecuador—Webinar with Attorney Hugo Echeverria." Center for Democratic and Environmental Rights, June 11, 2020. Video, 59:52. https://www.centerforenvironmentalrights.org/news/ecuador-video-hugo-echeverria.

Economy for the Common Good. "Common Good Matrix 5.0." https://www.econgood.org/apply-ecg/common-good-matrix/.

Economy of Love. "Barton Duvet Cover Sateen." https://economyoflove.net/products/barton-duvet-cover-sateen/.

———. "Certification." https://economyoflove.net/certification/.

Educate the Whole Child. "Our Schools." https://www.educatethewholechild.org/schools/.

———. "What Is Whole Child Education?" https://www.educatethewholechild.org/what-is-whole-child-education/.

———. "Why Certify?" https://www.educatethewholechild.org/Why-Certify/.

Edutopia. "Project-Based Learning (PBL)." https://www.edutopia.org/project-based-learning.

Eisler, Riane. "Caring for People and Nature First." In *The New Possible*, edited by Philip Clayton et. al., 71–79. Eugene, OR: Cascade, 2021.

Elkind, David. *Miseducation: Preschoolers at Risk*. New York: Knopf Doubleday, 1987.

Emerson, Ralph Waldo. "Politics." In *The Complete Works of Ralph Waldo Emerson*. Centenary ed., 3:215–16. Boston: Houghton Mifflin, 1904.

Evergreen Cooperatives, "About." https://www.evgoh.com/about.

Faust, Sean T., dir. *The Finland Phenomenon: Inside the World's Most Surprising School System*. DVD. Memphis, TN: New School Films, 2011.

Feige, Edgar L. *Taxation for the 21st Century: The Automated Payment Transaction (APT) Tax*. Presented to the President's Advisory Panel on Federal Tax Reform, Apr. 28, 2005. https://govinfo.library.unt.edu/taxreformpanel/comments/_files/APT%20Tax.pdf.

Felber, Christian. "What If the Common Good Was the Goal of the Economy?" TEDx Talks, Dec. 1, 2015. YouTube video, 22:47. https://www.youtube.com/watch?v=dsO-bo_r-5Y.

Ferber, Linda. "Nature's Nation: The Hudson River School and American Landscape Painting, 1825–1876." The Gilder Lehrman Institute of American History. https://www.gilderlehrman.org/history-resources/essays/natures-nation-hudson-river-school-and-american-landscape-painting-1825.

Fernández, María. "Mondragón's Cooperative Model Adapts to Changing Times." *El País*, Apr. 20, 2016. https://english.elpais.com/elpais/2016/04/04/inenglish/1459777506_442063.html.

Fight the New Drug. "20 Must-Know Stats About the Porn Industry and Its Underage Consumers." Fight the New Drug. https://fightthenewdrug.org/10-porn-stats-that-will-blow-your-mind/.

Finnish National Agency for Education. "Average Group Sizes in Basic Education in Finland Below the OECD Average." Oct. 8, 2019. https://www.oph.fi/en/news/2019/average-group-sizes-basic-education-finland-below-oecd-average.

Flying Cloud Institute. "S.M.Art Schools." https://www.flyingcloudinstitute.org/smart-schools.

Francis, Philip. *When Art Disrupts Religion: Aesthetic Experience and the Evangelical Mind*. New York: Oxford, 2017.

Frankl, Viktor E. *Man's Search for Meaning: An Introduction to Logotherapy*. New York: Washington Square, 1963.

Fullerton, John. "An Introduction to Regenerative Economics." Regenerators, Sept. 12, 2022. YouTube video, 15:37. https://www.youtube.com/watch?v=ZCWqPIs4jGA.

———. *Regenerative Capitalism: How Universal Principles and Patterns Will Shape Our New Economy*. Boulder, CO: Capital Institute, 2015. https://capitalinstitute.org/wp-content/uploads/2015/04/2015-Regenerative-Capitalism-4-20-15-final.pdf.

Gakhal, Jaskiran, et al. "Forum Theatre." *Participedia*. Jun. 23, 2020. https://participedia.net/method/149.

Gelder, Tom van. "The Six Basic Exercises by Rudolf Steiner." Mar. 2011. https://tomvangelder.antrovista.com/pdf/basic.pdf.

Gelles, David. *The Man Who Broke Capitalism: How Jack Welch Gutted the Heartland and Crushed the Soul of Corporate America—and How to Undo His Legacy*. New York: Simon & Schuster, 2022.

Goethe, Johann Wolfgang von. From *My Life: Campaign in France 1792–Siege of Mainz*. Vol. 5 of *Goethe*. Edited by Thomas P. Saine and Jeffrey L. Sammons. Princeton, NJ: Princeton University Press, 1994.

Goodall, Jane. "In the Forests of Gombe." *Orion* (Spring 2000), 64–65.

Goodman, Peter S. "Co-Ops in Spain's Basque Region Soften Capitalism's Rough Edges." *New York Times*, Dec. 29, 2020. https://www.nytimes.com/2020/12/29/business/cooperatives-basque-spain-economy.html.

Graaf, John de, and Vivia Boe, dirs. *Affluenza*. Reading, PA: Bullfrog Films, 1997.

Greater Good in Action. "Walking Meditation." https://ggia.berkeley.edu/practice/walking_meditation.

Greene, Peter. "This Decade-Long Experiment in Teacher Evaluation Has Been an Unsurprising Failure." *Forbes*, Apr. 21, 2021. https://www.forbes.com/sites/petergreene/2021/11/30/this-decade-long-experiment-in-teacher-evaluation-is-a-failure/.

Guardian Staff and Agencies. "Florida and Texas Schools Defy Governors' Mask Mandate Bans as Cases Soar." *Guardian*, Aug. 11, 2021. https://www.theguardian.com/us-news/2021/aug/11/florida-texas-schools-mask-mandates-covid.

Haass, Richard. *The Bill of Obligations: The Ten Habits of Good Citizens*. New York: Penguin, 2023.

Hancock, LynNell. "Why Are Finland's Schools Successful?" *Smithsonian Magazine*, Sept. 2011. https://www.smithsonianmag.com/innovation/why-are-finlands-schools-successful-49859555/.

Harris-Perry, Melissa, host. "Is Egypt Ready for a Democracy?" *The Takeaway*. WNYCStudios, Feb. 4, 2011. https://www.wnycstudios.org/podcasts/takeaway/segments/113054-egypt-ready-democracy.

Harwood, A. C., *The Recovery of Man in Childhood: A Study in the Educational Work of Rudolf Steiner*. Great Barrington, MA: Myrin Institute, 2001.

Hassan, Basma. "It's Cotton Harvest Time in Egypt." *SEKEM*, Oct. 28, 2021. https://sekem.com/en/its-cotton-harvest-time-in-egypt/.

Heller, Cheryl. *The Intergalactic Design Guide: Harnessing the Creative Potential of Social Design*. Washington, DC: Island, 2018.

Henderson, Rebecca. *Reimagining Capitalism in a World on Fire*. New York: PublicAffairs, 2020.

Herrera, David. "Mondragon: A For-Profit Organization That Embodies Catholic Social Thought." *Review of Business* 25 (2004) 56–68. https://www.proquest.com/scholarly-journals/mondragon-profit-organization-that-embodies/docview/220965845/se-2.

Heubeck, Elizabeth. "He Comes From a Family of Teachers. Does He Want That for the Next Generation?" Education Week, Mar. 7, 2024. https://www.edweek.org/teaching-learning/he-comes-from-a-family-of-teachers-does-he-want-that-for-the-next-generation/2024/03.

Hobbes, Thomas. *Leviathan*. London: Penguin Classics, 2017.

Houston, Jean, and Anneloes Smitsman, hosts. "The Love and Caring Economy with Hazel Henderson." *The Future Humans Podcast*, Feb. 24, 2022. YouTube video, 57:16. https://www.youtube.com/watch?v=IvwUWb6u6eY.

Huber, Makenzie. "South Dakota Cashes in $1.79 Million on 2021 Sturgis Motorcycle Rally." *Sioux Falls Argus Leader*, Sept. 9, 2021. https://www.argusleader.com/story/news/2021/09/09/2021-sturgis-motorcycle-rally-attendance-and-south-dakota-tax-revenue-covid-pandemic/8255253002/.

Hughes, Gertrude Reif. "Rudolf Steiner's Activist Epistemology and Feminist Thought in America." In *American Philosophy and Rudolf Steiner*, edited by Robert A. McDermott, 245–47. Great Barrington, MA: Lindisfarne, 2012.

Hugill, Johnny, and Matija Franklin. "The Wisdom of a Universal Basic Income." Behavioral Scientist, Oct. 19, 2017. https://behavioralscientist.org/wisdom-universal-basic-income/.

Immerwahr, Daniel. "The Pitchfork History." *New Yorker*, Oct. 23, 2023.

Impact Terms. "Steward Ownership." https://www.impactterms.org/Steward-Ownership/.

Ingram, Noble. "Is the Teaching Profession in Decline?" ASCD, Jan. 18, 2023. https://ascd.org/blogs/is-the-teaching-profession-in-decline.

Inner Development Goals. "Framework." https://innerdevelopmentgoals.org/framework/.

Institute for Local Self-Reliance. "Small Schools vs. Big Schools." Mar. 19, 2012. https://ilsr.org/rule/small-schools-vs-big-schools/.

International Cooperative Alliance. "Cooperative Identity, Values, and Principles." https://ica.coop/en/Cooperatives/Cooperative-Identity.

Iuviene, Nicholas, et al. "Sustainable Economic Democracy: Worker Cooperatives for the 21st Century." MIT Community Innovators Lab, Oct. 2010. https://institute.coop/resources/sustainable-economic-democracy-worker-cooperatives-21st-century.

Jacob, Jemiya. "Be the Change." Genesis, Jun. 17, 2019. https://www.genesisca.org/single-post/2019/06/17/be-the-change.

Jefferson, Thomas. "From Thomas Jefferson to Uriah Forrest, with Enclosure, 31 December 1787." Founders Online. https://founders.archives.gov/documents/Jefferson/01-12-02-0490.

Johnson, Ayana Elizabeth. *What If We Get It Right?* New York: One World, 2024.

Jordan, Seth. "Welcome Back to Work. Now Please Hold Still While We Put Your Collar and Leash Back On." The Whole Social, Sept. 2, 2021. https://thewholesocial.substack.com/p/welcome-back-to-work-now-please-hold.

Jordan, Thomas, et al. "Inner Development Goals: Background, Method, and the IDG Framework." 2021. https://www.scribd.com/document/663335812/IDG-Report-Full.

Kagan, Robert. *The Jungle Grows Back: America and Our Imperiled World*. New York: Knopf, 2018.

Kakutani, Michiko. "The Lasting Power of Dr. King's Dream Speech." *New York Times*, Aug. 28, 2013. https://www.nytimes.com/2013/08/28/us/the-lasting-power-of-dr-kings-dream-speech.html.

Kardaras, Nicholas. "How Goethe's *Sorrows of Young Werther* Led to a Rare Suicide Cluster." Literary Hub, Sept. 15, 2022. https://lithub.com/how-goethes-sorrows-of-young-werther-led-to-a-rare-suicide-cluster/.

Karp, Robert. *Toward an Associative Economy in the Sustainable Food and Farming Movement*. Milwaukee: New Spirit Ventures, 2007. https://robertkarp.net/wp-content/uploads/2018/03/Toward-an-Associatve-Economy.pdf.

Kastel, Mark. "NGO Appeals to Biden Administration and Congress to Reverse Corporate Dominance and Consolidation in Organics." Organic Eye, Oct. 5, 2021. https://organiceye.org/ngo-appeals-to-biden-administration-and-congress-to-reverse-corporate-dominance-and-consolidation-in-organics/.

Kaur, Valerie. *See No Stranger: A Memoir and Manifesto of Revolutionary Love*. New York: One World, 2020.

Kawano, Emily. "Solidarity Economy: Building Economy for People and Planet." In *The New Systems Reader: Alternatives to a Failed Economy*, edited by James Gustave Speth and Kathleen Courrier, 285–302. London: Routledge, 2020.

Kegan, Robert, et al. *An Everyone Culture: Becoming a Deliberately Developmental Organization*. Cambridge: Harvard Business Review, 2016.

———. *The Evolving Self: Problem and Process in Human Development*. Cambridge: Harvard University Press, 1982.

Kegan, Robert, and Lisa Laskow Lahey. *An Everyone Culture: Becoming a Deliberately Developmental Organization*. Boston: Harvard Business Review, 2016.

Kelly, Marjorie. *Wealth Supremacy: How the Extractive Economy and Biased Rules of Capitalism Drive Today's Crises*. Oakland, CA: Berrett-Koehler, 2023.

Keltner, Dacher. *Awe: The New Science of Everyday Wonder and How It Can Transform Your Life*. New York: Random House, 2023.

Kennedy, Robert F. "Remarks at the University of Kansas." Mar. 18, 1968. https://www.jfklibrary.org/learn/about-jfk/the-kennedy-family/robert-f-kennedy/robert-f-kennedy-speeches/remarks-at-the-university-of-kansas-march-18-1968.

Kenner, Robert, dir. *Food, Inc*. Los Angeles, CA: Magnolia Pictures, 2008.

Kimmerer, Robin Wall. "The Gift of Strawberries." In *Braiding Sweetgrass: Indigenous Wisdom, Scientific Knowledge, and the Teachings of Plants*, 22–38. Minneapolis: Milkweed Editions, 2013.

———. *The Serviceberry: Abundance and Reciprocity in the Natural World*. New York: Scribner, 2024.

King, Martin Luther, Jr. "Keep Moving from This Mountain." Address at Spelman College, Apr. 10, 1960. https://kinginstitute.stanford.edu/king-papers/documents/keep-moving-mountain-address-spelman-college-10-april-1960.

Kirschenmann, Fred. "Fred Kirschenmann Oral History Interview." Interview by Jane Gates. Sustainable Agriculture Oral History Series. National Agricultural Library, USDA, 1990. https://www.nal.usda.gov/legacy/afsic/fred-kirschenmann.

———. "Soil: From Dirt to Lifeline." TEDx Talks, Feb. 4, 2012. YouTube video, 15:19. https://www.youtube.com/watch?v=VObLitSe3K0&list=PLCB19B14A57BBDA98.

Klein, Naomi. *This Changes Everything: Capitalism vs. The Climate*. New York: Simon & Schuster, 2015.

Kleinath, Sara. "Essential Elements of 4-H: Belonging." Michigan State University Extension, Nov. 8, 2019. https://www.canr.msu.edu/news/essential-elements-of-4-h-belonging.

Knowles, Hannah. "Covid Cases Are Linked to the Sturgis Motorcycle Rally, But the Full Impact May Never Be Known." *Washington Post*, Aug. 21, 2020. https://www.washingtonpost.com/nation/2020/08/20/sturgis-attendee-bar-coronavirus/.

Langworthy, George, dir. *Vanishing of the Bees*. Narrated by Ellen Page. London: Dogwood Pictures, 2009.

Large, Martin, ed. *Free, Equal, and Mutual*. Stroud, UK: Hawthorne, 2018.

Lent, Jeremy. *The Web of Meaning*. Gabriola Island, BC: New Society, 2021.

Leonnig, Carol, and Philip Rucker. "Transcript: Carol Leonnig and Philip Rucker." Face the Nation, Jul. 25, 2021. https://www.cbsnews.com/news/transcript-carol-leonnig-and-philip-rucker-on-face-the-nation-july-25-2021/.

Litman, Harry, host. "Making Ends Meat: Farmers Get Raw Deal." *Talking Feds*, Nov. 29, 2021. https://www.talkingfeds.com/episodes/00-00-2019/template-a7777-pk93k-37srg.

Lively, Kathryn J. "The Six Saboteurs of Self Change." Psychology Today, Nov. 17, 2013. https://www.psychologytoday.com/us/blog/smart-relationships/201311/the-six-saboteurs-self-change.

Lovins, L. Hunter, et al. *A Finer Future: Creating an Economy in Service to Life*. Gabriola Island, Canada: New Society, 2018.

Lynas, Mark. "Organic Farming Can Feed the World—Until You Read the Small Print." Alliance for Science, Nov. 22, 2017. https://allianceforscience.org/blog/2017/11/organic-farming-can-feed-the-world-until-you-read-the-small-print/.

Macy, Joanna. *World as Lover, World as Self*. 30th Anniversary Edition. Berkeley: Parallax, 2021.

Mancini, Meg, et al. "Principled Principal Development: The Greater Boston Principal Residency Network." *Horace* 24 (2008). https://web.archive.org/web/20080516150323/http://www.essentialschools.org/cs/resources/view/ces_res/502.

Markonnen, Juho. "Steward-Ownership Is Capitalism 2.0." Resilience, May 15, 2018. https://www.resilience.org/stories/2018-05-15/steward-ownership-is-capitalism-2-0/.

Martinelli, Luke. "Assessing the Case for a Universal Basic Income in the UK." Institute for Policy Research, Sept. 2017. https://www.bath.ac.uk/publications/assessing-the-case-for-a-universal-basic-income-in-the-uk/attachments/ipr-assessing-the-case-for-a-universal-basic-income-in-the-uk.pdf.

Mason, Charlotte. *The Original Home Schooling Series*. 4th ed. Bromley, England: Charlotte Mason Research Co., 1993.

Massei, Karsten. *Gifts of the Honeybees: Their Connection to Cosmos, Earth, and Humankind*. Translated by Ines Kinchen. New York: Steiner, 2022.

Massie, Robert K. *A Handbook on Faith and Money*. New Haven: Yale Divinity School, 2017.

Masters, Richard. *Rudolf Steiner and Social Reform: Threefolding and Other Proposals*. Forest Row, UK: Rudolf Steiner, 2022.

McGilchrist, Iain. *The Master and His Emissary: The Divided Brain and the Making of the Western World*. Exp. ed. New Haven: Yale University Press, 2019.

McGilchrist, Iain, and Phoebe Tickell. "Imagination: A Way to Remake the World." Perspectiva, Apr. 15, 2023. YouTube video, 1:37:19. https://www.youtube.com/watch?v=7c9vyj_0zSs.

McLaughlin, Gayle. "A Local Community Defines Its Destiny." In *Rebuilding After Collapse: Political Structures for Creative Response to the Ecological Crisis*, edited by John Culp, 187–96. Anoka, MN: Process Century, 2018.

Merton, Thomas. *Seeking Paradise: The Spirit of the Shakers*. Edited by Paul M. Pearson. Maryknoll, NY: Orbis, 2003.

Miksha, Ron. "EO Wilson, 92, Has Left the Lab." Bad Beekeeping Blog, Dec. 30, 2021. https://badbeekeepingblog.com/2021/12/30/eo-wilson-92-has-left-the-lab/.

Miller, D. Lee. "CAFOS: What We Don't Know Is Hurting Us." Natural Resources Defense Council, Sept. 2019. https://www.nrdc.org/sites/default/files/cafos-dont-know-hurting-us-report.pdf.

Minds at Work. "Facilitator's Workshop." https://mindsatwork.com/programs-services/coach-development/facilitators-workshop/.

Mondragon Corporation. "About Us." https://www.mondragon-corporation.com/en/about-us/.

———. "Our Code of Ethics." https://www.mondragon-corporation.com/wp-content/uploads/docs/DOC_codigo_etico_EN.pdf.

———. "Humanity at Work." https://www.mondragon-corporation.com/people/site/assets/files/103207/urteko-txostena-2023.pdfp.

Montbrial, Thierry de. "Letter from Europe: Disorder, Injustice and Our Current Crisis." Policy Magazine, Sept. 7, 2020. https://www.policymagazine.ca/letter-from-europe-disorder-injustice-and-our-current-crisis/.

Morse, Flo. *The Shakers and the World's People*. New York: Dodd, Mead, and Co., 1980.

———. *The Story of the Shakers*. Burlington, VT: Countryman, 1986.

Mullick, Nirvan. "Caine's Arcade." Apr. 9, 2012. YouTube video, 10:58. https://www.youtube.com/watch?v=faIFNkdq96U.

Muriel, Pablo A., and Alan J. Singer. *Supporting Civics Education with Student Activism: Citizens for a Democratic Society*. London: Routledge, 2021.

Murthy, Vivek H. "Our Epidemic of Loneliness and Isolation: The U.S. Surgeon General's Advisory on the Healing Effects of Social Connection and Community." US Department of Health and Human Services, 2023. https://www.hhs.gov/sites/default/files/surgeon-general-social-connection-advisory.pdf.

Musset, Pauline. "School Choice and Equity: Current Policies in OECD Countries and Literature Review." OECD Education Working Papers 66, Jan. 31, 2012. https://www.oecd.org/content/dam/oecd/en/publications/reports/2012/01/school-choice-and-equity_g17a20d7/5k9fq23507vc-en.pdf.

National Center on Education and the Economy (NCEE). "Top-Performing Countries: Finland." https://ncee.org/country/finland/.

National Center for Education Statistics. "Fast Facts." https://nces.ed.gov/fastfacts/display.asp?id=1.

Newton, Peter, et al. "What Is Regenerative Agriculture? A Review of Scholar and Practitioner Definitions Based on Processes and Outcomes." *Frontiers in Sustainable Food Systems* 4 (2020). https://doi.org/10.3389/fsufs.2020.577723.

Nidess, Dan. "Why a Universal Basic Income Would Be a Calamity." *Wall Street Journal*, Aug. 10, 2017. https://www.wsj.com/articles/why-a-universal-basic-income-would-be-a-calamity-1502403580.

Nightingale, Steven. *Granada—A Pomegranate in the Hand of God*. Berkeley: Counterpoint, 2015.

Nyoike, Vincent. "Countries That Have Tried Universal Basic Income." Basic Income Earth Network, Jul. 26, 2022. https://basicincome.org/news/2022/07/countries-that-have-tried-universal-basic-income/.

Ocean Spray. "About Us." https://www.oceanspray.com/about-us.

Ockham, William. "The Noosphere (Part I): Teilhard de Chardin's Vision." Teilhard de Chardin, Aug. 13, 2013. https://teilhard.com/2013/08/13/the-noosphere-part-i-teilhard-de-chardins-vision/.

Oikocredit. "About Oikocredit." https://www.oikocredit.org/about-oikocredit/.

O'Kane, Caitlin. "Jimmy Carter Had a Long History with Habitat for Humanity—Even Pitching in on Builds in His 90s." CBS News, Dec. 29, 2024. https://www.cbsnews.com/news/jimmy-carter-habitat-for-humanity-history-the-carter-work-project/.

Organic Valley. "Organic Grass-Fed Milk Is More Nutritious. It's Science." https://www.organicvalley.coop/resources/organic-grass-fed-milk-nutrition/.

Organisation for Economic Co-Operation and Development (OECD). "Better Life Initiative: Country Note—Norway." 2022. https://www.oecd.org/wise/Better-Life-Initiative-country-note-Norway.pdf (archived at https://web.archive.org/web/20240327050413/https://www.oecd.org/statistics/Better-Life-Initiative-country-note-Norway.pdf).

———. "High Performing Systems for Tomorrow: 2023 Conceptual Framework." Dec. 2023. https://issuu.com/oecd.publishing/docs/high_preforming_systems_for_tomorrow_2023_framewor.

P., Gene. "Benefits of Gratitude: 31 Reasons to be Grateful." Happier Human, Jun. 26, 2023. https://www.happierhuman.com/benefits-of-gratitude/.

Palmer, Parker. *Healing the Heart of Democracy*. San Francisco: Jossey-Bass, 2011.

Peterson, Trudy Huskamp. "The Universal Declaration of Human Rights: An Archival Commentary." International Council on Archives, Dec. 10, 2018. https://www.ica.org/resource/the-universal-declaration-of-human-rights-an-archival-commentary/.

Pollak, Susan M. "The Idea of the Beloved Community." Psychology Today, Jan. 13, 2023. https://www.psychologytoday.com/us/blog/the-art-of-now/202301/the-idea-of-the-beloved-community.

Presencing Institute. "Presencing." https://www.presencing.org/presencing.

Putnam, Robert D., and Shaylyn Romney Garrett. *The Upswing: How America Came Together a Century Ago and How We Can Do It Again*. New York: Simon & Schuster, 2020.

Quote Investigator. "Quote Origin: Be the Change You Wish to See in the World." Oct. 23, 2017. https://quoteinvestigator.com/2017/10/23/be-change/.

———. "Quote Origin: The Intuitive Mind Is a Sacred Gift and the Rational Mind Is a Faithful Servant." Sept. 18, 2013. https://quoteinvestigator.com/2013/09/18/intuitive-mind/.

Raworth, Kate. "Doughnut Economics at the City Scale." Shareable, Mar. 16, 2021. https://www.shareable.net/cities_tufts/kate-raworth-doughnut-economics-at-the-city-scale/.

———. "Three Horizons Framework—A Quick Introduction." Doughnut Economics Action Lab, Aug. 8, 2018. YouTube video, 6:52. https://www.youtube.com/watch?v=_5KfRQJqpPU.

Real Organic Project. "2022 Real Organic Symposium: Milk + Money." Real Organic Project, Jan. 30, 2022. YouTube video, 3:44. https://www.youtube.com/watch?v=negfqCHsO8g.

Reggio Children. "Reggio Emilia Approach." https://www.reggiochildren.it/en/Reggio-Emilia-Approach/.

Reich, Robert B. *The System: Who Rigged It, How We Fix It*. New York: Knopf, 2021.

Retif, Sherri. "The Integration of Sport and Spirituality." Spirituality Mind Body Institute, Oct. 24, 2022. YouTube video, 9:06. https://www.youtube.com/watch?v=FqS7Nk1O9Mg.

Rifkin, Jeremy. *The Empathic Civilization: The Race for Global Consciousness in a World in Crisis*. New York: TarcherPerigee, 2009.

Robinson, Ken. "Do Schools Kill Creativity?" TED Talk, Feb. 2006. 19:11. https://www.ted.com/talks/sir_ken_robinson_do_schools_kill_creativity.

Robinson, Kim Stanley. *The Ministry for the Future*. New York: Orbit, 2020.

Rockefeller, Steven. *Spiritual Democracy and Our Schools: Renewing the American Spirit with Education for the Whole Child*. New York: Clearview, 2022.

Rodale Institute. "Can Organic Feed the World?" https://rodaleinstitute.org/blog/can-organic-feed-the-world/.

Ross, Sean. "What Is the Human Capital Theory and How Is It Used?" Investopedia, Nov. 11, 2024. https://www.investopedia.com/ask/answers/032715/what-human-capital-and-how-it-used.asp.

Rossi, Jacqui. "Malala Yousafzai, Activist." Biography, Mar. 13, 2018. YouTube video, 3:17. https://www.youtube.com/watch?v=6by9NEhT9GM.

Rousseau, Jean-Jacques. *The Social Contract*. Translated by Maurice Cranston. New York: Penguin, 1968.

Rowson, Jonathan. "Four Ways of Knowing the Meta Crisis." Perspectiva, Jan. 25, 2022. YouTube video, 14:45. https://www.youtube.com/watch?v=NbBH1Hs_jLo.

Sachs, Robert. "The Mind as Computer Metaphor: Benson and the Mistaken Application of Mental Steps to Software (Part 3)." Fenwick Bilski Blog, Apr. 11, 2016. https://www.fenwick.com/bilski-blog/the-mind-as-computer-metaphor-benson-and-the-mistaken-application-of-mental-steps-to-software-part-3.

Safi, Michael, and Agencies. "Ganges and Yamuna Rivers Granted Same Legal Rights as Human Beings." *The Guardian*, Mar. 21, 2017. https://www.theguardian.com/world/2017/mar/21/ganges-and-yamuna-rivers-granted-same-legal-rights-as-human-beings.

Salk, Jonathan. "A New Reality: Human Evolution for a Sustainable Future." Talks at Google, Jul. 1, 2019. YouTube video, 43:43. https://www.youtube.com/watch?v=IgvawiWp_dc.

Sanders, Bernie. *It's OK to Be Angry About Capitalism*. New York: Crown, 2023.

Satin, Joseph, ed. *The 1950s: America's "Placid" Decade*. Boston: Houghton Mifflin, 1960.

Saunders, Eckenhoff. *Seed + Spark: Using Nature as a Model to Reimagine How We Learn and Live.* Chicago: Eckenhoff Saunders Architects / 180 Studio, 2020.

Scarcella, Mike. "Tyson, Other Poultry Processors to Pay $180 Million to Settle Workers' Wage Claims." Reuters, Dec. 24, 2024. https://www.reuters.com/legal/litigation/tyson-other-poultry-processors-pay-180-million-settle-workers-wage-claims-2024-12-24/.

Schaefer, Christopher. *Re-Imagining America: Finding Hope in Difficult Times.* Stroud, UK: Hawthorn, 2019.

Scharmer, Otto. "2023 in Eight Points: Meditating on Our Planetary Moment." Field of the Future, Dec. 30, 2023. https://medium.com/presencing-institute-blog/2023-in-eight-points-meditating-on-our-planetary-moment-3081cf51ed5d.

———. *Theory U: Leading from the Future as It Emerges.* Oakland, CA: Berrett-Koehler, 2009.

———. "Theory U—Learning from the Future as It Emerges." TEDx Talks, Oct. 26, 2016. YouTube video, 24:51. https://www.youtube.com/watch?v=GMJefS7s3lc&t=13s.

Scharmer, Otto, and Katrin Kaufer. *Leading from the Emerging Future: From Ego-System to Eco-System Economics.* Oakland: Berrett-Koehler, 2013.

———. *Presencing: 7 Practices for Transforming Self, Society, and Business.* Oakland, CA: Berrett-Koehler, 2025.

Schneider, Jack. "Small Schools: The Edu-Reform Failure That Wasn't." Education Week, Feb. 9, 2016. https://www.edweek.org/leadership/opinion-small-schools-the-edu-reform-failure-that-wasnt/2016/02.

Scholes, Mary C., and Robert J. Scholes. "Dust Unto Dust." *Science* 342 (2013) 565–66. https://doi.org/10.1126/science.1244579.

Scripture Central. "Where Does the Word 'Deseret' Come From?" Aug. 20, 2020. https://scripturecentral.org/knowhy/where-does-the-word-deseret-come-from.

Seeley, Thomas D. *Honeybee Democracy.* Princeton: Princeton University Press, 2010.

Seguinland Institute. "Alumni Testimonials." https://www.seguinlandinstitute.org/testimonials.

Seijen, Koen van, host. "Helmy Abouleish—How to Scale Regenerative Agriculture in Egypt from 2,000 Farmers to 40,000 in One Year Without Charging a Premium." Investing In Regenerative Agriculture and Food, Jul. 4, 2023. https://investinginregenerativeagriculture.com/2023/07/04/helmy-abouleish.

Sekem. "Cultural Life." https://sekem.com/en/Cultural-Life/.

———. "Dr. Ibrahim Abouleish." https://sekem.com/en/About/Founders/Dr-Ibrahim-Abouleish/.

———. "History." https://sekem.com/en/about/history/.

———. "Sekem Companies." https://sekem.com/en/Economy/Sekem-Companies/.

———. "SEKEM Inspirations. Movement and Growth." https://sekem.com/en/Sekem-Inspirations-Movement-and-Growth/.

Semple, Kirk, et al. "Meet the People Getting Paid to Kill Our Planet." *New York Times,* Feb. 1, 2022. https://www.nytimes.com/2022/02/01/opinion/climate-sustainability-agriculture-lobby.html.

Senge, Peter, et al. *Presence: Human Purpose and the Field of the Future.* New York: Crown, 2004.

Shanahan, Ed. "Herman Daly, 84, Who Challenged the Economic Gospel of Growth, Dies." *New York Times,* Nov. 8, 2022. https://www.nytimes.com/2022/11/08/business/economy/herman-daly-dead.html.

Shelton, Richard. "Prince Albert in the Can." *Rain Shadow Review* (2022) 77–83.

Shiva, Vandana. "Seeds of Suicide and Slavery Versus Seeds of Life and Freedom." *Al Jazeera*, Mar. 30, 2013. https://www.aljazeera.com/opinions/2013/3/30/seeds-of-suicide-and-slavery-versus-seeds-of-life-and-freedom.

Siegel, Robert. "Origins of Bridge to Nowhere Explained." NPR, Sept. 10, 2008. https://www.npr.org/2008/09/10/94481285/origins-of-bridge-to-nowhere-explained.

Simon-Delso, N. et al. "Systemic Insecticides (Neonicotinoids and Fipronil): Trends, Uses, Mode of Action, and Metabolites." *Environmental Science and Pollution Research International* 22 (2015) 5–34. https://link.springer.com/article/10.1007/s11356-014-3470-y.

Skipper, Clay. "'Hope Is a Muscle': Why Krista Tippett Wants You to Keep the Faith." *GQ*, Jul. 21, 2022. https://www.gq.com/story/krista-tippett-on-being-interview.

Smith, Gregory A., and David Sobel. *Place- and Community-Based Education in Schools*. London: Routledge, 2010.

Smith, Jamil, host. "Revolutionary Love." *The Grey Area with Sean Illing*. Vox Conversations, Sept. 23, 2021. Podcast, 57:00. https://podcasts.apple.com/ca/podcast/revolutionary-love/id1081584611?i=1000536432524.

Snyder, Timothy. *On Freedom*. New York: Crown, 2024.

Sobel, David. *Place-Based Education*. Great Barrington, MA: Orion Society, 2004.

———. "Swimming Upstream Against the Current: Changing the School Improvement Paradigm." Community Works Journal, Jun. 8, 2019. https://medium.com/communityworksjournal/swimming-upstream-against-the-current-changing-the-school-improvement-paradigm-941c3159b8cd.

Soil Health Institute. "Connections Between Soil Health and Human Health." https://soilhealthinstitute.org/our-work/initiatives/connections-between-soil-health-and-human-health/.

Solnit, Rebecca. *A Paradise Built in Hell: Extraordinary Communities That Arise in Disaster*. New York: Viking, 2009.

Speth, James Gustave, and Kathleen Courrier, eds. *The New Systems Reader: Alternatives to a Failed Economy*. London: Routledge, 2020.

State of Vermont Agency of Education. "Public High School Choice." https://education.vermont.gov/vermont-schools/school-operations/public-schools/public-high-school-choice.

Stegner, Wallace. *The Sound of Mountain Water*. New York: Doubleday, 1997.

Stein, Zachary. *Education in a Time Between Worlds: Essays on the Future of Schools, Technology, and Society*. New York: Bright Alliance, 2019.

———. "If Education Is Not the Answer, You Are Asking the Wrong Question: Why It's Time to See Planetary Crises as a Species-Wide Learning Opportunity." Perspectiva, 2019. https://drive.google.com/file/d/1z8GJmn3FWRhg20YuHosqznKt2_uBZnC4/view.

Steiner, Rudolf. *Rethinking Economics: Lectures and Seminars on World Economics*. New York: Steiner, 2013.

———. *Towards Social Renewal*. Forest Row, UK: Rudolf Steiner, 1977.

Steuernagel, Armin. "Transforming Ownership to Create a Better Economy." TEDx Talks, Feb. 9, 2018. YouTube video: 19:18. https://www.youtube.com/watch?v=Z2Uy_ODDiZo.

Stoll, Timothy. "Forming Humanity: Redeeming the German Bildung Tradition." Review of *Forming Humanity: Redeeming the German Bildung Tradition* by Jennifer A. Herdt. Notre Dame Philosophical Reviews, Jan. 1, 2020. https://ndpr.nd.edu/reviews/forming-humanity-redeeming-the-german-bildung-tradition/.

Strauss, Valerie. "How A Fabulous Principal Lost Her Job—and More Damage the Misuse of Test Scores Has Caused." *Washington Post*, Oct. 5, 2017. https://www.washingtonpost.com/news/answer-sheet/wp/2017/10/05/how-a-fabulous-principal-lost-her-job-and-more-damage-the-misuse-of-test-scores-has-caused/.

Tanner, Lindsey, and Jocelyn Gecker. "CDC Data Shows U.S. Teen Girls 'in Crisis' with Unprecedented Rise in Suicidal Behavior." PBS News, Feb. 13, 2023. https://www.pbs.org/newshour/health/cdc-data-shows-u-s-teen-girls-in-crisis-with-unprecedented-rise-in-suicidal-behavior.

Tata-Cornell Institute. "Study Reveals Complex Links Between Soil and Human Health." Aug. 23, 2021. https://tci.cornell.edu/?news=study-reveals-complex-links-between-soil-and-human-health.

Teaching-Certification.com. "Education Spending by State—How Does Your State Compare?" https://www.teaching-certification.com/teaching/education-spending-by-state.html.

Teigen, Lloyd D. "Agricultural Parity: Historical Review and Alternative Calculations." ERIC Institute of Education Sciences. https://eric.ed.gov/?id=ED282982.

Teilhard de Chardin, Pierre. *Christianity and Evolution*. New York: Harcourt, 1969.

Topa (Four Arrows), Wahinkpe, and Darcia Narvaez. *Restoring the Kinship Worldview: Indigenous Voices Introduce 28 Precepts for Rebalancing Life on Planet Earth*. Berkeley: North Atlantic, 2022.

Trainer, Ted. "Kurdist Rojava: A Social Model for Our Future." Resilience, Jan. 3, 2020. https://www.resilience.org/stories/2020-01-03/kurdist-rojava-a-social-model-for-our-future/.

Transforming Center. "Spiritual Direction." https://transformingcenter.org/spiritual-direction-4/.

Travis, Mark. *In Union: The People, Places, and Stories of Canterbury Shaker Village*. Canterbury, NH: Canterbury Shaker Village, 2019.

Udell, Edward H. *Agent of Social Transformation: Rudolf Steiner during World War I and the German Revolution*. Published by the author, 2024.

United Nations. "History of the Declaration." https://www.un.org/en/about-us/udhr/history-of-the-declaration.

———. "Universal Declaration of Human Rights." https://www.un.org/en/about-us/universal-declaration-of-human-rights.

United Nations Office of the High Commissioner. "Human Rights Indicators: A Guide to Measurement and Implementation." https://digitallibrary.un.org/record/765918/files/Human_rights_indicators_en.pdf.

University of California Agriculture and Natural Resources. "About Worm Castings." https://ucanr.edu/sites/default/files/2018-07/286155.pdf.

US Department of Agriculture (USDA). "Value Added Producer Grant," Jan. 2020. https://www.rd.usda.gov/sites/default/files/fact-sheet/508_RD_FS_RBS_VAPG.pdf.

Valens, Tom, and Amy Valens. "Chapter 1: Why We're Here." A Year at Mission Hill, Jan. 31, 2013. YouTube video, 4:52. https://www.youtube.com/watch?v=LzXOmDVHXug.

———. "Chapter 5: The Eye of the Dragon." A Year at Mission Hill, Mar. 28, 2013. YouTube video, 6:11. https://www.youtube.com/watch?v=iSrlG6HSSaw.

Vouloumanos, Victoria. "'I Quit at That Moment': Teachers Who Quit Are Sharing the Moment They Realized It Wasn't for Them." Buzzfeed, Nov. 24, 2023. https://www.buzzfeed.com/victoriavouloumanos/former-teachers-reveal-breaking-point-quit.

Wagamese, Richard. *Embers: One Ojibway's Meditations*. Madeira Park, BC: Douglas & McIntyre, 2017.

Walker, Darren. "UVM 2019 Commencement Address: Darren Walker." University of Vermont, Jun. 25, 2019. YouTube, 16:37. https://www.youtube.com/watch?v=JmavhjmpTqA.

Warrick, Joby. "'They Die Piece by Piece.'" *Washington Post*, Apr. 9, 2001. https://www.washingtonpost.com/archive/politics/2001/04/10/they-die-piece-by-piece/f172dd3c-0383-49f8-b6d8-347e04b68da1/.

Waterman, Charles. *The Three Spheres of Society*. London: Faber & Faber, 1946.

Wheatley, Margaret. *Who Do We Choose to Be? Facing Reality, Claiming Leadership, Restoring Sanity*. Oakland, CA: Berrett Koeler, 2017.

Whoriskey, Peter. "Why Your 'Organic' Milk May Not be Organic." *Washington Post*, May 1, 2017. https://www.washingtonpost.com/business/economy/why-your-organic-milk-may-not-be-organic/2017/05/01/708ce5bc-ed76-11e6-9662-6eedf1627882_story.html.

Whyte, William Foote, and Katherine King Whyte. *Making Mondragon: The Growth and Dynamics of the Worker Cooperative Complex*. 2nd ed. Ithaca, NY: ILR, 1991.

Wikiquote. "W. H. Murray." Aug. 5, 2021. https://en.wikiquote.org/wiki/W._H._Murray.

Wilkinson, Richard, and Kate Pickett. T*he Spirit Level: Why Greater Equality Makes Societies Stronger*. New York: Bloomsbury, 2010.

Will, Madeline. "Some Positive Signs for the Teacher Pipeline, But It's Not All Good. What 3 Studies Say." Education Week, Mar. 25, 2024. https://www.edweek.org/leadership/some-positive-signs-for-the-teacher-pipeline-but-its-not-all-good-what-3-studies-say/2024/03.

Williams, Mark. "The Role of the Worker Bee." PerfectBee, May 16, 2025. https://www.perfectbee.com/beekeeping-articles/the-role-of-the-worker-bee.

Williams-Siegfredsen, Jane. "Forest Schools in Early Years—What They Are, Where They Started and Their Ethos." Teach Early Years. https://www.teachearlyyears.com/enabling-environments/view/danish-forest-schools.

———. *Understanding the Danish Forest School Approach: Early Years Education in Practice*. 2nd ed. London: Routledge, 2017.

Winiecki, Martin. "Unremitting Turkish Attacks Leave Rojava in Peril—and in Need of Solidarity." Truthout, Feb. 15, 2024. https://truthout.org/articles/unremitting-turkish-attacks-leave-rojava-in-peril-and-in-need-of-solidarity/.

Winkler, Franz. "The American Dream." Unpublished manuscript. Great Barrington, MA: Myrin Institute.

———. *Man: The Bridge Between Two Worlds*. New York: Harper & Brothers, 1960.

———. "A Memorial for Rudolf Steiner." Lecture, New York, Mar. 29, 1959.

———. "Training in Intuition." *Myrin Institute Proceedings* 39. Great Barrington, MA: Myrin Institute, 2022.

Wisevoter. "Per Pupil Spending by State." *Wisevoter*. https://wisevoter.com/state-rankings/per-pupil-spending-by-state/.

World Population Review. "Countries with Universal Basic Income 2025." https://worldpopulationreview.com/country-rankings/countries-with-universal-basic-income.

Xian, Tong, et al. "Stress Effects on Meat Quality: A Mechanistic Perspective." *Comprehensive Reviews in Food Science and Food Safety* 18 (2019) 380–401. https://doi.org/10.1111/1541-4337.12417.

Yad Vashem. "Janusz Korczak." https://www.yadvashem.org/education/educational-materials/lesson-plans/janusz-korczak/korczak-bio.html.

Zaiets, Karina, et al. "Mass Killing Database: Revealing Trends, Details, and Anguish of Every US Event Since 2006." USA Today, Aug. 18, 2022. https://www.usatoday.com/in-depth/graphics/2022/08/18/mass-killings-database-us-events-since-2006/9705311002/.

INDEX

4-H youth development program, 127
50-Year Farm Bill, 111

Abouleish, Ibrahim, 41, 150, 171–72, 178 *see also* Sekem
Abrahamic Initiative, 42 *see also* Chautauqua
addiction to growth, 158 *see also* Doughnut Economics
affluenza, 215n4
Agilent Technologies, 181
agriculture, 109–32, 163, 198, 217
    Agricultural Adjustment Act and parity, 123
    alternative and sustainable visions for, 118–32 *see also* regenerative agriculture
    blighted paradigms in modern agriculture, 110–16
    contributions to the climate crisis, 118–19, 127
Alperovitz, Gar, 139, 140n17, 171n2
    "A Pluralistic Commonwealth," essay, 139
alternative education approaches, 74–82
altruism, 22, 50–51, 138
    as a motivator, 138
American constitution, a new kind of, 195, 198
    elements of, 197
animal welfare in farming, 112–15
    Aurora Organic Dairy and treatment of cows, 115–16
    concentrated animal feeding operations (CAFOs), 112
    Monsanto's war on bees, 113–14
    Tyson and chicken abuse, 112–13
art, 43, 58, 81, 173–75
    arts integration in education, 76, 81, 102, 106, 175
    potential to shape future and affect consciousness, 173
    value at Sekem, 173
aspirations, 194–210
    author's aspirations for society, 195
    for the cultural sphere, 206–8
    for the economic sphere, 200–202
    for the political sphere, 203–6
    role in visioning, 195
Aurora Organic Dairy, 115
authentic assessments in education, 101

balance in society, 169–82
    community examples of, 175–76
    economic examples of, 180–81
    fourfold conceptual framework and diagram, 179
    political examples of, 181–82
    threefold conceptual framework and diagram, 178
bees, 113, 183–91
    bee democracy, 185
    lessons for human society, 183–91
    Monsanto's war on, 113–14
    teamwork and social roles, 184

belonging, 17, 48–52, 62, 87–88 *see also* circles of belonging
    role in prompting altruism, 50–51, 88
    sense of, 17, 48–52, 62, 87–88
Beloved Community, 4, 50, 65–66, 197
    as a growth environment for citizens, 197
    exercise for building a, 65–66
    relationship to belonging, 50
Berry, John M., Sr., 224
Berry, Mary, 224
Berry, Wendell, 60, 64, 111, 129
    50-Year Farm Bill, 111
    "The Peace of Wild Things," 64
bildung, 102
biodynamic farming, 118, 154 *see also* regenerative agriculture
Björkman, Tomas and Lene Rachel Andersen, 86–88
    The Nordic Secret, 86–87
Brown, Jeffrey, 136–37, 156
Burley Tobacco Growers Co-Operative, 120, 124, 126, 223–24
    tobacco price and production management, 223–24

capitalism, 11, 22, 28, 32, 72, 73, 116, 134–67, 176
    alternatives to prevailing version of, 134–56
    coexistence with cooperation and examples, 139–56
    critique of profit maximization and inequality, 134–35
    defense and limitations, 135
    impact on the environment, 72, 135
    impact on social attitudes, 73
    in agriculture and hierarchies of domination, 116
    motives in a productive system, 156–58
    structural issues and competition, 164
carbon credits, 153–54
charter schools, 98, 105, 180
Chautauqua (community), 40, 42–44, 49
    interfaith participation, 42–43
    lessons from, 43–44
circles of belonging, 48, 88
    definition and diagram, 48
    expanding social identity in education, 88
Citizens United decision, 170, 176
City Neighbors school, 214
Civil Rights Movement, 4, 11, 52, 86, 181
civilization, new visions, 28–29, 52, 54–55, 58–59, 60–62, 66, 82, 109–10, 116, 117, 138, 139–41, 170, 175, 188, 191, 192–200, 207, 209–10, 213–17
    agriculture's place in, 110, 117
    capitalism and cooperation in, 140–41
    citizen responsibilities to create, 209–10
    education as a necessary component, 82, 86, 192–200, 207
    five immediate actions to contribute to, 213–16
    foundations for social change, 82
    love as a redirectional tool in, 60–62
    stages of, 58, 66
    two models for, 28
climate change, 3, 11, 72, 118, 119, 125n34, 127, 131, 140, 207n20
    agriculture's contribution to, 119, 127
    government's responsibility in mitigation, 140, 207n20
Colony Collapse Disorder (CCD), 113, 183
Commodity Credit Corporation (CCC), 223
community building, 6, 8, 39–47 *see also convivencia*
    at Chautauqua, 43–44
    at Granada, 39–41
    at Sekem, 41–42
    for the American Shakers, 44–47
Community Supported Agriculture (CSA), 110, 121–22, 131, 138, 164, 214
    model and benefits, 121–22

INDEX

Community Wealth Building (CWB), 162
Compass School in Vermont, 96n10, 98–99
compliance culture in schools, 94–95, 213
concentrated animal feeding operations (CAFOs), 112–13, 116, 119
consumer associations, 155n58)
convivencia, 29n24, 38–52, 54, 66, 113–14, 122, 126, 141, 146, 187, 197, 202, 215
    definition, 38–39
    examples of, 39–47
    in economy, 139–41, 146, 215
    violations of, 113–14
cooperative economy, 133–66
    three horizons thinking diagram, 165
cooperatives, 139, 144–50, 163, 165n74, 202–3
    additional cooperative models, 165n74, 180–81
    coexistence with capitalism, 139–40
    Mondragón as an example of, 144–50
COVID-19 pandemic, 28, 58, 71, 72, 104, 113, 136, 146
creativity, 15–16, 17, 32, 44, 45, 46–47, 47n16, 50, 52, 71, 74–76, 80–81, 92–97, 101, 105, 149, 155, 162, 177, 178, 196
    in cooperatives, 148, 154
    in education, example of, 80–81
    in Shaker life and principles, according to BARD, 47n16
    in student education, 71, 74–76, 162
    in teaching, 92–97, 101, 105, 177, 196
    relationship to intuition, 15–16
    relationship to worship in the American Shakers, 46–47
crop insurance, negative effects, 111–12
cultural sphere, 29–33, 36, 93, 172–77, 206–8 *see also* three spheres of society
    as part of the three spheres of society, 31–33, 36, 176–77

components and role in society, 173–77
role in safeguarding freedom, 36

Danish Folk Schools, 48, 61, 86, 217
decommodification of labor, 172 *see also* Shakers
deeply transformative learning, 6, 162, 217 *see also* Gap Year Programs
democracy, xi, 5, 10, 17, 20, 26, 33–35, 61, 70, 73–74, 104, 135, 139, 144, 149n40, 151, 181, 185, 198
    bee democracy, 187
    economic democracy, 149n40
    relation to education and current challenges in the United States, 73–74
    under capitalism, 135, 139
    worker democracy in cooperatives, 144
democratic schools, 106
Dignity of Risk, 86
disaster response, 50–51, 161 *see also* altruism
Doerr, Anthony, 173–74
    All the Light We Cannot See, 173–74
Doughnut Economics, 152, 158–59
    conceptual framework by Kate Raworth, 158
    the Doughnut diagram, 159

economic sphere, 30–32, 142, 170–73, 176–77, 178–79, 180–81, 200–202 *see also* three spheres of society
    as part of the three spheres of society, 31–33, 178–79
    relationship to cultural sphere, 30–32
    relationship to political sphere, 170
    responsibilities and relationship to mutuality, 200–202
Economy of Love, 150–53, 202 *see also* Sekem
    principles and implementation at Sekem, 150–53
educate the whole child (concept), 69–89

Educate the Whole Child (organization), 7, 13, 75, 76, 81
education, 7, 13, 16, 69–106
    central role in future change, 7, 16, 69
    connection to cultural sphere and individual development, 193
    role in cultivating empathy, 62–65
    public education, 13, 70, 92–95
        failing paradigms, 70
        four major problems in funding and governing, 92–95
egotism, 35, 36, 40, 49, 54, 57, 72, 142, 176, 215
    of the group, 40, 49
    on a continuum with love, 57
    relationship to individualism, 35
Eisler, Riane, 116
    "Whole Systems Change," essay, 116
emerging complexity, ix
Emerson, Ralph Waldo, 26–27
    "Politics," essay, 26
empathy, 53–55, 57, 61–66, 76–77, 122, 130, 197 *see also* love, Peace Table
    development in early childhood, 62–66
equality, 29, 31–32, 45, 47n16, 62, 93–94, 170, 176, 181–82, 195, 199, 203
    ideal in political/legal sphere and democratic practices, 181–82, 203
    state responsibility to level playing field, 199
evolved society, visions of, 217–18

fair trade, 152–53, 202
farm price stability and control, 122–23 *see also* Burley Tobacco Growers Co-Operative
fear, x, 14, 58–59, 61, 70, 181
    as opposite of love, 61
    as opposite of open will, 14
    as a tool in governments, 59
    in education, 70
    in corporate structures, 181

Federal Reserve, 201
    example of effective operation, 201
Finland's approach to education, 51, 84, 96–97, 102–4
five intelligences, 76, 83 *see also* whole-child education
forest kindergartens, 84 *see also* Scandinavian education, lessons from
Forum Theater, 163
four levels of problem-solving, 13–14, 131
    diagram with examples, 14
Fourteenth Amendment, 93
Frankl, Viktor, 23, 25–26, 35, 51, 222
    Man's Search for Meaning, 23
Free, Equal, and Mutual (Large), 177
freedom, 19–37, theme throughout *see also* inner freedom
    elements of, 21–23
    relationship to individualism, 34–36
freedom, equality, and mutuality, 29, 170, 176 *see also* liberté, egalité, fraternité
freedom to teach, 90–106 *see also* education
funding inequities in education, 91–96, 104–5, 214
    in the United States, 91–95
    solutions and examples, 96, 104–5, 214

gap year programs, 6, 73, 88, 162, 217, 225–26
    components of effective programs, 225
    student experiences and educational impact, 225
Gelles, David, 135–36
    The Man Who Broke Capitalism, 135
generosity, 50, 127, 160, 187, 199
gift economy, 134, 160
Goethe, Johann Wolfgang von, 56, 102, 27, 203, 211
    Sorrows of Young Werther and mental health, 174
government, modern limitations, 11, 22, 27, 50, 66, 74, 79, 92–94, 100,

104, 105, 123–26, 169–70, 171, 173, 201, 203, 204, 206, 207n20
   a reenvisioned constitution's effects on, 204
   effective and ineffective interventions in agriculture, 123–26
   government bureaucracy and effects on education, 74, 93–94, 100
   in disasters, 50
   in moderating climate change, 207n20
   micromanaging public education, 79, 92–94, 104
   summary of, 171
government-sponsored service programs, examples, 226 *see also* gap year programs
Granada, 39–40, 43, 49, 52, 54, 66, 197
gratitude, 51n21, 63–65, 73, 127–29, 131, 156, 160, 187, 194 *see also* empathy
   relationship to happiness, 51n21, 63n20
   relationship to land and farming, 127–29, 131
Goodall, Jane, 60, 82, 218

Henderson, Hazel, 157
Henderson, Rebecca, 156
   Reimagining Capitalism in a World on Fire, 156
homeschooling, 75 *see also* alternative education approaches
honey, 184, 188–90 *see also* bees
   symbol of transformation, 186–88
hope, 8, 11, 28, 52, 56, 64, 218
   as a muscle to be exercised, 218
   effects of lack thereof, 28
   for the future, theme throughout
Hudson River School, 175 *see also* cultural sphere
Human Capital Theory, 101
human consciousness, 25, 71, 126, 164, 173
human evolution, 20, 23–25, 28, 52, 60, 157, 189, 210 *see also* freedom

human nature, 12, 50, 161, 176, 194
   two contrasting visions of, 194
human rights, 49, 202, 209 *see also* Universal Declaration of Human Rights

ideals, 9, 29, 41, 44, 56, 195, 197–99 *see also* freedom, equality, and mutuality
   definition, 56
   examples related to the three spheres framework, 29
   relationship to responsibilities, 197–98
   role in transforming society, 9
individualism, 34–35, 46, 143, 164
   ethical individualism (individualism 2.0), 35
   individualism 1.0 characteristics, 34
   rugged individualism, 143, 164
industrial agriculture, 111, 153
inequality, 51–52, 56, 62, 134, 138, 147
   social and health consequences, 51
   strategies for reduction, 52
Inner Development Goals, 162n69, 189, 190, 197, 210, 215–16
   graphics, 190
   five areas of inner growth, 190
   relationship to imagination, 216
   relationship to Sustainable Development Goals, 210
inner freedom, 20, 22, 23–25, 27, 35, 36, 66, 151, 197
   in the face of suffering, 23–25, 197
   relationship to love and empathy, 66
   role in humanity, 20
   threats to, 27
intuition, 15–16, 21, 193
   definition, 15–16
   role in creativity and presencing, 15–16
Irvine, Joyce, 93–94 *see also* Wheeler Elementary School
islands of coherence, 60 *see also* six stages of civilization

INDEX

justice, 29, 56, 62, 93, 146, 176, 197–99, 203–6
    relationship to the political sphere, 203–6

Kimmerer, Robin Wall, 134, 160, 194
    Braiding Sweetgrass, 160
    The Serviceberry, 134
King, Martin Luther, Jr., 4, 10, 194, 197
Kirschenmann, Fred, 120

Large, Martin, 177
    Free, Equal, and Mutual, 177
    threefold diagram, 178
liberté, egalité, fraternité, 29 see also freedom, equality, and mutuality
love, 53–66, theme throughout see also Beloved Community
    as force for societal good, 60–62
    connection to justice, 56–57
    cultivation in children, 62–65
    in Shaker practices, 55–56
    love and equality, 62
    love/egotism continuum, 57–60
    philia, 54

Macy, Joanna, 60, 82
    "The Great Turning" and changes in sense of self, 60
Maslow's Hierarchy of Needs, 196–97
    pyramid diagram, 196
materialistic thinking, 95, 101
    in education, 101 see also Human Capital Theory
Metacrisis, 7, 217
Mondragón Cooperative, 9, 140, 144–50, 161, 173, 187
    education and worker empowerment, 148
    founding and historical background, 144
    producer and consumer cooperatives, 145
    Rochdale Principles and cooperative identity, 145
    scale, sustainability, and challenges, 146–48

Monsanto, 114
moral decay in modern civilization, 59
mutuality, 29–31, 39, 42, 141, 170, 176, 180–81, 200, 215 see also ideals
    in the economic sphere, 180–81, 200

national education standards, recommendations, 105
Native American farming philosophy, 131 see also gratitude
Nature Deficit Disorder, 81–82
neonicotinoids, 114 see also Monsanto
New England town meeting, 181 see also democracy
No Child Left Behind program, 71, 103
no-till farming, 118
Nordic Secret, The (Björkman and Andersen), 48, 86

open mind, open heart, and open will, ix, 6, 12, 14, 15
    oppositions to each, 14
organic farming productivity, defense of, 119
organic fraud, 115, 117
Orion Magazine, 7, 12, 77, 82

Paradise Built in Hell, A (Solnit), 50, 161
Paris Climate Accord, 72, 204
Pay It Forward (film), 163, 174, 217
Peace Table, 63, 76–77 see also empathy
Peace of Wild Things, The (Berry), 64
PISA and NAEP tests, 97 see also Finland's approach to education
place-based education, 75, 77–78
    case study of Crellin Elementary School, 77–78
political sphere, 30–32, 94, 171, 199, 203–6, see also Three spheres of society
    as part of the three spheres of society, 30–32
    rights, aspirations, and responsibilities, 203–6
    role in education, 94

Post-World War II international cooperation and the "Placid Decade", 176
presencing, 12–18, 21, 69, 130, 131, 138, 165, 193 *see also* open mind, open heart, and open will
  application in problem-solving, 12–18
  definition, 12
  obstacles to, 14
problem-solving, 13–15, 45n11, 131, 150 *see also* presencing
  chart, four levels of problem-solving, 14
project-based learning, 75, 78–81, 92
Public High School Choice program, 98

Raworth, Kate, 152, 157–58, 158n61, 159, 165 *see also* Doughnut Economics
  Doughnut Economics: Seven Ways to Think Like a 21st-Century Economist, 152
Real Organic Project, 214
regenerative agriculture, 119–32
  examples of, 119–22
Reggio Emilia schools, 75, 214, 216
responsibilities of the citizen, 27, 165, 199–210, 211 see also Inner Development Goals
  to move economy in the direction of cooperation, list of, 165
  to prompt societal change, list of, 211
  in the cultural sphere, 208–10
  in the economic sphere, 202–4
  in the political sphere, 205–8
responsibilities of the state, 199–10
  in the cultural sphere, 208–10
  in the economic sphere, 202–4
  in the political sphere, 205–8
rights of nature (legal concept), 207–8
Robinson, Kim Stanley, 7n3, 207, 215
  The Ministry for the Future, 7n3, 207, 215
Rockefeller, Steven, 35
  Spiritual Democracy and Our Schools, 35

San Antonio v. Rodriguez, 93
Sanders, Bernie, 138–39
  It's OK to Be Angry about Capitalism, 138
Scandinavian education, lessons from, 84–88
Scharmer, Otto, 12, 60, 130, 138 *see also* presencing
Sekem, ix, x, 4, 9, 40, 41–42, 119, 140, 150–56, 171–73, 179, 187, 191
  Economy of Love, 150–55
  economic structure of, 151–52
  history and founding, 41, 150–51
  Sekem's Four Spheres fourfold diagram, 179
self-change, 8–10, 27, 43, 83, 140, 191, 210 *see also* inner freedom
Shakers, 3, 9, 18, 40, 44–47, 49, 52, 55, 129, 140, 141–44, 172
  challenges of celibacy and decline, 141
  historical overview and values, 44
  work as prayer and decommodification, 142
Shambala warriors, Buddhist tradition, 61
Six Month Exercises, 83, 219–22
  exercises to try, 219–22
six stages of civilization, 58–59
social and emotional learning, 76, 88, 102, 205, 209
  classroom example, 76
  relation to bildung, 102
soil health, 117–18, 131
  connection to human health, 117
  role in regenerative agriculture, 118
Solnit, Rebecca, 50, 161
  A Paradise Built in Hell, 50, 161
standardized curricula, critique of, 13, 32, 71, 79, 93, 97
  impact on teaching individuality, 93
  limitations for creativity and individual attention, 79
STEAM programs, 81
Stein, Zak, 5, 8, 18, 72
  Education in a Time Between Worlds, 72
Steiner, Rudolf, 172

steward ownership, 139
  definition and European model, 139
  examples of companies embracing model, 139
Strafford Organic Creamery, 119 *see also* regenerative farming

teaching, 70–88, 102–4
  alternative schools and approaches to, 74–81
  preparing teachers, 102–4
  systemic issues for teachers in the US, 70–74
  Scandinavian approaches, 84–88
  teacher inner life and health, 83
  teacher turnover, 71
The Great Turning, 60–61 *see also* Macy, Joanna
Three Horizons Thinking, 165–66
  graphic, 165
three spheres of society, 30–32, 93, 170, 176, 177, 200–208
  aspirations, responsibilities, and rights of each sphere, 200–208
  definition and attribution, 30–32
  diagram, 31
True Price, 153n49, 173
  definition and attribution, 153
  role in future societies, 173
Trump, Donald, 33, 58, 137
truth, 33–35
  role in facilitating freedom, 33–35
Tyson, 112–13
  control of chicken industry and farming conditions, 112
  labor practices and political influence, 113

Unity of Revelation (concept), 40
Universal Basic Income, 143n22, 206
  applications in potential to eliminate poverty, 206
  comparisons in Shaker society, 143n22

Universal Declaration of Human Rights, 202, 209 *see also* human rights
  Article 1 and implementations in economics, 202
  Article 29 and implementations in community, 209
USDA organic label, 115–17, 214
  flaws and fraud in organic certification, 115–16
  restoring integrity, 117
US Department of Agriculture (USDA), 111, 115, 117, 119, 120, 124, 214, 223–24
Utopian communities, examples, 4–5, 9, 44, 142 *see also* Mondragón Cooperative, Sekem, Shakers

visioning, 5–8, 11, 15, 18, 138, 218

Waldorf, schools and education, 75, 106
Welch, Jack, 35, 135–36, 156, 180
  impact on corporate culture at GE, 180
  "Neutron Jack" and cost cuts at GE, 135–36
Wheatley, Margaret, 58, 175 *see also* six stages of civilization
Who Do We Choose to Be? (Wheatley), 58
Wheeler Elementary School, 94
whole-child education, 69–88
  application and approaches, 74–75 *see also* alternative education approaches
  balance between standards and teacher agency, 106
  definition and overview, 74
  five intelligences as they relate to whole-child education, 76
Winkler, Franz E., 16n20, 25–26, 29, 31, 35, 64–65, 219
  For Freedom Destined, 25
  Man—the Bridge between Two Worlds, 64
worker cooperative federations, 146 *see also* Mondragón Cooperative

Yousafzai, Malala, 24, 25, 100

www.ingramcontent.com/pod-product-compliance
Lightning Source LLC
Chambersburg PA
CBHW060558230426
43670CB00011B/1874